For Nadine —

I've tried to
capture your unique
experiences and
wisdom in these
pages.

In deep appreciation,

Nadine

SUCCEEDING IN HIGH TECH

SUCCEEDING
IN HIGH TECH

A Guide to Building
Your Career

═══ MARLENE SHIGEKAWA

JOHN WILEY & SONS
New York • Chichester • Brisbane • Toronto • Singapore

This publication is designed to provide accurate and
authoritative information in regard to the subject
matter covered. It is sold with the understanding that
the publisher is not engaged in rendering legal, accounting,
or other professional service. If legal advice or other
expert assistance is required, the services of a competent
professional person should be sought. *From a Declaration
of Principles jointly adopted by a Committee of the
American Bar Association and a Committee of Publishers.*

Library of Congress Cataloging in Publication Data:

Shigekawa, Marlene, 1944-
  Succeeding in high tech.

  Bibliography: p.
  Includes index.
  1. High technology industries—Management.
  I. Title.

HD62.37.S52 1987   650.1   86-33953
ISBN 0-471-85636-3

Printed in the United States of America

10 9 8 7 6 5 4 3 2 1

For Gene
whose support and encouragement
gave birth to this work
and to Mom and Dad
who have been my greatest teachers

PREFACE

It is no secret that high technology companies are plagued by instability: short product life cycles, high risk, and rapid change. These harsh realities demand an inventive and innovative workforce that organizes itself so a fusion of brainpower occurs, producing innovative products and services that meet customer needs. Operating functions work together collaboratively and generate the free flow and exchange of information, material, and resources. Role ambiguity is an accepted state of affairs. Traditional reporting lines are broken for overlapping boundaries and assignments. Complexity and change are as natural to the environment as silicon is to the microchip.

This book is about how to survive and, ultimately, be personally effective and successful in the high-tech world. It's about how to manage yourself and your job in an environment where change is the single constant and collaborative problem solving is a valuable commodity. To succeed in high-tech environments, you really need to become a mini entrepreneur—a person who is in charge of his or her career and treats the job as if it were his or her own business. Mini-entrepreneurs succeed because they rely on their technical skills and their personal integrity, their passion to accomplish things, and powers of influence to carry them through dire straits. Unlike external entrepreneurs who cherish their independence, mini-entrepreneurs recognize the critical need for teamwork in a company that demands interdependence to survive.

I have focused on high-tech companies because they are relatively new to American business. They are a laboratory for a new strain of management philosophy and practices evolving out of an information society. Until recently, high-tech companies have been characterized by high growth and fierce competition. Their reliance on people at all levels to give their personal best with rewards for success puts them in a unique position. But what was once unique and a luxury is fast becoming a necessity, as we compete in the global marketplace. In addition no work environment over the next decade will be untouched by high tech in some fashion. Computers are weaving the fabric of the information age. Much can be learned from what excellent high-tech companies have produced in both product and people development.

The current buzzwords heard in the corporate hallways of America are: "innovative," "excellent," and "entrepreneurial." All of us have some notion of what these labels mean. Tom Peters and Robert Waterman in *In Search of Excellence* paint a picture of what excellence looks like and how it works. Peter Drucker assures us that these characteristics are not the provinces of lonely, half-mad individuals with flashes of genius. They are competencies that can be learned and managed. I contend that they result from applying a whole list of self-management roles, skills, and competencies from which the mini-entrepreneur draws.

As mini-entrepreneurs, we can be as innovative and creative in generating excellent products and services as the managers to whom we report. "Intrapreneurs" and product champions are not the only ones who can improve upon existing products and services. Everyone, from the machinist to the software specialist to the finance manager, who has the brainpower and imagination to make things better can get involved. Each one can make a difference in the long run by pulling America out of its productivity slump. If change and transformation are to take root, it's got to be from the bottom up, as well as from the top down, beginning with top executives.

I am continually amazed by the overemphasis placed on managers and supervisors as leverage points for success. What management consultants and executives often ignore is the other half of the equation. They assume that leadership involves injecting shots of motivation, open communication, and problem solving into the blood of their employees, hoping that some magical transformation will ensue. This by and of itself is not enough. A learning process is needed to change perceptions and perspectives, and to rid ourselves of obsolete behaviors that no longer work in the new information age.

This book will serve as a road map to success for the professional/technical individual. It includes systematic steps for becoming more entrepreneurial and innovative. Managing yourself toward these ends requires discipline, forethought, honest self-assessment, and a command of purpose that can be personally and professionally satisfying and productive to your organization. To succeed in a high-tech environment of excellence and become a mini-entrepreneur is a three-part process (which outlines the text):

Part I: Fitting into the Entrepreneurial Culture
Part II: Fine Tuning Your Power Skills
Part III: Managing for Success

To help you along in the process a number of exercises, inventories, and questionnaires have been included. If you have the time and patience to complete them, personal insight and an "A ha" experience will result. The examples of mini-entrepreneurs in action will help you recognize blind spots and reverse any counterproductive patterns. Although sections of the book are independent sources of information, the step-by-step process that unfolds is designed to help you reach an optimal level of performance.

Definitions of success are really a matter of individual choice and lifestyle. For some, success means moving up the corporate ladder into management. For others, it may mean moving laterally into a different functional area, staying in a technical area, or just living a more balanced existence between career and family. To give you a taste of high-tech success, as well as to help you along in this tough yet rewarding process, I have drawn upon the experiences of high-tech top performers: mini-entrepreneurs. These individuals have all made mistakes, but in the end have prevailed and been recognized as valuable contributors to their companies. They have made a difference, and so can you.

MARLENE SHIGEKAWA

Oakland, California
March 1987

ACKNOWLEDGMENTS

This book has truly been a collaborative effort, evolving from the work and inspiration of many. The following companies have provided interview time and contributed to the research supporting this work: Apple Computer, Cognos Corporation, Hewlett-Packard, ROLM, Signetics, and Tandem. I am grateful to the following individuals who opened doors for me at these companies: Nancy Dixon, Mary Ann Easley, Gene Godin, Anne Martin, Christie Miller, Ramesh Sekar, Dan Scharf, Richard Springs, Tom Waldrop, Lane Webster, and John Wood.

I am also appreciative of experts in the publishing field who have fine tuned this work. Phil Cecchettini, my first editor, helped conceive this work, nurtured me during the embryonic phase, and provided guidance and support. Others who aided me in this work include Hal Strauss and my current editor, Mike Hamilton from John Wiley & Sons. Mike's confidence in my work and his vision of success have made this book a reality.

Without the cooperation, openness, and candor of many high-tech people, this work would not have been possible. Their real life experiences validated existing theories and concepts and substantiated hunches. They include: Rich Abreu, Richard Brooks, Elizabeth Chew, Gordon Crompton, Nancy Dixon, Jim Ericson, Nadine Grant, Sandy Irving, Cathy Jordan, Jim Kaldem, Sherman Malone, Lloyd Mealer, Robin McKenna, Tom McQuade, Catherine

Nunes, Ralph Posmoga, Michael Potter, Bev Rindfleisch, Rob Rovetta, Dan Scharf, Richard Springs, Terry Steves, Marjorie Swiatowiec, Tom Waldrop, Laura Wilson, and John Wood.

I am especially grateful to Michael Potter, chairman and chief executive officer of Cognos Corporation, for spending interview time with me. Robert Scavullo, president of Noesis Computer Company, has generously donated computer time and photocopying facilities, and I am appreciative of his sharing of resources and enthusiasm for this work.

Last but not least, my husband, life's partner, and dearest friend, Gene Godin, helped shape and mold this work by serving as my most admirable critic.

I thank the universe for bringing us all together to exchange perspectives, learn, and share life's surprises. I have relished the journey.

M.S.

CONTENTS

SUCCEEDING IN HIGH TECH

FITTING INTO THE ENTREPRENEURIAL CULTURE

1

IN SEARCH OF THE ENTREPRENEURIAL SPIRIT

Excellence in the Corporate Culture

CULTURE SHOCK

Carol Callahan, a cost estimator, is contemplating looking for a similar job at another company. She is not completely dissatisfied with her current position nor with the company, LBT, a manufacturer of computer systems for the military. Having been in her position for four years, she feels comfortable, but she would also like a new challenge. She decides to contact a former co-worker, Craig McMillen, who recently was hired by one of the more progressively managed companies in Silicon Valley. She and Craig plan to meet for lunch at his new company.

Craig arranges an informal luncheon meeting with Jennifer, a personnel representative. Jennifer explains to Carol how she felt when she first came to this company. "I came from a very large semiconductor company. It's been a 360-degree change from there to here. I was in culture shock for my first 360 days here. People would say to me, 'OK here is what we want you to accomplish and here are your tools, now go do it.'"

Jennifer further emphasizes, "This attitude is passed down from top management to the worker. We are all told the same thing, 'Here's your job, this is what I expect, go do it.' It's a real incentive for people to be creative."

Craig joins in, "This is really shocking. I'm pretty much filling the same role I did at LBT, but I now have responsibility for the budget. So I've had to learn the accounting structure and I've become really dollar conscious. Before, at LBT, my manager would tell me to let the vice president worry about that. So here you have to have a broader view of your job."

Jennifer adds. "Here they give you a lot more flexibility to get your job done. For example, we have 'flex' hours. They don't care how long it takes to do the job, just so it gets done. People have that flexibility. They know what is expected of them, and they just go off and do it. They like that flexibility. They like that freedom."

After listening to these exciting testimonies, Carol feels attracted to this work environment, this different culture. She asks herself if she has the skills, the drive, and the willingness to succeed here. Also she wonders: "What other information about high-tech environments should I gather, not only about this company but other companies and job market trends in general? How important is understanding the corporate culture compared to my feeling satisfied and competent in a job?"

Excellent companies, including high-tech companies, give birth to and nourish the entrepreneurial spirit. The survival of high-tech companies depends on innovative and rapid change in product, technology, and competitive positioning in the marketplace. The collective efforts of committed, creative, and adaptable people make these changes possible. Company success, then, depends upon taking full advantage of its people resources by granting individuals the freedom to succeed. Change and individual career success demand taking risks and welcoming new challenges, while dealing with uncertainties. Top management expects and nurtures these qualitities of the corporate entrepreneur. Managing your career in excellent high-tech companies then means, in part, managing change—bending with the winds of ever changing business priorities, accepting sudden shifts in work goals and cutbacks in work hours, tolerating the ambiguity surrounding a first and only job role. Above all, it means job ownership, treating your job as if it were your own small business enterprise.

THE DUAL REVOLUTION: TECHNOLOGICAL AND SOCIAL

When was the last time you saw anyone using a slide rule? Or when was the last time you saw an advertisement for a key punch operator?

The explosive growth of high technology has changed dramatically and continues to impact our lives. Robots and voice synthesizers are with us now. The invention of the integrated circuit, the microchip, seriously has changed the office environment and mechanized information processing in ways that only science fiction writers thought of 15 to 20 years ago. Electronic mail decreases paper flow; personal computers become learning tools supplementing classroom training; telecommuters set up offices in their homes; and robots take over routine and hazardous jobs.

The invention of the chip in 1959 spawned a special breed of corporate innovators who have kept alive the entrepreneurial spirit. By developing a new technology, they built a new society. Now we are at a pivotal point, leaving behind an industrial society producing goods and fast becoming an information society providing services. Daniel Bell in *The Coming of Post-Industrial Society* stresses that we are shifting from manufacturing and manual occupations to service, technical, and professional occupations.

By a narrow margin, more Americans in 1970 were employed in business and professional services than in manufacturing (production of goods and construction). New information occupations include: systems analysts who design the general requirements of a data processing job or automation project; computer programmers who translate instructions into orders which computers understand; computer operators who run computers; and data entry clerks (originally key punch operators) who feed data into computers.

The computer has invaded the areas of manufacturing and design engineering and created more service and technical jobs. Previous manual record-keeping of inventory and production scheduling now is automated. So today you see help-wanted advertisements for machine shop schedulers, asking for experience with automated material requirements planning (MRP) systems and organization skills. CAD/CAM (computer-aided design and computer-aided manufacturing) is replacing manual engineering design and is forcing the design engineer to make the quantum leap from drawing board to computer terminal. This shift makes the design engineer and the drafter with computer knowledge highly employable.

These changes prompt us to ask where we are going with our increased technology and what sort of impact it is making on our professional lives. D. Bruce Merrifield, head of the Commerce Department Office of Productivity, Technology, and Innovation, contends that 90 percent of everything we know in the sciences we learned in the past 30 years. Our knowledge is going to double again in the next 10 to 15 years. What is it that technology can teach us beyond giving faster, more efficient tools and techniques for communicating data? Beyond artificial intelligence, what social technologies, such as humanistic management practices, have emerged and taken hold in the high-technology environments?

Management of all excellent companies, including high-tech companies, perhaps like women's consciousness raising groups in the 1970s, has raised its consciousness about how people want to be treated in the workplace. When it comes down to the wire, high-tech survival needs drive competition in two main arenas: developing technology and attracting, motivating, and retaining quality people. Because of these needs they try to treat their people as first-class citizens in a democratic society worthy of personal and professional growth opportunities.

A recently promoted accounting supervisor in a high-tech company expresses her personal goals for becoming an effective supervisor:

> *As a new supervisor, I want to be able to succeed at the management level. It is a real challenge to allow my people to grow and allow them a personal life outside of work. I want to make them feel that they are a valuable person both personally and on the job. If their self-esteem is good, they'll perform better.*

To make the most of their people resources, some high-tech companies are forming partnerships for excellence. These partnerships incorporate job ownership, trust in competence and job discretion, and flexibility toward achieving mutual goals. Enlightened management injects the entrepreneurial spirit into individual workers, believing that this shot in the arm will help carry the company through hard times. Other industries also practice this; it is just more obvious in high tech due to its fast-moving pace and competitive nature.

Like all trends, the high growth rate of high-technology companies is not following a linear pattern. Rapid growth eventually reaches a tipping point causing a downward slide in sales, profit, and hiring of employees. During the worst times, companies lay off employees and cut back work hours. These changes, however, do not necessarily dampen the entrepreneurial spirit; but they strengthen it. Values are not thrown out the window with layoffs, reorganization, and changes in leadership; they stick to those values which have earned them the label of excellence.

Throughout this book, the exercises will help determine your level of understanding of "excellence": those attributes associated with the excellent companies. As you complete Exercise 1-1, you will be able to assess your knowledge of management practices of excellent companies. In the course of this book, you may test this knowledge, determine how you can become personally effective, and build your high-tech career.

EXERCISE 1-1. Assessing Your Viewpoints of Excellence

DIRECTIONS: Check the response that best reflects your viewpoint. See the key at the end of this chapter for an interpretation of your answers.

1. In excellent companies, the corporate hierarchy is:
   (a) acknowledged by employees following the chain of command;
   (b) demonstrated by a distinct separation of management and labor;
   (c) deemphasized by worker participation in problem solving.

2. In excellent companies, channels of communication are:
   (a) formal with a reliance on memos, written procedures, and committees organized by executives;
   (b) informal with a vast network of open communication and a practice of keeping in touch;
   (c) one way with decision-making stemming from the top.

3. The task force in excellent companies serves the purpose of:
   (a) a longitudinal study for developing strategic plans;
   (b) enabling individuals from various functional areas to solve problems which affect the entire company (cost reduction, employee turnover, layoff policy);
   (c) achieving organizational fluidity, gathering resources for problem-solving, and treating ad hoc behavior as more normal than bureaucratic.

4. Experimentation, the willingness to try out things, in excellent companies:
   (a) comes after careful analysis and debate;
   (b) is encouraged by creating an environment and attitudes which support testing and learning;
   (c) is avoided to eliminate parallel and possibly redundant development and cost overruns.

5. In excellent companies, the responsibility for new product development falls to:
   (a) the Research and Development staff, as this is their function;
   (b) the Marketing Department, as they are most sensitive to customer needs;
   (c) a team consisting of the inventor, the entrepreneur inside the company, and the executive champions who protect others from the bureaucracy.

6. The management style in excellent companies is:
   (a) getting everyone involved and working hard to keep things simple;

EXERCISE 1-1. *(Continued)*

   (b) characterized by a reliance on numbers, hard data, and control reports;

   (c) characterized by a preoccupation with conformity to protocol and written procedures.

7. Productivity gains and financial rewards in excellent companies are achieved through:

   (a) sound fiscal control systems and elaborate automated systems;

   (b) treating people as the most important asset and respecting the individual;

   (c) control systems which hold each employee accountable for time spent during the work day.

8. Goal setting in excellent companies usually occurs:

   (a) on a one-to-one basis between boss and subordinate;

   (b) with the boss setting goals for a team;

   (c) with the team members setting realistic goals for themselves.

9. Excellent companies believe that corporate success depends:

   (a) on a company's people acting on the values stated in its corporate philosophy;

   (b) on the appropriate organizational structure;

   (c) on the administrative skills of managers.

10. The process of orienting new employees in excellent companies:

   (a) is lengthy and involves learning the technical terms of the business;

   (b) focuses on employee benefits such as medical and insurance benefits and stock option plans;

   (c) involves the sharing of the corporate philosophy and parables for success through stories, myths, and legends.

HIGH-TECH EXCELLENCE

Let's take a closer look at the makings of excellent high-tech companies. Not all high-tech companies can be considered excellent, but companies that have earned this label have certain common characteristics. Even though slumps in the high-tech industry have resulted in layoffs, there are some important lessons to be learned from excellent companies.

Their need to stay competitive in the marketplace forces companies to stay innovative both in product design and organizational development. The characteristics that earn a company a label of "excellence" are true for any company, not just high tech. To create an environment responsive to customer and employee needs, they cultivate a breeding ground for mini-entre-preneurs.

By decentralizing authority and responsibility, the company gives employ-ees opportunities to give their personal best to the team with rewards for doing so. Job ownership results in both pride in workmanship and an esprit de corps, which lay the groundwork for a culture of excellence. This nurtur-ing of the entrepreneurial spirit produces qualitative and quantitative differ-ences in productivity and services. Qualitative differences, sometimes immea-surable in the short run, are the building blocks of a culture of excellence.

The corporate philosophy of ROLM, a Silicon Valley company, fosters a "great place to work" reputation in order to attract and motivate the best and brightest people. To give credence to this "great place to work" slogan, the company designed an environment conducive to creativity—partitioned of-fices, a recreation center with pool and tennis courts. This company, as well as other excellent companies, through the environment breed a personally effective individual worker, the mini-entrepreneur.

What Are Mini-Entrepreneurs?

Before breaking down the meaning of excellence, let's define the term, "mini-entrepreneur." Similar to the entrepreneurs who take risks starting a new business, mini-entrepreneurs work within corporations to invent new methods, open new channels of communications, and work as teams to accomplish group goals. Instead of starting new businesses, they overhaul and fine-tune them by thinking of their job as if it were their own small business. With a vision of a better product and a better world, mini-entrepre-neurs use brainpower to push themselves to excel, grow, and succeed.

Their work takes on greater meaning that just a paycheck. A couple of mini-entrepreneurs tell it in their own words:

> Your concentration eight hours a day is these products. Socializing is talking about the products. Unlike other places, we don't spend five hours working and three hours taking a coffee break.

> There's a feeling of we're going to make it or break it, and we're going to make it. Everyone wants to be successful.

> There's a desire here for quality products. Everyone wants us to be the best.

You will be able to get a more detailed picture of the mini-entrepreneur in Chapter 2.

What Is Excellence?

Employees and management consultants provide two perspectives of excel-lence. Management consultants define excellence in terms of innovation, financial performance, and employee benefits or opportunities for professional growth. What is significant at this point in the evolution of American business is the shift from heavy reliance on concrete, quantitative data, such as profits as a sole measure of success, to human resource practices, the people side of business. After all, business is first and foremost a human activity, so it seems natural to come to this conclusion: businesses are created by humans for human benefit.

As defined in *In Search of Excellence*, Tom Peters and Robert Waterman link excellence to the capability of remaining continuously innovative and keeping close to the customer. Innovation is the ability to respond and adapt to changes in the environment, customer needs, employee needs, skills of competitors, and government regulations. In other words, the key to excellence is a culture which fosters innovation. The secret to an innovative culture lies in shared values passed down from corporate leaders over time.

Rosabeth Kanter Moss in *The Change Masters* uses a different set of criteria to define excellence. Emphasizing participative work systems, she describes innovation as the degree to which opportunity to use power effectively is granted or withheld from individuals.

For her survey, she selected 47 progressive companies based on implementing systems and applying practices to people such as effective human resource systems, participatory workplace alternatives, and affirmative action programs. Kanter Moss stresses that company success depends on allowing the entrepreneurial spirit to flourish. Similar to Peters and Waterman, the survey found that the companies with reputations for progressive human resource practices were significantly higher in long-term profitability and financial growth.

Employees judge excellence according to pay, fringe benefits, work environment, job security, and opportunities to grow professionally. For some employees the opportunity to grow outweighs job security. An employee of an excellent high-tech company explains her signposts of excellence:

> It's an opportunity to grow and an opportunity to fail. An opportunity to grow means that a company cares enough about you as a person to let you expand to your potential. It's allowing you to make a change commensurate with what you want to do, what you've learned and where you want to go.
>
> Having an opportunity to fail means that they give you an environment where you feel comfortable taking risks. If you don't take risks and you don't make mistakes, you don't learn. A lot of companies require such a high level of approval to do a project that you never get the opportunity to do it.

Sudden financial reverses and changes in top leadership affect attitudes toward the company. This is unavoidable. One employee explains how attitudes can change during the worst of times:

When the whole company changes and you've got best friends that were laid off and you are with a completely new group, you wonder if it is all worth it. A lot of people got caught up in saying, "It's not fun anymore. It's not the old company." Some of those people left.

How these companies deal with their people during hard times uphold their stature of excellence. Constant communication about the reasons for change, generous severance pay, and outplacement efforts soften the blow. One employee explains:

The company did a really good job of explaining to us the company's objectives. They needed to reduce operating expenses. Because most employees have ownership in the company via stock or bonus plans, they want to give back to the company.

Of all my friends that got laid off, I haven't heard a negative comment. The company had an outplacement service with resume writing and career consultant. They had other companies come in and interview the laid-off people. A lot of people saw it as an opportunity go do other things.

The company kept us informed about changes before they hit the press.

Mini-entrepreneurs know that their companies will experience low growth periods. Respecting people during the worst of times makes up the acid test of excellence.

ELEMENTS OF AN ENTREPRENEURIAL CULTURE

Let's find out what makes up an entrepreneurial culture or a culture of excellence. Figure 1-1 highlights a culture of excellence.

Shared Values

Shared values, like glue, hold together all operational aspects of the business during the worst of times as well as during the best of times. In the high-tech entrepreneurial culture, the means, "the way we do things around here," are as important as the ends (productivity and profitability). This is true for all organizations regardless of cultural type. Some companies just do a better job of articulating their shared values.

At the heart of shared values stands a belief that everyone will do the best possible job with their capabilities, given the right opportunities. Without this trust, individuals would not be given the leverage or the freedom to

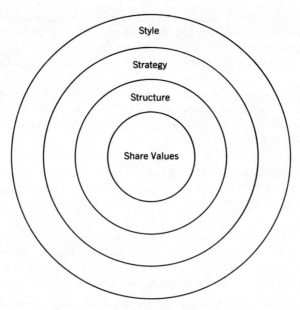

FIGURE 1-1. Dynamics of an Entrepreneurial Culture.

accomplish things, and with it, they will. The formula that follows reflects how trust in people relates to results:

$$\frac{\text{People} + \text{Respect}}{\text{Technology}} = \frac{\text{Innovation}}{\text{Quality}}$$

This formula for hard humanism is currently driving certain companies toward excellence. Michael Potter is Chairman and Chief Executive Officer of Cognos Corporation, an international software company with an annual growth rate of 40 percent over the last several years, and he reveals this trust: "Here we are working with machines, yet our chief assets are people and brainpower. We are anything but an organization of machines. We have been successful because we have relied on our people." Furthermore this formula stirs up a sense of mutuality, of give and take, as witnessed in profit-sharing plans of many high-tech companies. After all, what's good for the company is good for the employee and vice versa. Given the right opportunities and incentives, people will give their personal best.

During the best times, profit sharing within the high-tech entrepreneurial culture makes the hard side of humanism visible. Splitting the bounty of success yields two messages: results are rewarded; and we need everyone's expertise and effort to be successful. The reward system of pay incentives provides the structure and reinforces shared values, belief in positive outcomes, and belief in rewarding winners. So granting freedom to individuals, in turn, creates a sense of internal competition, a striving for personal excellence. Trust, accountability, and giving time and attention to mini-entrepreneurs make things happen. They reinforce one another.

Transmitting Values

Real leverage within the high-tech entrepreneurial culture stems from building from the top down and bottom up. In other words, management attempts to clue people in on what really counts and to value everyone's contribution regardless of formal rank. Without top down—bottom up flow of power, top management would just be paying lip service to shared values. Instead of coercing people into complying with standards of conduct, they give them breathing space to identify with shared values. For example, ROLM's corporate philosophy states that it does its best to maintain an entrepreneurial spirit and to avoid bureaucracy through broad decentralization of responsibility and authority. ROLM believes this is the only environment that provides the individual freedom required for creative thinking and rapid response to the changing needs of the markeplace. To reinforce the entrepreneurial aspect, new employees experience a six-week orientation, during which new employee meet various managers on a one-to-one basis. They also meet the company president. Top and bottom ranks make contact ensuring socialization and learning the ropes. Shared values infiltrate every aspect of organizational life from formal training, to celebrations, to circulation of divisional goals to the lowest level.

An employee of a high-tech company which manufacturers mainframe computers reveals just how top management gains employee commitment by stepping off the management pedestal:

> Managers don't assume that they have all the right answers. When working with their employees, they don't say, "Go do it this way." They let them do it their own way.
>
> That's one way of acknowledging fallibility from the top. I've seen the president acknowledge fallibility. They set an example by showing humility. Here might doesn't make right. That's because management and people in the company are all the same. Nobody is more or less important. The CEO has a job like anybody else in the company. Our company philosophy states that everyone has a right to fail and not be considered a failure.

Not everyone, however, can perform effectively with so much job freedom. For some, the lack of structure and absence of formal authority creates a disorientation and discomfort resulting in an inability to adapt to this environment. As one product marketing manager put it, "You either buy into these values, or you leave." But withdrawal leaves behind an even more potent body of mini-entrepreneurs.

Conversely, companies that pay lip service to people orientation, do not communicate face to face with workers. They give directives or chastise through memo writing. They withhold information from their employees as a means of keeping control rather than sharing information and brainpower to be innovative.

In excellent companies, people are given the benefit of the doubt. They are trusted and seen as desirous and capable of succeeding along with the company. They are given a long leash to question; for by questioning the usual way of doing things, the spirit of innovation prevails. Listen to Brook Tierney, a sales program developer for a high-tech company:

> *Our credo to the public is that we want to be a technology leader. In order to do that we need innovative people with new ideas. There are no stupid ideas. To make things better you've got to question why things are done a certain way. You can't accept the statement, "We're doing it this way, because we've always done it this way." That just breeds stagnation. I don't accept that answer. It's part of the culture to question. You know you're not going to get in trouble for doing so. You know you've not going to be labeled a trouble-maker or rebel rouser.*
>
> *The spirit of innovation is valued here. What is innovation? It's often questioning to make things better.*

Table 1-1 compares traditional business values and those influencing excellent high-tech companies.

STRUCTURE

High-tech companies create an environment nourishing creativity and innovation while maintaining a coherence to stay competitive in the marketplace. Including workers on all levels, the accounting clerk to the engineering design manager, makes this possible. Joint problem solving and decision making serve the dual purpose of meeting company goals and developing mini-entrepreneurs.

While excellent companies attempt to include all parties in decision making, no organization is devoid of elitism. Undoubtedly you have seen certain people gain status and carte blanche to do as they please. The connection between their special knowledge, innovations, and ideas and the bottom line gives them an elite status. This is true for engineers in high tech, actuaries in insurance, and authors in publishing.

TABLE 1-1

A Comparison of Traditional Business Values and New Values

Assumptions Underlying Traditional Business Values	Assumptions Underlying New Values
People to fit jobs, rigidity.	Jobs to fit people. Form and flow.
Imposed goals, top-down decision making.	Autonomy encouraged. Self-actualization.
Hierarchy, bureaucracy.	Worker participation, democratization. Shared goals, consensus.
Fragmentation, compartmentalization in work and roles. Emphasis on specialized tasks. Sharply defined job descriptions.	Cross-fertilization by specialists seeing wider relevance of their field of expertise. Choice and change in job roles encouraged.
Aggression, competition, "Business is business."	Cooperation. Human values transcend "winning."
Struggle for stability, station, security.	Sense of change, becoming. Willingness to risk. Entrepreneurial attitude.
Quantitative quotas, status symbols, level of income, profits, "raises," Gross National Product, tangible assets.	Qualitative as well as quantitative. Sense of achievement, mutual effort for mutual enrichment. Value intangible assets (creativity, fulfillment) as well as tangible.
Polarized: labor versus management, consumer versus manufacturer, etc.	Transcends polarities. Shared goals, values.
Centralized operations.	Decentralized operations wherever possible. Human scale.
Runaway, unbridled technology. Subservience to technology	Appropriate technology Technology as tool, not tyrant.

Adapted with permission from Marilyn Ferguson, *The Aquarian Conspiracy: Personal and Social Transformation in the 1980's.* Los Angeles: J.P. Tarcher, 1980.

Smashing the Pyramid

Top management in excellent companies is restructuring its environment by smashing the pyramid. This outdated structure, in use since the turn of the century, represents the division of labor and hierarchical management. The high-tech environment rejects the rigid hierarchy, because it thwarts creative energies; it obstructs the information flow. A participative management style replaces the pyramid for better exchange of information and resources. People, regardless of level and department, are thrown together in project teams to discuss common problems. Michael Potter, Chairman and Chief Executive Officer of Cognos Corporation, affirms his faith in his employees when he tells them, "You're the ones who know your jobs the best, so go ahead and work on your ideas." Borrowing from Peter Drucker, he points out, "The one question which we need to continually ask our people is, 'How can we make you more effective in your job?'" He emphatically points out that, "We attribute our success to the fact that our people have come up with new ideas and have made them work. We just provide a supportive environment." The participative management style then becomes a matter of survival, a solution for confronting a turbulent internal and external environment.

Team Play

In many high-tech companies, teams enable both individual and organization to be nimble, to remain responsive and adaptive to their environment. The formation of a team depends on how it is generated. For example, a team may include people from engineering, marketing, and manufacturing with a goal of product development. The customer's name often identifies it: The Atari Team, the H-P Team, The Coleco Team. These product teams meet on a regular basis to discuss product status relative to customer needs. However, an identified problem resulting from a product team meeting can generate a corrective action team, which is organized on an impromptu and temporary basis. Reflecting the organization's quick reaction time, these autonomous and adaptive work teams encourage the mini-entrepreneur to remain innovative in problem solving and decision making.

One team that developed a prototype for a personal computer was given the freedom to innovate and the privacy to create by working in a separate facility. As if in a cocoon, they built cohesiveness and linked brainpower, eventually emerging with their new product. The Jolly Roger that flew over their building was the symbol of the team's modus operandi—"acting like pirates outside of corporate law."

However, drawbacks to team cohesiveness occur when power is unequally distributed, as one manager explains:

Organizationally speaking, we weren't as effective as we could have been. We had our chairman of the board also acting as a vice president of an operating division. So he pretty much got his own way. He had created a special sort of environment with that division. It created a lot of jealousy. They got preferential treatment, and it really alienated other groups.

So when they decided to reorganize and got rid of the two divisions, it became easier to work.

The danger of excessive team cohesiveness will be discussed further in Chapter 7.

Strategy

Strategy is a company's planned actions in response to or in anticipation of changes to its external environment such as customers and competitors. It includes an analysis of the external environment, competition, customer needs, and the company's strengths and weaknesses in achieving goals. By definition high-tech companies are dynamic; product life cycles are short, technology changes, and position in the marketplace is precarious. They usually devote time and attention to long-range planning for a five-year period or more, based on a tight fit between customer needs and company capabilities and resources. This proactive stance attempts to minimize a reactive posture later on.

The driving forces of experimentation and internal competition keep high-tech companies adaptive, innovative, and consequently, competitive by encouraging mini-entrepreneurs to play to win. At Data General, as described by Tracy Kidder in *Soul Of A New Machine*, this game is called "competition for resources." The president of Data General, Ed de Castro, likes to stir up competition among teams, which he believes leads to sorting out bad ideas and eliminating ideas that don't work. He prefers testing the product inside the company instead of using the customer. This games encourages mini-entrepreneurs to keep on their toes and be innovative.

Other companies (IBM, Hewlett-Packard, Digital, Wang), also create internal competition. The reasoning behind the strategy stems from the laws of probability. In other words, as you increase your number of experiments, you inevitably increase your successes. This is how innovative companies increase their chances for a success, and how they are able to convince mini-entrepreneurs to take risks. The environment, more than the individual, makes the biggest difference in the amount of innovative activity.

By-products of internal competition become opportunities for the individual entrepreneur, the chance to test, learn, and fail or succeed. Tolerance of mistakes and unexpected changes is part of the strategy. An unspoken belief in the entrepreneurial culture implies that "It is better to have tried and failed than to not have taken the risk." This is the up side. The down side of this strategy conveys the message, "But you better make darn sure that you don't repeat the same mistake."

Structure, strategy, and shared values overlap, creating the dynamics of the entrepreneurial culture. With structure and strategy interlocking, style activates the social machinery, the culture.

Style

How managers spend their time and the kind of symbolic behavior they display is a measure of an organization's style. An entrepreneurial culture then is reflected in management's behavior. An employee from an entrepreneurial culture explains: "The executive vice presidents are always walking the halls and asking what's going on and what are the issues."

Theories of management style can be explained quite simply in terms of the differences between two concerns: the concern for people and the concern for productivity. Robert Blake and Jane Mouton, in *The Managerial Grid*, illustrate various styles of achieving productivity through people. Earlier, this chapter introduced the participative management style. The grid in Figure 1-2 gives you a sense of what participation means by displaying management theories emerging in the late 1950s. The first dimension is the concern for productivity, which means achieving a result directly or through workers. The second dimension is concern for the worker as a human being. The third dimension summarizes the manager's beliefs when the first two concerns come together in varying degrees.

Top management in excellent high-tech companies tries to integrate and balance concern for people with concern for production. One channel for addressing "people needs," (finding out what people have on their minds) is an informal communication network. An informal communication system eliminates barriers between top management and the worker on the shop floor. Senior managers make time to find out what is really happening. At Digital Equipment, the chief executive meets regularly with an engineering committee of people from all levels. At ROLM and Cognos, the presidents are available to meet with employees at their requests.

Opportunities for informal communication occur in various places throughout the company and carry a flavor of "Let's hash it out." A tolerance for locking horns and a committment to problem solving drive behavior. Andrew Grove, president of Intel, describes it as a "confrontation-oriented management style," meaning bluntness and straightforwardness.

Getting out of the office and keeping in touch is also part of the informal communications network. At Hewlett-Packard (H-P) they call it MBWA— Management By Wandering Around. The physical surroundings invite infor-

How Managers Think

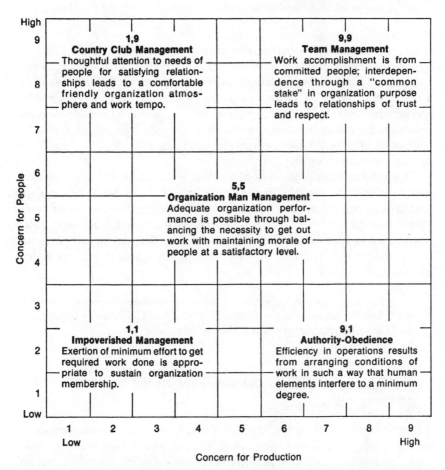

FIGURE 1-2. The Managerial Grid. *Source*: Robert R. Blake and Jane S. Mouton. *The Managerial Grid III*. Houston, TX: Gulf Publishing Co., 1985, p. 12.

mal exchanges with an excess of conference rooms with blackboards for problem solving. At ROLM and Tandem, the recreation facilities such as tennis courts, swimming pools, and a gym allow for casual yet meaningful and worthwhile exchanges.

Craig McMillen, a project coordinator, explains how he made contact and actually solved a problem in the dressing room of the recreation center.

There are all sorts of ways of communicating around here. Not just in meetings.
I bumped into my project manager in the "Rec" center and we struck up a

conversation in the shower of all places. We actually got to be friends after that, and it was much easier for me to get the information I needed to get my job done.

In the entrepreneurial culture, management makes people feel like they are winners by rewarding them with more than a paycheck or bonus. They give recognition and chances to celebrate. At Tandem, outstanding employees win a weekend trip to New Orleans, Hawaii, or Canada. At ROLM, assembly workers are rewarded for extra effort to meet a deadline by a celebration and unlimited amounts of ice cream on the shop floor. At Signetics, as part of the Corporate Quality Program, employees celebrate a "Z−D Day," for "zero defects standard of quality."

This informal atmosphere is casual but not relaxed, for mini-entrepreneurs are held accountable for their performance. Craig McMillen explains that he was hired because he was considered a "driver," saying, "whatever it takes to get the job done, I'll do it." Underneath this informal atmosphere lies a style carried out to maximize innovation. Tony Scarsdale, a sales program manager for a manufacturer of personal computers, points out how style is perpetuated:

Everyone here is top notch. They are worth much more than any single person at the top. The culture is in the people. This is achieved by a kind of organizational breeding. People hire others that are like them.

ENTREPRENEURIALISM AND INDIVIDUAL RESPONSIBILITY

Excellent high-tech companies create an environment intertwining structure, strategy, style, and shared values in such a way that it empowers the mini-entrepreneur. It enables that person to become personally effective in achieving both individual and organizational goals. Having laid the groundwork for people to succeed, companies affirm a hard humanism. This humanism pushes individuals to stand up and be counted as valuable contributors and also holds them accountable for results. This environment takes advantage of a natural inclination to be creative, to problem solve, and to succeed.

Knowledge Power Versus Position Power

Participative management creates high expectations of workers on all levels. Due to the absence of a rigid hierarchical structure and formal communications systems, the mini-entrepreneur must rely on building cooperative working relationships with peers inside and outside the home department. By crossing organizational boundaries, mini-entrepreneurs become knowledge workers with knowledge power (information, resources, materials) as opposed to having position power (supervisory, managerial title). An expansion of roles for the boss and the employee accompanies rising expectations.

A growing number of managers prefer to be catalysts or developers of people rather than just power wielders, for the real power lies in these qualities. Assuming the role of team leader or coach, the manager motivates mini-entrepreneurs by explaining team plans and goals as opposed to using formal authority that turns requests into demands. This shift in management style can be disconcerting to those who prefer to remain dependent on the traditional boss. They would rather be passive than take on new responsibilities or create their own work plans, which can frustrate the manager who is no longer a traditional boss but a member of the team.

Top management can humanize the workplace and create semi-autonomous work teams, but the individual must be willing to develop personally and to acquire the knowledge and interpersonal skills needed to function as a mini-entrepreneur.

Interpersonal Know-How

As traditional notions of power use change, the importance of interpersonal skills and personal effectiveness increases. In traditional companies, lines of authority are clear, tasks are specific, and the chain of command sets in motion decision making. However in excellent high-tech companies, mini-entrepreneurs deal with vague assignments, overlapping territories, uncertain authority and resources, and a team orientation to reaching goals.

Mini-entrepreneurs are able to overcome obstacles, open new channels, and develop positive working relationships by sharing new concepts and a common language which link various departments rather than separates them. The mini-entrepreneur relies less on technical know-how and more on personal effectiveness to build bridges of understanding in reaching common objectives.

Marta Dunlap, operating under severe deadlines in her new job in customer marketing, takes the time to build positive working relationships with her new coworkers. In gathering technical information to write sales brochures, she is highly dependent on others. She explains how she relies on her interpersonal influence.

> *Right now I am in a sticky situation because I don't have the time to get to know people I am working with on this project. So I have to use every bit of poise, grace, and convincing to get along well with people who have never dealt with*

me before in order to pull information from them. What I am asking them to do is not in their job description, and they are already overloaded with work from their boss. What I try to do is to show them what's in it for them. So I'll show them my first draft and ask them to tell me where I am off target.

Only those who are aware of the dynamics of the workplace, connected to others by mutual respect and motivated to achieve common goals, can make a contribution to the company and feel fulfilled in the process.

CONCLUSION

The culture shock of moving from a traditionally run company to one managed like excellent companies so much in the news these days can be awesome. The dynamics and requirements of the marketplace have made high-tech companies the breeding ground for entrepreneurialism, but this phenomenon is not restricted to such organizations. Managers in increasing numbers of companies in an array of fields are realizing that management style affects productivity. The internal company entrepreneurial spirit may have begun in high tech, but it is now appearing all over.

Four elements make up an entrepreneurial culture: shared values, structure, strategy, and style. They overlap and interact to create an atmosphere in which people can work to their potential and create the best products, working environment, and company possible. How you can benefit from this environment and contribute the most to your company makes up the rest of this book.

ANSWERS TO EXERCISE 1-1. Assessing Your Viewpoints of Excellence

DIRECTIONS: Check the space to the left of the answer that corresponds to your response for each of the 10 items. For example, if your response to item 1 was "a," place a check beside "1a". When you have checked all the items, add the number of checks and write the total for each category in the "total" line.

Category A	Category B	Category C
_____ 1c	_____ 1a	_____ 1b
_____ 2b	_____ 2a	_____ 2c
_____ 3c	_____ 3b	_____ 3a

ANSWERS TO EXERCISE 1-1. *(Continued)*

Category A	Category B	Category C
_____ 4b	_____ 4a	_____ 4c
_____ 5c	_____ 5b	_____ 5a
_____ 6a	_____ 6b	_____ 6c
_____ 7b	_____ 7a	_____ 7c
_____ 8c	_____ 8b	_____ 8a
_____ 9a	_____ 9c	_____ 9b
_____ 10c	_____ 10a	_____ 10b
_____ Total	_____ Total	_____ Total

Scoring Interpretation:

Category A: If you scored 7–10 points, congratulations, you have a thorough comprehension of the management practices of excellent companies.

Category B: If you scored 7–10 points, you have made a good beginning of acquainting yourself with the workings of the excellent companies, but you need to dig more to thoroughly comprehend their characteristics.

Category C: If you scored 7–10 points, you have a considerable amount of research ahead. This includes more reading, discussing the ideas presented with individuals who are employed in excellent high-tech companies, and observing management practices in your own company.

PORTRAIT OF A MINI-ENTREPRENEUR
Trying Harder and Succeeding More

BEYOND TECHNICAL KNOW-HOW

Larry Buxton has written new business proposals for an excellent company in Silicon Valley for three years. After graduating with a Bachelor of Science degree in electrical engineering, he worked in an engineering design area for another company. He decided to change jobs to broaden his experience.

Stan Leland, a newly hired engineer also with a Bachelor of Science degree in electrical engineering, works in the same area as Larry. He approaches Larry for some advice because Stan feels frustrated by his attempts to get technical information from one of the software engineers.

STAN: I just asked Jim to give me some design information on the Phantom system, and he spills out this technical jargon, half of which I don't understand and I don't need for the proposal I'm writing.

LARRY: Listen Stan, don't feel bad. When I first came into this job, I faced the same problem.

STAN: Oh really. Well how did you deal with it?

LARRY: When I felt that Jim was talking over my head, I listened patiently. Then later I got one of the systems engineers, Kate, who I know works well with Jim, to sit in on another meeting with Jim and me. They discussed the design requirements and I just sat there, took notes and listened for key words that I wanted to use in the proposal. When we left the meeting with Jim, I asked Kate to write a synopsis of what was said. When I got that synopsis, I read it from layman's point of view to see if it would be understandable to others.

STAN: So essentially what you did to handle the situation was to use Kate as an interpreter for you.

LARRY: Yes, you need everyone's help to get the proposal written. It's a team effort especially in our job. You also need to rely on your communication skills.

STAN: Nobody ever told me that when I was in engineering school. I though I could depend on my technical expertise to solve problems and get the job done. It seems the more I find out things, the more I need to learn.

As Stan returns to his desk he begins to wonder about what other competencies he needs to learn to become as effective as Larry.

Top performers within excellent high-tech environments can be considered mini-entrepreneurs. They work at all corporate levels and within all areas, manufacturing, finance, human resources, engineering. It is not where they work that is so significant but how they use their personal power, their personal effectiveness. They use it to propel themselves forward and upward by taking risks, being innovative, and managing themselves and others. In the final analysis, the more entrepreneurial you become, the more effective you become as a human being. Let's begin pinpointing the characteristics, work behavior, and values of mini-entrepreneurs.

To begin, you can first assess your knowledge of mini-entrepreneurial practices by completing Exercise 2-1. This inventory can serve as a self-assessment tool for determining your skill level relative to the competencies of mini-entrepreneurs. It can also be used as a communication tool for seeking feedback from coworkers and your supervisor. You may ask these individuals to rate you, and then you can compare the two sets of ratings.

Although it will take some time to complete this inventory, your responses will be helpful to you in understanding the ideas proposed throughout this book and relating them to your specific situation. Also, it will help you gain insight into your specific strengths and areas for improvement as they relate to high-tech excellence. Time devoted to this exercise now will benefit you later, as you continue to build upon this knowledge.

EXERCISE 2-1. Mini-Entrepreneurial Skills Inventory

DIRECTIONS: Complete this exercise to identify your strongest skills and those which need further development. Rate yourself based on your own self-perceptions and feedback you have received from others. There are no right or wrong answers. Rate yourself as honestly and accurately as you can using the following rating scale.

```
5 = OUTSTANDING SKILLS

4 = A STRENGTH

3 = AVERAGE SKILLS

2 = BELOW AVERAGE SKILLS

1 = LEAST SKILLED AREA
```

	RATING
1. Setting reachable job goals.	
2. Asking the right questions to get the answers needed.	
3. Analyzing a situation and identifying the important issues.	
4. Questioning the usual way of doing things.	
5. Actively listening to others.	
6. Helping others to see mutual interests and goals.	
7. Assuming new tasks beyond normal job duties.	

EXERCISE 2-1. *(Continued)*

	RATING
8. Outlining action steps for achieving results within time frames.	
9. Resolving conflicts between yourself and others.	
10. Explaining another person's viewpoint to others.	
11. Informing other team members of information that may help them.	
12. Reality checking suggestions and new ideas of others.	
13. Researching new methods, procedures, and concepts to be applied on the job.	
14. Implementing new concepts and ideas despite adversity.	
15. Identifying my strengths and weaknesses and outlining steps for improvement.	
16. Establishing priorities after reaching agreement with others.	
17. Initiating corrective action as problems arise.	
18. Enabling others to see my vision using terms that are attractive to them.	
19. Pinpointing the needs and objectives of others.	

EXERCISE 2-1. *(Continued)*

	RATING
20. Working jointly with others inside and outside my work unit to accomplish a task.	
21. Talking yourself into taking limited risks.	
22. Identifying potential obstacles to reaching goals.	
23. Anticipating problems before they occur.	
24. Diagnosing a situation and maintaining an objective viewpoint by seeing all sides of the problem.	
25. Communicating effectively with people within various departments and at different organizational levels.	
26. Observing the work behavior of others to collect data and draw conclusions.	
27. Using language (metaphors, stories, and examples) familiar to the listener.	
28. Negotiating agreements within a group.	
29. Keeping a balance between concern for people and concern for production.	
30. Taking action on my own authority without asking permission.	
31. Introducing new ideas and projects that are precedent setting and represent concept leaps.	

EXERCISE 2-1. *(Continued)*

	RATING
32. Gaining the support of others for my project.	
33. Adapting to changing priorities and circumstances beyond my control.	
34. Envisioning the end product/result before the project begins and communicating the vision to others.	
35. Sharing the responsibility and credit for tasks or projects.	

Now turn to the end of this chapter for an interpretation of your results.

THE EVOLUTION OF MINI-ENTREPRENEURSHIP

Now that you have had a chance to assess your entrepreneurial skill level, let's trace the evolution of the mini-entrepreneur. In Chapter 1 you were introduced to the high-tech environment and the dynamics of the entrepreneurial culture. Now you will be able to gain a broader perspective of both the changing business world and the characteristic behaviors and values that make up the new breed of workers, the mini-entrepreneurs.

What whirlwind of social forces produced the mini-entrepreneur? Three intertwining social and economic currents evolving over the last 30 to 40 years have changed the face of American business, revolutionized technology, and handed over power to the worker: the microelectronics revolution, the shift from an industrial society to an information society, and the emerging new breed of worker. We have already reviewed briefly the history of the microelectronics revolution in Chapter 1, as well as recognized the coming of an information society. An understanding of the evolution of a new breed of worker will show you that mini-entrepreneurs are like ripe fruit, waiting to be plucked by employers in an information society. The marriage of entrepreneurialism and high technology produced a new breed of worker whose values are rooted in the counterculture of the 1960s. The new breed, the mini-entrepreneur, rose out of the ashes of the human potential movement. With their birth arrived a revised work ethic. The values of mini-entrepreneurs lie at the core of the entrepreneurial culture. In understanding how their values evolved, you can match your career values with those of the entrepreneurial culture.

A Baby-Boomer Lineage

Social analysts, futurists, and management consultants point out that we are experiencing an entrepreneurial explosion that is probably related to the "baby boomers," the large number of children born between 1946–1965 constitutes a "megageneration." The term was coined by John Naisbitt in *Megatrends*. By 1990, they will make up one-third of the total population. In the 1960s some baby boomers were in college and demonstrated a strong anticorporate feeling on issues related to the environment, civil rights, and Vietnam. Much of this anticorporate feeling was buried during the 1970s as graduates went to work in corporations. Within the corporation, the baby boomers were saving money, learning about operating a business, and planning to become entrepreneurs, as the thought of their 1960s independence lingered in their minds. The number of executives who moved from big to small firms doubled during the last half of the 1970s. This shift was reportedly accompanied by greater job satisfaction and more independence.

Entrepreneurialism, like an epidemic, spread throughout the high-tech industry as risk takers left secure jobs to start their own companies. Figure 2-1 demonstrates spin-off patterns and lines of ancestry linking "mother" company to "spawned" company. Although this family tree of entrepreneurs uses high-tech examples, the phenomenon is not limited to such companies.

From Individual to Shared Values

The values and beliefs of corporate executives who founded and are currently heading high-tech companies are rooted in the values of the post-World War II generation, the baby boomers. These leaders are shaping a new corporate culture and becoming role models for others inside and outside the corporation. They are paving the way for the next generation, the mini-entrepreneurs, and are giving them the same independence, worker rights, and sense of personal power that they were seeking in the 1960s. In 1973 Jim Treybig, president and chief executive officer of Tandem Computers and a former marketing manager at Hewlett-Packard, founded Tandem and lured other Hewlett-Packard employees to his company. With humanistic values, they constructed a people-oriented environment with a company swimming pool, flexible hours, and a participative management program. In *Business Week* (July 14, 1980), Treybig at age 39, states, "The human side of the company is most important to make the $1 billion mark." Lee Felsenstein, designer of the

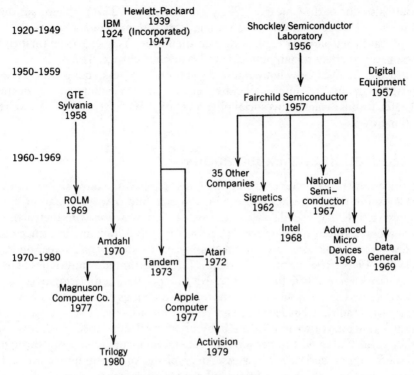

FIGURE 2-1. Lines of High-Tech Ancestry.

Osborne computer, was also designer of the bullhorns for "Stop the Draft Week" in 1967.

This counterculture engineer, Lee Felsenstein, and others of the Homebrew Computer Club with antiwar, antiestablishment attitudes of the 1960s, set in motion a revolution of computers built by people for people. Believing that computers should be used for, not against people, they spawned several companies such as Northstar, Vector Graphics, and Apple, and their computer-to-the-people movement carried over into the free and open exchange of technical information among companies and an informal management style.

The most dramatic example of this shift in values is Jerry Rubin, one of the Chicago 7. A 1960s activist and Yippie, he led thousands of youths to the streets, rioting at the 1968 Democratic National Convention. A converted entrepreneur, he established his own stock brokerage and has entered the entertainment business, performing with his former compatriot, Abbie Hoffman, also one of the Chicago 7. They call their show "The Yippie versus the Yuppie." Through humorous bantering, Jerry Rubin accounts for his philosophical turnaround by explaining that the former Yippies lacked financial resources to effect social, political, and economic change. Today thousands of former Yippies, now baby-boom generation Yuppies (Young Urban Professionals), have become small entrepreneurs and the genuine heroes of the 1980s. Rubin explains this social phenomenon, "We haven't sold out, we're taking over."

Education and Expectations

Baby boomers are better educated than their parents and have higher expectations for their careers. Those who did not find a work situation that supported their values displayed a sense of dissatisfaction with their work. Opinion Research Corporation (an Arthur D. Little company in Princeton, New Jersey), conducted a survey of employee attitudes over a 25-year period (1950–1975). They uncovered a major shift in the attitudes and values of the U.S. work force. Their findings confirm the speculation that employees are discontented and that they expect more from their jobs now than they have in the past. Traditional incentives to get people to work—security, fear, sense of duty—don't carry weight for the baby boomers. Unlike their predecessors, they value and expect to get intrinsic satisfaction from their work through respect, equity, and responsiveness. An employee of an entrepreneurial culture expresses it this way: "I think all people work for recognition. A lot of people work for money, but another one of our top priorities is recognition. That way we still all strive to do better."

Workers at all levels, not only managers, are openly demanding that their needs for achievement, recognition, and job challenge be met. The well-educated baby boomers have revived the spirit of individualism by questioning dogmatic thinking and authority. Perry Pascarella in *The New Achievers* comments on the extent of their personal search: "Even in the recession years of the early 1980s, people who were beginning careers sought employment with companies that had a reputation of offering an opportunity for self-fulfillment." In short, workers are asking to be treated as human beings with brainpower, not just machines with horsepower.

CORPORATE CULTURE WITH BABY-BOOMER APPEAL

For the most part, the founders of high-tech companies established in the 1970s are living out baby-boomer values. Through their efforts to retain quality employees, corporate founders have built organizations to meet individual needs and values. Steve Wozniak and Steve Jobs, founders of Apple Computer, made history not only with the wizardry of their personal computer but also with their sense of social responsibility. Through a bill passed by the California legislature, Steve Jobs has given a computer to every school in the state. Steve Wozniak organized a rock concert with the theme of UNISON (Unite Us in Song), called the US Festival, aimed at bringing music and technology together. Other high-tech companies demonstrate their loyalty to the individual employee through certain established policies: a no-layoff policy at IBM, Hewlett-Packard, and Digital Equipment Corporation and retraining for employees at IBM and Hewlett-Packard. Succeeding generations of entrepreneurs fostered an informal management style and a playground for high achievers. The difference between Data General and Digital Equipment, according to *Forbes* magazine, can be seen in the "hippie long hair" of some of Data General's top brass. At Data General, Tom West, a project manager, compares the addictive feeling attached to creating a computer to playing pinball, "You win one game and you get to play another."

Management practices at companies in Silicon Valley follow suit with some nontraditional touches. When Renn Zaphiropoulos was president of Versatic, now a subsidiary of Xerox, employees dined at his home on a meal that he prepared. If you were a member of the task force that created the MacIntosh at Apple Computer, your signature is enscribed in the casing of each computer.

Appealing to values baby-boomer values, the corporate leader provides recognition for mini-entrepreneurs making them feel a part of a shared vision and a valuable contributor in making it a reality. In describing the attributes of a great leader, Steve Jobs asserts: "Leadership is having a vision, being able to articulate it so that people around you can understand it, and getting consensus on a common vision." Steve Jobs brought Apple Computer out of the garage into the marketplace. Because of his vision, today Apple stands among the corporate computer giants. Even though his ungraceful departure from Apple may have caused some to question his leadership ability, no one can argue with success. The change can be viewed simply as "an end of an era at Apple," as one employee put it. Sharing a common vision is like playing dominoes; you line up your common values and the power of commitment once tapped gets things moving in the right direction. Let's now examine the values of the mini-entrepreneur.

A Revised Work Ethic

A revised work ethic, which found its way into the more innovative companies, satisfies two needs of the baby-boom generation: (1) the opportunity to grow, to be challenged, and learn something new and (2) the right to be treated as a first-class citizen living in a democratic society. Baby boomers, raised in an affluent society in the late 1940s to early 1960s, are now questioning whether a materialistic society emphasizing the external was suited to meet inner values. Michael Maccoby in *The Leader* sees us moving toward a "self-development ethic," while Daniel Yankelovich calls it an "ethic of commitment." In other words, the desire for personal growth naturally leads many to commit themselves to things outside of themselves— the work group, a clean environment, the community, world peace. The shift in emphasis from external to internal values became a turning point creating a corporate cultural revolution, one that cannot go unnoticed. A 1977 Harris poll showed that 79 percent of the population favored better use of basic resources rather than reaching higher material standards of living. A similar percentage preferred to spend more time on human interaction rather than improved technological communication.

The 25-year survey conducted by Opinion Research Corporation also indicates that there has been a growing awareness of individual rights, a decreasing tolerance of inequity, and a concern for Affirmative Action (hiring and promoting women and minorities). These findings, cited in the *Harvard Business Review*, January 1979, showed both managers and employees feel this way. In 1950, the percentage of managers was far less.

The structure and style of the high-tech environment unshackles mini-entrepreneurs from traditional constraints by granting them the freedom to find meaningful relationships at work, give their best, become involved productively in the company. Individual development, a sense of human rights, mutual respect, and participation form the cornerstones of the renewed work ethic.

New Roles/Different Skills

How then do these values and expectations, when properly meshed, shape work roles? High growth, a turbulent internal environment, and the competitive marketplace discussed earlier demand worker participation, more team work, closer communication, and more individual initiative than required by more bureaucratic work environments. For these reasons as well as societal changes at large (moving from an industrial society to an information society), the mini-entrepreneur assumes the primary roles of quasi-manager and knowledge worker.

Knowledge Workers

Knowledge workers use brainpower to get things done. Job duties within the information society require the use of higher level, more abstract work such as coordinating people and projects and gathering and communicating this information both verbally and in writing. The mini-entrepreneur qualifies as, what Peter Drucker calls, a "knowledge worker." As such, the mini-entrepreneur becomes a resource for new ideas, an innovator, a problem solver. By crossing over the traditional job boundaries, the mini-entrepreneur becomes a quasi-manager or know-how manager. Skills used by the mini-entrepreneur functioning as knowledge worker fall within the category of "data" and "people," the skills outlined in the *Dictionary of Occupational Titles*. See Figure 2-2 for worker functions falling within these categories. More importantly, these skills are transferable because they can be transferred from one job category to another. For example, a purchasing specialist and a production coordinator both use the skills of serving, persuading, compiling, and analyzing. Specialized and technical knowledge, although important to their

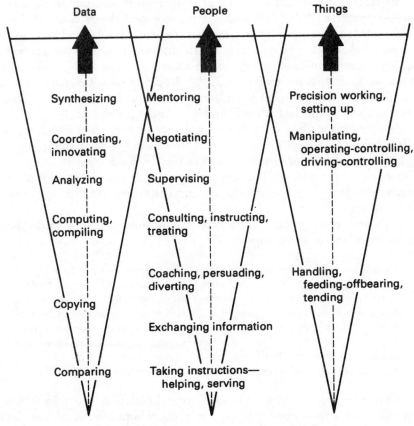

FIGURE 2-2. Three Categories of Functional Skills.

jobs, is not enough, in and of itself, to give them enough leverage to achieve the desired results.

By moving from an industrial society to an information society, the knowledge worker becomes the backbone of business operations. High-tech companies depend more on brainpower, using information (concepts, ideas, theories) for task completion, rather than muscle power and industrial machines. Today, fewer than one worker in four is employed in manufacturing.

Quasi-Managers/Individual Contributors

The mini-entrepreneur, using people and data skills, sees what needs to be done and seeks out information and resources by overstepping artificial boundaries between departments. Similar to a line manager, the mini-entrepreneur moves the company closer to achieving its goals (making a profit and winning in the marketplace) and in so doing, becomes both a quasi-manager (a manager in action not in title) and an individual contributor. Both the quasi-manager and the individual contributor gets things done. But the quasi-manager does so by pulling in others to problem solve and make joint efforts workable. Individuals who initiate informal group problem solving become quasi-managers by influencing others regardless of job title and position. In fact, every individual is, by definition, a self-manager and a contributor (either for good or bad) to the organization's welfare. In high-tech companies, this fact is made known to more people.

The power source of mini-entrepreneurs stems from their interpersonal effectiveness. Effective use of personal power means exercising interpersonal competence—the ability to express ideas clearly, listen, understand group dynamics, and negotiate. The mini-entrepreneur earns the title of quasi-manager and individual contributor through risk taking and eliciting support from others.

Let's now examine how Larry Buxton functions as both an individual contributor and quasi-manager:

> *Because writing new business proposals requires the expertise of people from systems engineering, finance, and technical publications, I need to build a rapport with them and gain their trust and respect. Initially I started out in this job as an individual contributor. But it's turning into a quasi-management position. The scope of what I am doing is getting so big that there has to be delegation. But there is a blurry line between being an individual contributor and a quasi-manager. There are certain aspects of what we do which are individual contributor oriented and others which are not.*

Mini-entrepreneurs draw upon interpersonal skills instead of relying upon technical know-how alone and are able to reach both job effectiveness and career satisfaction. They rely upon an internal power, the ability to set and achieve personal and professional goals, rather than waiting for and depending upon external power from job titles or top management approval. The shift from position power to personal power enables the mini-entrepreneur to become a know-how manager. Although position power and personal power are not mutually exclusive, they overlap more in well-run companies. Let's now break down the many roles of the mini-entrepreneur and list those skills or competencies needed.

Closeup of a Mini-Entrepreneur

Mini-entrepreneurs share some common characteristics with their company founders, the entrepreneurial prototypes of the organization. They wear some of the same hats and play the same roles. Two primary roles that they both assume are needs assessor and needs satisfier. As an inventor of a product or service, the entrepreneur surveys the market and finds a gap that will satisfy a customer's need. For example, Jim Treybig, a founder and president of Tandem, identified the need to have emergency backup computer services in the event a computer become inoperative. He came up with the idea of having two computers in one, hence the brand name "Tandem."

Having identified a need, the entrepreneur invents a product or service to satisfy the need. The ability to assess the need could mean success or failure for the entrepreneur. Theodore Levitt uses the term "market myopia" to explain misreading of customers. He points out that customers buy need satisfactions, not products. Why did the railroads of this nation, once prosperous businesses, fail to sustain themselves? Railroad businesspeople failed to see that their customers were really buying transportation not rail transit.

Peter Drucker, also pointing out the danger of market myopia, differentiates the scientist from the technologist. The technologist is that person who understands what new knowledge is becoming available and works on converting it into technology—into new processes and products. The technologist, unlike the scientist who develops new knowledge, applies this knowledge to different fields. Drucker argues, regardless of job position as line manager or research scientist, businesspeople need to scan the environment, be alert to new insights, and see the potential application of technology. A layperson, with a good "feel" for science and technology does this better than the highly trained specialist in a technical or scientific field who "is likely to become the prisoner of his own advanced knowledge." The layperson may be better because, like the specialist, he or she is also a prisoner of knowledge but a lot more people share that average knowledge. There is a bigger potential best for what might result. Also the layperson is not artificially restricted to thinking about applications, while the specialist tends to be.

Working inside the corporation, mini-entrepreneurs assume the dual roles of needs assessor and needs satisfier by using existing resources of information, people, and material to solve problems. They also run the risk of marketing myopia by discounting or ignoring information and ideas, technical in nature yet seemingly unrelated to their technical expertise. Lou Ann Bender, a manufacturing cost analyst, explains both the difficulties overcoming artificial boundaries of technical knowledge and the benefits of sharing brainpower to solve problems that cut across several work areas:

> *It is so easy to get stuck in your little job, your goals, that you forget that another department may cross paths with you. What they have to tell you may have implications for what you are doing.*

> *For example, a person in manufacturing brought up a problem on the positive inventory system. I listened. Then I realized that this problem affects the accounting interface with positive inventory. If the numbers are incorrect, the material won't be ready to ship. So even though positive inventory isn't my area, I arranged a meeting with a supervisor in the inventory area to research the problems.*

In this situation, Lou Ann assessed a need/problem and took steps toward satisfying/resolving it, even if it meant getting involved in an area for which she is not formally responsible. Internal corporate customers all have differing needs to be satisfied including managers, supervisors, peers, and team members. Mini-entrepreneurs, aware of the multiple needs of internal customers, take steps to become personally effective.

Mini-Entrepreneurial Action Steps

Let's look at the steps outlined in the learning/working cycle to comprehend how the mini-entrepreneur utilizes multiple roles to be personally effective. Figure 2-3 outlines the action steps and accompanying roles necessary to become personally effective, steps for building your career. The various roles, which the mini-entrepreneur undertakes, are listed beneath each action step. These roles can be broken down further into skills, the same skills listed in Exercise 2-1 in the Mini-Entrepreneurial Skills Inventory. Chapter 3 discusses those skills in more detail.

This success cycle of learning/working becomes a map to follow. It can also serve as an entry plan for individuals who are newcomers to a entrepreneurial high-tech environment.

Now let's turn to the career path of Marta Dunlap, who has become personally effective, promotable, and career satisfied. Her case illustrates how the success cycle operates and can also work for you.

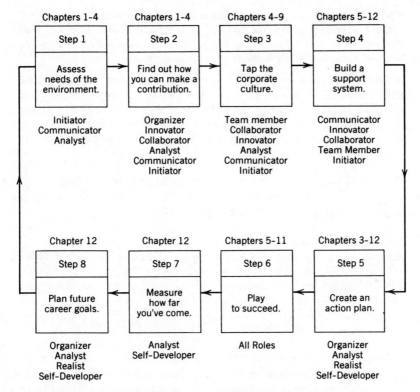

FIGURE 2-3. Steps for Building Your Career.

Marta first entered the company with an MBA as a senior financial analyst, fully aware of her desire to transfer to a marketing position. After five months, Marta transferred to the marketing function as a new business planner and just recently was promoted to the job of manager of product marketing. In effect, she created her current position for herself. In the process of so doing, Marta acted as a mini-entrepreneur by assessing a need and satisfying it. She adds:

The need for the job was apparent months back. There are lots of ways to highlight a need for a job. When a certain function isn't being done in an organization, it becomes fairly obvious to certain people at a management level. So when a situation comes up, and something isn't being done, one way to start that selling process early is to make sure that people recognize that that particular position needs to be filled, certain functions need to be done, and that they could be part of a new job.

When I knew that my new job was done and we were going to reorganize, I started talking to people in the division about what needed to be done, what they thought I could do. These were people who were friends, not in the personal sense, but in the business sense, managers who I could trust.

I asked them, "Can you help me formulate not only my career path but let's talk about some ideas, where am I going?" Also I asked them to match my needs with those of the organization. We did some of that. When my job was being worked out by the layer of management above me, I already knew I was going to get the job, because of the informal communication I had done with my manager and others.

Marta has successfully completed the cycle outlined in Figure 2-3 by moving from a less desirable position to a more desirable one. As she shifts from Step 8 to Step 1, again she begins the cycle:

As soon as we firmed up the job, that afternoon I met with all the sales managers, since they happened to be in town. I called a meeting and explained my new job. They were pleased for me. I said to them, "These are the things we could be doing, but what do you need to have done by a person in this capacity?" They gave me three things and then I asked for more. They said, "No, no, no. You don't understand. If you do two of the three things, you'll be doing a great job." So I said, OK

To become a mini-entrepreneur, you need to assume multiple roles of organizer, initiator, analyst, innovator, communicator, collaborator, team member, optimist, and self-developer. The skills, however, are only part of what it takes to become personally effective. Chapter 3 gives you a chance to focus on the inner power of mini-entrepreneurs.

CONCLUSION

Existing within an entrepreneurial culture, top performers within excellent high-tech environments can be viewed as mini-entrepreneurs. Like their company founders, they utilize similar skills and assume multiple roles to reach job accomplishment and career satisfaction and become personally effective. In becoming entrepreneurial, the mini-entrepreneur, in essence, becomes an effective human being.

For the most part, holding nonmanagerial positions, mini-entrepreneurs are members of a changing work force whose values reflect those of the baby-boom generation. They value opportunities to express themselves, prove themselves competent, and learn and grow professionally and personally. Baby-boomers will compose one-third of the population by 1990 and currently are making an impact on management practices and the work force. Many have become entrepreneurs by starting new businesses and have incorporated the activist philosophy of the 1960s into the workplace. They have carved out a revised work ethic based on their values, their innovative drive, and discontent with an overemphasis on materialism. This work ethic values worker rights, mutual respect between management and worker, self/career development, and participation in decision making. These qualities concoct "the right stuff" for entrepreneurial cultures of excellence.

As we shift from an industrial society to an information society, the mini-entrepreneur becomes a knowledge worker. Relying less on the muscle power required by a manufacturing environment producing goods, the mini-entrepreneur depends on skills to move data and people towards goal completion.

Moving beyond the formal constraints of the job (authority and job title), the mini-entrepreneur uses influence and personal power to become personally effective—job effective and career satisfied. The mini-entrepreneur follows specific action steps and employs specific skills, both of which can be learned.

ANSWERS TO EXERCISE 2-1. Mini-Entrepreneurial Skills Inventory

DIRECTIONS: Transfer your numerical rating from Exercise 2-1 to the duplicate items. Total your scores for each role category, then divide by number indicated. Your final scores for each category will give your relative strengths.

	RATING
I. BEING AN ORGANIZER: Goal Setting, Planning and Implementing Skills	
1. Setting reachable work goals.	
8. Outlining action steps for achieving results within time frames.	
16. Establishing priorities after reaching agreement with others.	

ANSWERS TO EXERCISE 2-1. *(Continued)*

	RATING
22. Identifying potential obstacles to reaching goals.	
Total Scores	
Final Scores: Divide by 4 =	
II. BEING AN INITIATOR: Information seeking and problem solving skills	
2. Asking the right questions to get needed information and to determine the source.	
17. Initiating corrective action as problems arise.	
23. Anticipating problems before they occur.	
30. Taking action on my own authority without asking permission.	
Total Score	
Final Score: Divide by 4 =	
III. BEING AN ANALYST: Conceptualizing, organizing thought and activities.	
3. Analyzing a situation and identifying the important issues.	
24. Diagnosing a situation in maintaining an objective viewpoint by seeing all sides of the problem.	

ANSWERS TO EXERCISE 2-1. *(Continued)*

	RATING
26. Observing the work behavior of others to collect data and draw conclusions.	
Total Score	
Final Score: Divide by 3 =	
IV. BEING AN INNOVATOR: Taking risks, thinking creatively, setting company precedents.	
4. Questioning the usual way of doing things.	
14. Implementing new concepts and ideas despite adversity.	
18. Enabling others to see my vision using terms that are attractive to them.	
31. Introducing new ideas and projects that are precedent setting and represent concept leaps.	
Total Score	
Final Score: Divide by 4 =	
V. BEING A COMMUNICATOR: Using communication and interpersonal skills.	
5. Actively listening to others.	
9. Resolving conflicts between yourself and others.	

ANSWERS TO EXERCISE 2-1. *(Continued)*

	RATING
19. Pinpointing the needs and objectives of others.	
25. Communicating effectively with people within various departments and at different organizational levels.	
27. Using language (metaphors, stories and examples) familiar to the listener.	
Total Score	
Final Score: Divide by 5 =	
VI. BEING A COLLABORATOR: Using group process, facilitating skills.	
10. Explaining another person's viewpoint to others.	
20. Working jointly with others inside and outside my work unit to accomplish a task.	
28. Negotiating agreements within a group.	
32. Gaining the support of others for my project.	
Total Score	
Final Score: Divide by 4 =	
VII. BEING A TEAM MEMBER: Building alliances, networks, coalitions, or teams.	

ANSWERS TO EXERCISE 2-1. *(Continued)*

	RATING
6. Helping others to see mutual interests and goals.	
11. Informing other team members of information that may help them.	
29. Keeping a balance between concern for people and concern for production.	
35. Sharing responsibility and credit for tasks or projects.	
Total Score	
Final Score: Divide by 4 =	
VIII. BEING A REALIST: Empowering, positively influencing others.	
12. Reality checking suggestions and new ideas of others.	
21. Talking yourself into taking limited risks.	
34. Envisioning the end product/result before the project begins and communicating the vision to others.	
33. Adapting to changing priorities and circumstances beyond my control.	
Total Score	
Final Score: Divide by 4 =	

ANSWERS TO EXERCISE 2-1. *(Continued)*

	RATING
IX. BEING A SELF-DEVELOPER: Improving self, seeking new learning experiences.	
7. Assuming new tasks beyond normal job duties.	
13. Researching new methods, procedures, and concepts to be applied on the job.	
15. Identifying my strengths and weaknesses and outlining steps for improvement.	
Total Score	
Final Score: Divide by 3 =	

INTERPRETATION OF SCORES

Each of the skills in the inventory have been assigned to a particular role, listed in Figure 2-4. Each of these roles is equally important to the mini-entrepreneur in achieving personal effectiveness. The amount of time spent assuming the various roles and using the supporting skills depends on your job and workplace circumstances.

Interpretation of Final Scores

Rank your scores by placing a "1" next to the highest score, a "2" next to the second highest score, a "3" next to the third highest score, and so forth (see Figure 2-4).

The role with the highest score indicates that you perform the duties of this role very well. To determine which specific skills are your strongest, look for skills that you rated yourself a "5". If you have very few "5s," look at your "4s."

ROLE	FINAL SCORE	RANK
Organizer		
Initiator		
Analyst		
Innovator		
Communicator		
Collaborator		
Team Member		
Realist		
Self-Developer		

FIGURE 2-4.

Special Considerations

The role categories of "realist" and "self-developer," while important aspects of being a mini-entrepreneur, are difficult categories in which to compare scores because it is difficult to see a direct relationship to short-term job goals. Also a skill, such as number 7 (assuming new tasks beyond normal job duties), that may be important to you personally may not be important in your current job.

3

BECOMING A MINI-ENTREPRENEUR

Investing in YOU, Inc.

INNER POWER

Mitch Stein is a technician in the manufacturing area of a high-tech company that produces integrated circuits. A new supervisor, Leroy Grayson, has been assigned to his unit.

With a long-term goal of becoming a supervisor, Mitch has enrolled in a presupervisory training program sponsored jointly by the company and the local community college.

Arriving one morning at the plant, Mitch sees a crowd gathered on the shop floor. He hears a loud voice and notices another supervisor, Joe, shouting at and abusing Leroy. Mitch sees that Leroy is calm and in control. The crowd watches Leroy walk into Joe's office as Joe follows. They close the door. Later, when they returned to the shop floor, Mitch noticed that the two supervisors, Leroy and Joe, were congenial and respectful of one another.

That afternoon Mitch approached Leroy out of concern and curiosity:

MITCH: I want to commend you on your conduct this morning. If I were you, I would have decked Joe.

LEROY: Ten years ago I might have done just that. But now I know that would have gotten us nowhere except find ourselves without jobs.

MITCH: What did you do? What did you do to calm him down?

LEROY: Well, I waited until he calmed down. In fact I was laughing at him. I told him that when he was rational we could start being productive.

MITCH: How could you remain so calm, so rational?

LEROY: Look, I consider myself to be a professional. As long as I choose to remain in this realm, I need to carry myself in a certain manner, no matter what I am faced with, even negative confrontations. Someday you will be in this position. That's what I am grooming you for, so benefit from what you see.

As Mitch leaves Leroy's office, he wonders if he has the self-control and inner strength to handle this kind of conflict.

Now that you have gained an insight into what it means to be personally effective in a high-tech environment, you can begin looking at a process to become more entrepreneurial. For beginners, you can see if you have the knowledge, skills, and abilities needed by the high-tech entrepreneurial culture. You will need to gauge whether your work style needs realignment, whether your values conflict with those of the corporate culture, and if your goals fit in well with those of the organization.

You can begin building a Personal Effectiveness Plan (PEP) to determine your strengths, areas of improvement, personal and corporate values, work style, and action steps for any desired changes. The first step in building your PEP is to examine what it means to be personally effective. You can assess some assumptions you may have about the use of power by mini-entrepreneurs within the high-tech environment by completing Exercise 3-1.

EXERCISE 3-1. Assessing Your Power Assumptions

DIRECTIONS: This exercise will assist you in examining fallacious assumptions concerning use of power, for fallacious assumptions lead to ineffective behavior. Check the response that best reflects your assumption. For an interpretation of your answers, see the key at the end of this chapter.

1. As a mini-entrepreneur, the first step you can take toward becoming more powerful is by:
   (a) taking a leadership role to gain control over others;
   (b) becoming aware of your needs, desires, and values;
   (c) following the advice of people in positions of power.

EXERCISE 3-1. (Continued)

2. Within the high performance environment exists the assumption:
   (a) Power can be shared to enrich the individual, others, and the company;
   (b) The people at the top have access to real power for they set the vision for the company;
   (c) Managers are the real source of power because they get things done through others.
3. In order to have an impact on others, as a mini-entrepreneur, you can:
   (a) withhold information from others so that when the right times comes you can reveal it and be seen as powerful;
   (b) convince others to do things in ways which are most beneficial to you;
   (c) work as a team member in problem solving and reaching group goals.
4. As a mini-entrepreneur, you feel powerful when:
   (a) you can act on clear, specific directives from your supervisor;
   (b) opportunities exist for you to apply your expertise and influence others in ways that are mutually beneficial;
   (c) you can use your job title and authority to achieve results.
5. A second step you can take toward becoming more powerful is by:
   (a) interacting with others in ways that leave both people feeling more powerful;
   (b) sharing important information but making sure that the other person does not have the advantage;
   (c) taking precautions with those who are not considered members of your own work unit.

Now let's take some time to determine what is meant by personal effectiveness. How does personal effectiveness shape the role of the mini-entrepreneur?

PERSONAL EFFECTIVENESS AND YOU, INC.

You are personally effective when you achieve mutually agreed upon results through the shared expectations of two parties within the organization. A joint feeling of celebration is the barometer for personal effectiveness. If you feel like celebrating over a drink with your coworkers, you definitely feel a sense of achievement and personal satisfaction. Recognition also makes people feel personally effective. As a new business planner, Marta and her marketing manager designed and organized the program, materials, and group assignments for a long-range planning session involving more than 100 people. She describes her feeling of accomplishment: "I was really pleased when our division manager congratulated my manager and myself for doing such a great job. Bob, my manager, was the titular head, but our division manager acknowledged both of our efforts in front of everyone." The parties involved may include you and your supervisor, you and team members, or you and coworkers.

Becoming personal effective allows you to acknowledge your own skills, values, and goals, as well as the goals and values of the organization, and align your personal style with the corporate culture. To put it simply, you must be "in touch" with the needs of coworkers at all levels and be "in tune" with the proper way of doing things within the organization.

To tap your talents, creativity, and expertise, first you must become aware of your strengths as well as your weaknesses, your values as they relate to your career, and the goals you would like to achieve. These goals may be both personal and professional. Because this information is subjective, only you can lay the foundation for being personally effective. But remember that first you must get in touch with your personal power before becoming personally effective.

Developing your personal and interpersonal power is essentially what this book is all about—tapping your reserves of creativity, insight, and innovation and putting them to work. You can increase your effectiveness by developing action plans and identifying specific steps to follow. Also, you can deepen your understanding of interpersonal power by identifying what excites you about being a part of your organization. Whether you are perceived as job successful by top management and personally effective depends on the degree to which you identify with the organization's corporate culture. If you find certain management practices personally offensive, counterproductive, and unrewarding, then you may spend your time and energy protecting yourself or engaging in team play that serves no end. This behavior results in job dullness and stagnancy, as opposed to working with others toward excellence. A new employee just entering an entrepreneurial culture after leaving an authoritative culture explains this difference.

> *"Withholding information which may be useful to someone else from another department was part of the rules of the game in company X. It was part of a silly real estate game—protecting your turf. But here it is intolerable. Here they place a high value on team work and collaborative problem solving."*

If your job performance is defined by corporate culture, then personal effectiveness demands examining yourself in relationship to your personal needs and those of the organization.

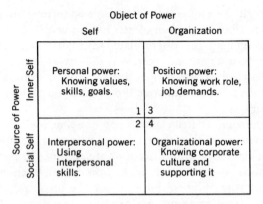

FIGURE 3-1. Power and Personal Effectiveness.

Figure 3-1 gives a framework for understanding how you can gain greater control over your career and use personal power. How you accomplish this depends on your sense of individual responsibility, your desires, capabilities, and values. It also depends on pressures which exist outside yourself such as organizational goals and expectations of coworkers, managers, and supervisors. Within any realistic and high performance environment, power is used in ways that leave others feeling stronger. Power is not used to dominate others, as an authorization to abuse others, or for personal aggrandizement. Rather it is used to empower others, arouse confidence in others, influence others, and generate a team spirit.

As an employee, your success is dependent on the success of the organization. Since the organization simply is made up of people, ultimately your success is dependent on facilitating the success of others. Power is accorded to you by others when it is in their best interest. Therefore, the exercise of power, by definition, means helping others to succeed.

To better understand the dynamics of personal power, personal effectiveness, and organizational effectiveness, let's look at the quadrants in Figure 3-1.

Personal Power and Self-Control

You are the source of your own power. After all, you make choices depending on personal needs, values, capabilities, and goals. Quadrant 1 in Figure 3-1 reflects choices emerging from your inner self. Individuals feel a sense of self-control or internal power, of knowing themselves, when they can say, "I feel certain and I am clear about my needs, values, goals, and my capabilities in satisfying them. I am able to direct, control, and strengthen myself."

Interpersonal Power and Concern for Others

Quadrant 2 focuses on the connection between personal power and your ability to influence or persuade. You can achieve mutual satisfaction and find common ground if you communicate clearly, listen attentively, and reach mutually satisfying agreements. You are interpersonally competent when you can say, "I feel powerful when I make an impact on others, when I can share my expertise and influence others in accomplishing a task or reaching group goals."

Position Power and Objectivity

In quadrants 3 and 4, the focus of the object of power shifts from the individual to the organization. Everyone working within an organization depends to some degree upon external supports such as the authority of a job title or place in the hierarchy. Depending upon the corporate culture, individuals use the prestige and authority of a job role as a way of influencing others to get the job done. Reliance upon external supports as opposed to personal power is referred to as position power, "position" meaning place in the organizational hierarchy. To exert your position power, define the parameters of your work role and respond to specific job demands. In more bureaucratic and authoritarian companies where position power is frequently used, you are likely to feel that the organization strengthens you because of corporate trappings you possess, such as a corner office, a parking space, a managerial job title.

In the high performance environment, position power is deemphasized resulting in a seemingly more egalitarian work climate. And in this climate image, title, and formal authority usually are deemphasized. Supporting this environment is a mixture of people whose positions, in reality, identify responsibilities and roles for achievement. Position, by itself, does not and cannot imbue an individual with more power. If you understand this, you will behave in ways that affirm others and allow each person to exercise their role and responsibilities toward achieving goals.

Identifying with Organizational Power

Quadrant 4 of Figure 3-1 focuses on how organizational power can benefit everyone. Corporate culture determines how organizational power is shared. As discussed in Chapter 1, the high-tech entrepreneurial culture smashes the pyramid and involves people at all levels in problem solving and decision making. In this culture, you will undoubtedly receive recognition for your efforts and be considered a winner. By owning a share of organizational power, you will feel strengthened because you are contributing to the organization. By identifying with the corporate culture, you are likely to say, "The company has enabled me to use my talents to serve others or influence others in ways which are both productive for the company and meaningful to me personally."

In reality, personal success and corporate success are not separate from one another. We can only look out for ourselves by looking out for others. A former Apple Computer marketing manager who worked on the *MacIntosh* computer expresses the reason behind all his efforts: "I certainly was not doing it for Steve Jobs. I was doing it for something much greater than that, and that was to change something really, honestly, truly for the better."

SHAPING "YOU", INC.

One way of understanding yourself in relation to the organization is to view it as a partnership. Like all partnerships, marriage, living arrangements, and joint business ventures, a clear definition of self and others needs to be defined. Figure 3-2 presents a way of understanding personal effectiveness and organizational effectiveness and illustrates the give-and-take required in any partnership.

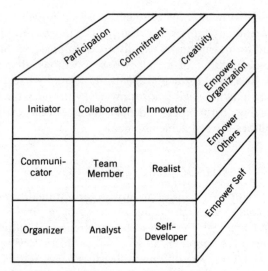

FIGURE 3-2. Building Blocks of Personal Effectiveness.

First let's consider organizational effectiveness in this model. Organizational effectiveness evolves from a culture of excellence. Let's now begin to break down this culture of excellence into manageable parts so that you can see the relationship between organizational and personal effectiveness. Figure 3-2 shows that the basic foundation of an entrepreneurial culture or culture of excellence is the structure comprised of opportunities to participate, to give your best as a mini-entrepreneur. Granted the power and flexibility to get your job done, you are also given opportunities to participate in decision making. These opportunities may include product teams, quality circles, or planning sessions, all of which require preparing and taking action. For you, participating first involves getting organized (setting goals, objectives, and actions plans), showing initiative rather than waiting for information or direction from others, and responding to others through communication. You can participate in this culture of excellence by assuming the roles of organizer, communicator, and initiator.

At the heart of any personal or professional relationship, lies the two-way process of commitment. Shared values make commitments durable to withstand time and circumstances. In the culture of excellence, people at all levels coach others to give their personal best and create a corporate culture that calls upon everyone's commitment. Commitment demands first analyzing what responsibilities are crucial to your job, demonstrating your commitment to other team members, and collaborating (working it out through joint efforts) with them. By being an analyst, team member, and collaborator, you demonstrate your commitment to the organization.

Another shared value, a value out of which the industry grew, is creativity. Creativity is born out of a reorientation and shift in perspective in job methods, services, and technology. In the work world, creativity demands more than originality of thought. It requires innovation, making the original idea a reality. It means realism, recognizing the upside as well as the downside of a situation and weighing the odds. Creativity tempered with realism makes one an innovator. Confronted with challenges and uncertainties, mini-entrepreneurs take on new responsibilities as a matter of course, and in the process, earn the label of self-developer, one who learns new aspects of a job and at the same time prepares themself for the next career move. When you undertake the roles of self-developer, realist, and innovator, you are adding your creativity to the organization.

In summary, an organization opens its doors to effectiveness by allowing its people to participate in decision making, showing a commitment to treating people as adults, and providing opportunities for creativity. Each of these organization or corporate cultural traits appears at the top of the block-type model in Figure 3-2. You can take advantage of these opportunities by assuming certain roles that will contribute to both job and organization effectiveness. Remember, "passing the buck," or hoarding important information violates the code of participation, commitment and creativity, diminishes organization excellence, and prevents you from being successful.

If you take on these mini-entrepreneur roles that occupy a block in the model, you will be working your way toward personal effectiveness. Figure 3-2 is similar to the hierarchy of skills in Figure 2-2 in that the skills required to fulfill the roles to "empower self" at the bottom form the foundation for the roles to "empower others." Similarly, the skills needed to "empower others" become stepping stones to the higher-level roles of "empowering the organization." Shifting focus from yourself to others also accompanies this progression. By taking advantage of the opportunities extended and accepting unique challenges, you will make an impact on three different levels; you will empower yourself, empower others, and empower the organization. Ultimately these all go together and are perspectives on what real power is. In this partnership, then, first you will need to know your own competencies and career values before you can make an impact on the organization.

Each block of Figure 3-2 represents a role you assume within the culture of the organization. These roles correspond to the role categories of the Mini-Entrepreneurial Skills Inventory in Chapter 2. What is acceptable to others depends on approach and thorough and accurate data presentation. Then effectiveness requires you to assume multiple roles and accurately assess your skills. The next step is to examine the type of skills required to play these various roles.

BUILDING YOUR PERSONAL POWER

Since personal power depends on judiciously exercising personal strengths and capabilities, first let's discuss some tools for assessing your strengths.

Skills Support

Chapter 2 helped to assess your strengths in the Mini-Entrepreneurial Skills Inventory and offered information about how jobs are classified in the *Dictionary of Occupational Titles*, according to whether a person works primarily with data, people, or things. Figure 2-2 listed examples of skills used within each of these job categories. To gain leverage in achieving your goals, you will need to become familiar with three types of skills—work-content, functional, and self-management.

Work-content skills, like technical skills, are competencies required to perform a particular job. They frequently include theories, concepts, or procedures that are highly specific and not transferrable to another job outside of a functional area. For example, a dentist needs to know crown preparation or a root canal treatment. A computer programmer needs to know various computer languages. These practices are job specific.

Unlike work-content skills, functional skills are transferrable to another type of job. In other words, you can apply these skills to another job once you have mastered them. For example, a technical writer can apply writing skills to a new position within the management development department, writing learning objectives and case studies for management training seminars. Systems engineers who communicate with customers and marketing personnel can transfer their verbal communication and interpersonal skills to a marketing position.

The third type of skills, called self-management or adaptive, are usually thought of as personal character traits acquired early in life. Richard Bolles in *The Three Boxes of Life* defines self-management skills by how you get along with others, how you relate to authority, and how you relate to time and space and control your impulses. This kind of skill is displayed by Leroy Grayson in the beginning of the chapter. Because self-management skills (managing time, stress, and your boss) help you adapt to a particular environment, they are called adaptive skills. Not only do these skills help you adapt to an environment, but they also help you create an environment where you and others are more likely to succeed.

When you apply functional and self-management skills, you are drawing from the well of personal effectiveness. Top performers within high-tech companies, while possessing work-content skills or technical skills, rely heavily on functional and adaptive skills to perform their jobs. The skills listed in the Mini-Entrepreneurial Skills Inventory are functional and self-management. To develop as a mini-entrepreneur, you need to be aware of and develop two growth processes: (1) positive use of power, (2) style that helps build a culture of excellence from the ground up. The following processes lay the foundation for the building blocks of personal effectiveness shown in Figure 3-2:

A. How to Develop and Use Power Positively

1. Empower self
2. Empower others
3. Empower organization

B. How to Develop a Style for Excellence

1. Participate in the work environment
2. Commit yourself to others
3. Use your creativity

The skills listed in the Mini-Entrepreneurial Skills Inventory break down each of the roles (initiator, collaborator, innovator, etc.) occupying a box in Figure 3-2. By effectively applying these skills, you can follow in the footsteps of top performers in cultures of excellence.

Now let's determine how top performers of high-tech companies apply these skills.

Mini-Entrepreneurial Skills in Action

Let's take a closer look at Larry Buxton, our top performer from Chapter 2. Larry has a technical background and relies heavily upon functional and self-management skills to get his job done. With a Bachelor of Science degree in electrical engineering and a desire to broaden his career, Larry moved from a design engineer in another company to an applications engineer responsible for writing new business proposals. To get his job done, Larry has learned to build bridges of understanding and cooperation with technical experts from various functions such as systems engineering, finance, and technical publications. Lacking position power (the formal authority to delegate responsibilities for writing various parts of the proposal), Larry relies on his interpersonal skills of communicating, collaborating, and team building. Now let's relate the skills listed in the Mini-Entrepreneurial Skills Inventory to the personal effectiveness of a top performer, Larry Buxton.

Skills Used

> 5. *Actively Listening to Others.*

> *This is very important in my job. A lot of this depends upon my level of understanding going into the situation. Some of the technical knowledge of the engineers is so high powered that only they can understand each other. If they are talking over my head I will usually try to stop them as soon as I can and get someone else more qualified to listen to them or explain it to them or ask them to write it down.*

> 11. *Informing Other Team Members of Information That May Help Them.*

> *We are the people at the plant, the home base, who interface directly with the sales people in the field. So we are always on the phone to the sale people. They will give us insight into what the issues are, what should go into the proposal, where the proposal should be the strongest, where the pricing should be.*

> 32. *Gaining the Support of Others for My Project.*

> *I feel that I do my job well. And if people recognize that then people are more willing to help. I think that it is easier to get help from someone if they respect*

you first of all. And it is easier still if they both respect you, like you, and enjoy being around you. I generally enjoy people anyway so that I will go out of my way to do small things for people, to listen to them. Although it isn't done to get more work out of somebody directly, being supportive is kind of a natural result of that rapport and friendship you've built.

29. **Keeping a Balance Between Concern for People and Concern for Production.**

I think if you are aware of their problems both work-related and nonwork-related, you have a better perspective of how well they are going to support you. If you're in tune with them at a feeling level, then you can understand why they have said what they have said.

If they tell you that they can't get something to you by 5 o'clock and you don't make an effort to understand why, then you are cutting your own throat. Maybe they are having marital problems and have to go see a lawyer. So you make other arrangements. They may be willing to come back after 5:00 to do the work. The traditional manager may say, 'I need this by 5:00 and I don't care what it takes to get it done.' The person will do it begrudgingly and probably do a poorer job than if someone showed some understanding and flexibility.

By examining Larry Buxton's skills in action, you will better understand the various types of skills needed to support the multiple roles of the mini-entrepreneur. However, to further determine your ability to identify these roles, complete Exercise 3-2.

EXERCISE 3-2. Identification of Mini-Entrepreneurial Roles
Part A

First read the following series of incidents comprising the case study of Mark Malone. Then using the Mini-Entrepreneurial Skills Inventory at the end of Chapter 2, indicate in the spaces provided the roles utilized. Two primary skills are used in each incident. Although multiple skills are used, identify the primary role used to accomplish the described task. It is helpful to underline the action verbs. After completing the exercise, check your responses against the key at the end of this chapter.

Mark Malone is a purchasing specialist at a Silicon Valley company that makes integrated circuits. He is responsible for procuring quality raw materials by working with suppliers, ensuring that materials purchased meet company specifications and testing standards.

EXERCISE 3-2. (Continued)

I. I spend the majority of my time answering phone calls, communicating with our overseas manufacturing plants via TELEX, addressing quality issues of materials that come in and don't meet the specifications. If the parts don't meet our specifications, then I get the vendor to acknowledge that they don't meet my specifications. Then we can agree on what to do about it.

II. We interface very closely with the incoming quality areas, the Engineering department, Accounting department that pays for the parts, the Traffic department that receives the parts in here or ships them either back to the vendor or to our offshore plants, and to the Stores people who keep inventory of the parts. Yes, we do interface with a lot of other groups, both inside and outside of our division, the Manufacturing group. I do a lot of negotiating with the people within the group to get what I want accomplished.

III. Priorities are another thing that change hourly. You may be working on one project then all of a sudden we'll receive a TELEX, or we'll get a call from an engineer, and our set of priorities change. We'll start working on something else. It means being very flexible, to take all these changes in stride and not let them get to you. You have to be able to stand back and keep everything in perspective. Afterall, we are all human.

IV. We try to prevent problems rather than operating with a Band-Aid approach. This relates to our Corporate Quality Program. We buy all the raw materials—the package, the silicon chip, the wire, the box. We have taken great strides to prevent the problems from occurring in the first place. Prevention as Phil Crosby points out in his book, *Quality if Free*, is one of the key absolutes of quality. I am problem solving everyday with all the suppliers.

V. From a purchasing point of view, our internal customers consist of our factories overseas in Bangkok and in Korea. They use the raw materials which we buy and inspect. We have some materials right now which don't meet our specifications and have been rejected. So I'll call in the salesman and the engineer on the vendor side. I will coordinate the visit. I will act as the mediator and the interpreter between the engineer from vendor side and our quality assurance people, inspection people, and our engineers. In this interface with the supplier, I collaborate with other team members: the purchasing guy, the quality guy, and the engineer. It is our objective to make sure that all the material that comes in the door meets the standard of zero defects. We collaborate and decide as a team whether to continue to do business with a supplier or not to.

EXERCISE 3-2. *(Continued)*

Roles Assumed	
Situation	Role
I.	_____
II.	_____
III.	_____
IV.	_____
V.	_____

PART B

Now review your own Mini-Entrepreneurial Skills Inventory. Select 3–5 skills that you rated "4" or "5." On a sheet of paper, describe the corresponding role that you found yourself playing.

As you can see from these experiences of top performers, they treat their job as if it were their own business ensuring standards of quality are met, treating coworkers as inhouse customers, seeking the advice of experts outside their immediate work area. What internal resources do they tap to become personally effective? To answer this question, our focus will shift to a discussion of personal power and risk taking.

Risk Taking

Those who have tapped reserves of personal power have done so by making conscious choices to take intelligent action that contributes to the quality of work life, service, or product of an organization. The result of taking appropriate and/or intelligent action affirms your personal competence and control. Even though you might have made some mistakes in the past, most likely, you are able to objectively look at what parts did work and what you have learned. As a result of your objectivity as well as feedback from others, you move ahead with self-confidence knowing that the same mistakes will not be repeated. While you may have felt some frustration and anxiety while taking the risk, you do not allow these feelings to stop you from acting again and forging ahead to meet your goals.

Tim Allen is a mini-entrepreneur who can adapt and be realistic and objective. These qualities keep his self-confidence and self-esteem from being shattered by a change of circumstances or the harsh judgments of others:

> *I take everything seriously, but if things don't go my way I don't worry about them. I'm not very good at worrying. If tomorrow management says, 'You're not going to be a product marketing engineer you are going to be a production control person,' I'd probably say, 'Fine.' I'm happy today, and I'm going to be happy tomorrow. If I'm happy then that's good. I'm very malleable. I question change, but if the decision is made then I'll accept it. I'll do a good job over there. Hopefully I'm going to learn, and I'll be realistic. After all change is the nature of things, especially in this business.*

> *If top management says, 'Tim, you're number one prioritiy has been dropped to number three.' I'll question it just so that I understand it and can relay it on to the customer. I usually live with the situation which is presented. I stay sort of 'loosey-goosey.'*

An exploratory study of 294 career changers conducted by Ellen Siegelman and documented in her book, *Personal Risk*, found that 83 percent experienced increased self-esteem, felt "more proud" or "more confident" as a result of undertaking a risky direction. More importantly, some individuals who described unsuccessful outcomes (mixed outcomes were 15 percent, negative outcomes were 13.5 percent) experienced positive feelings about themselves as a result of taking that risk. Taking the risk, deciding to take action, paid back more in self-esteem rather than outcome, the consequences of the making the decision. The cyclical pattern of building self-esteem, self-confidence, and personal power is illustrated in Figure 3.3.

Total Self-Esteem

Personal effectiveness of mini-entrepreneurs transcends the boundaries of the work world. In other words, mini-entrepreneurs do not solely rely upon what happens in their job to make them feel personally effective. Personal effectiveness can be viewed subjectively, for only you know what is personally satisfying. It can also be measured objectively by a company by productivity increases, sales, or services rendered. A risk-taker can fail in some objective way, make a wrong decision, and still view themselves as worthwhile. The value of undertaking an experience can far outweigh the outcome. The positive feelings that result from risk taking are seeing yourself as a survivor, learning about yourself in the process, and acquiring new skills.

Risk taking, by definition, means to expose oneself to a potential hazard or danger. It requires you to draw upon your skills and capabilities and question your negative thoughts ("I can't do this".) It broadens the perspective and

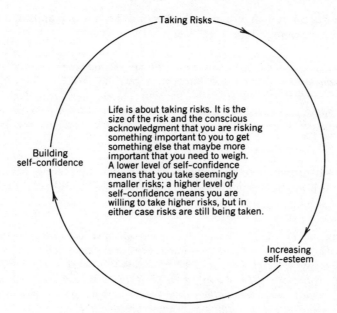

Taking Risks

Building
self-confidence

Life is about taking risks. It is the
size of the risk and the conscious
acknowledgment that you are risking
something important to you to get
something else that maybe more
important that you need to weigh.
A lower level of self-confidence
means that you take seemingly
smaller risks; a higher level of
self-confidence means you are
willing to take higher risks, but in
either case risks are still being taken.

Increasing
self-esteem

FIGURE 3-3. Building Self-Esteem.

depth of understanding. In short, it produces growth on emotional and intellectual levels. Risking taking arises from the uncertainty of life, and by dealing with these uncertainties, you become more competent and self-confident.

Two Examples

Now let's examine the risk taking experience of mini-entrepreneurs. While each experience varies from job to job, the underlying characteristics remain the same:

- Taking action to achieve results rather than not acting to avoid making mistakes. (Inaction can be a higher price to pay for missed opportunities to excel);
- Acting out a personal sense of what needs to be done rather than being told what needs to be done;
- Stretching; being strong enough to be vulnerable;
- Accepting the risks involved.

Steve recently received a promotion within the productivity improvement area and recalls a risk he took when he worked as a quality control supervisor. Relying upon own judgment, he responded to the demands of a critical situation confronting him:

I decided not to ship the product on a Saturday. Nobody else was around. We had a quality problem. We had ceramic packages that leaked. I decided to take a chance on that one and stop the shipments. It went over better than I had anticipated. I expected to be on one the trains out of town the next day. I literally came in feeling that I would be fired. But I was told that it was a good decision.

Recently promoted to a management position in marketing, Marta Dunlap recalls how she pushed herself to take risks. She describes risk taking in terms of her inner self:

I think that what I didn't have going for me was some technical background. But what could overcome that is my ability to ask questions and to go out and make myself vulnerable and find the information I wanted. It's almost like a compounding effect. I laid a lot of the groundwork the first year that really didn't come to fruition until the second year. You've just got to live and work with people over time. I didn't fully appreciate that at first.

Marta's experience is like discovering the natural growth and learning process that is part of all human experience. Now you can begin to relate your risk taking behavior to your working style by completing Exercise 3-3.

EXERCISE 3-3. Determining Your Risk Taking Behavior

DIRECTIONS: Recall a situation in your work life in which you confronted a challenge, a risky situation, with an outcome that was important to you. Write down your answers on a separate sheet of paper to the following:

1. Describe the situation or incident.
2. What did you expect to gain or lose by taking action?
3. What did you see as barriers or obstacles?
4. Describe the feelings you experienced before you reached a final decision.
5. Describe your actions to gain support or gather more information before reaching a decision.
6. What were the results?
7. How do you feel about yourself as a result of taking the risk?
8. List new skills used in the process.

FROM PERSONAL POWER TO INTERPERSONAL POWER

So far you have been evaluating your attitudes and skills. Before shifting from building personal power to interpersonal power, let's define interpersonal power. Interpersonal power requires you to get cooperation from others to reach group goals. It means influencing others to act in ways that are mutually beneficial to you and others. It involves making an impact on others in ways that leave them feeling more competent and self-confident. Interpersonal power is productive power, resulting from the exchange of information, material, or support.

Oppressive power, however, lies at the opposite end of the spectrum of productive or interpersonal power. Individuals who act aggressively dominate others by using power negatively. They are likely to treat others as if they were pawns in a chess game; they pull rank on subordinates; they hide behind their position within the hierarchy feeling that the authority of their position safeguards them against any questions or challenges.

As the pyramid collapsed, line/staff demarcations in the entrepreneurial culture became blurred. As a result power became available to those who influenced others. With their interpersonal power, these mini-entrepreneurs sell organizational goals, as opposed to using their formal authority to gain leverage in pulling together to get things done. Marta is an example of a mini-entrepreneur who has established an interpersonal power base.

In a marketing position, Marta relies upon building a rapport with engineers in order to reach company goals:

> One thing I do no matter who I'm talking to is to make clear what my purpose is in talking to them and be fairly frank and honest about where I am and what I'm doing. With the engineers, I am up front about my lack of technical expertise. I explain why it is I am asking them the questions and why I have come to them personally. I also admit that I don't know the answer. It has been pointed out to me that that works fairly well. I'm far more willing to make myself vulnerable and get shot down and admit what I don't know than a lot of other people. It works to my advantage. It makes it easier to approach people who are far above me in management level or way beyond me in technical expertise.

> I went to ask Ted to give me some comments on what I had written explaining this engineering diagram for a computer model. He knows that I rely upon him and his engineering expertise. I don't have to explain to him what I don't know. We have built up a rapport which saves us both time.

Todd, a senior personnel representative, however, uses a different tactic to build interpersonal power. He finds himself being confrontive, assertive, and painfully honest when he deals with employee relations problems. He describes his roles as similar to a consultant:

> *Sometimes you just have to get down and start yelling and screaming with people. I've done that before. I have given them all the data, and they agree that something needs to be done. And a month later nothing is done. So you really have to force the issues. Part of my role is to go out there and force the issues. So I will go out and talk to the managers and make them feel the pain, showing them that there is going to be some impact. It will reflect on them personally. But I am not willing to go out there and push the issue to the extreme.*

Because the high-tech entrepreneurial culture reinforces team work and collaborative problem solving, Todd has license to use persuasive communication skills to achieve results. In so doing, he, as a mini-entrepreneur, employs interpersonal power to strengthen himself, others, and the company.

TAPPING ORGANIZATIONAL POWER

Mini-entrepreneurs plug into existing organizational or cultural mechanisms to make their jobs easier, to develop their careers, and to meet organizational goals. They are "in tune" with the corporate culture, the way things are done within the organization. Mini-entrepreneurs also have the knack of both adapting to, and at the same time, questioning obsolete policies and procedures. They dare to play the part of the loyal opposition. How do mini-entrepreneurs use the culture to work to their advantage? Marta describes how she determines how to achieve personal and professional goals:

> *It's a matter of pulling together the resources around you. It is more about deciding what you want, who around you can help you, and then how to move people and the organization to get what you want than any set of specific job skills.*

She describes the critical aspect of working as a team, being a team player:

> *This is a verbal organization. People work together in groups. When you have a meeting it's a dynamic meeting and people get things done together. There is a tremendous amount which gets done in groups here. You have to learn how to move a group and work with a group to get things done. I think that it is an acquired skill. People acquire it because of the culture or they leave.*

Another example of the degree to which mini-entrepreneurs take advantage of available organizational power is Craig McMillen, a project coordinator. When asked about the "usual way of doing things around here," he responded with:

> *We are the company. We act as a team. Upper management says to us, 'OK you guys go down and find out what's going on.' It's like MBO. They'll say; "Set some objective. What do you need to do those? You have thought about it, now what are you going to do?" Then we'll say that we need this and this. We see if it is all right with everyone's budgets and then we go ahead. We don't question what they are doing. We know that they are doing everything to try to make us happy here.*

Tapping organizational power, in effect, requires you to use your individual initiative and team spirit to work collaboratively.

DEVELOPING YOUR PERSONAL EFFECTIVENESS PLAN (PEP)

Now that we have explored the various dimensions of personal effectiveness and roles needed to play, you can begin to develop your own Personal Effectiveness Plan (PEP). You already have begun to accumulate data by completing the Mini-Entrepreneurial Skills Inventory. Let's take the information from the inventory and begin building a PEP in Exercise 3-4. But first let's look at Larry Buxton's PEP. As an application engineer, he interfaces with numerous departments. In so doing he relies upon his communication and collaboration skills. His preliminary PEP in Figure 3-4 reveals that his strengths and areas for improvement fall within these areas.

EXERCISE 3-4. Building a Personal Effectiveness Plan (PEP)

DIRECTIONS: You will continue to build your Personal Effectiveness Plan as you accumulate more self-assessment data from the following chapters. By the last chapter, you will have completed a Personal Effectiveness Plan that includes action steps. A blank preliminary PEP is provided for you in Figure 3-5. Now you will be able to complete the skills assessment portion of the PEP.

Skills Assessment

To determine your strengths and areas for improvement, use the following procedures:

1. Identify your strengths by circling those skills which you rated yourself a "5." If you do not have any 5s circle the 4s.

EXERCISE 3-4. *(Continued)*

2. On the PEP write in the roles, skill numbers, and skill descriptions that make up a strength. Use sample form Figure 3-5.
3. Identify your areas of improvement by placing a check next to those skills that rated "1" or "2."
4. Select the role category (Analyst, Team Member) with the greatest number of areas for improvement.
5. On the PEP write in the roles, skill numbers, and skill description in the section, "Areas for Improvement."

STRENGTHS

R O L E	SKILL #	SKILL DESCRIPTION
Communicator	5	Actively listening to others.
	25	Communicating effectively with people within various depts & at different organzational levels.
Collaborator	20	Working joinly with others inside & outside my work unit to accomplish a task.
	28	Negotiating agreements within a group.

AREAS FOR IMPROVEMENT

R O L E	SKILL #	SKILL DESCRIPTION
Innovator	31	Introducing new ideas & projects that are precedent setting & represent concept leaps.
	14	Implementing new concepts and ideas despite adversity.

FIGURE 3-4. Larry Buxton's PEP.

STRENGTHS

R O L E	SKILL #	SKILL DESCRIPTION

AREAS FOR IMPROVEMENT

R O L E	SKILL #	SKILL DESCRIPTION

FIGURE 3-5. Preliminary Personal Effectiveness Plan (PEP).

CONCLUSION

Personal effectiveness within high-tech entrepreneurial environments goes beyond work-content skills or technical knowledge. It requires acknowledgement and development of your power by using inner strength, being interpersonally competent, using position power appropriately, and identifying with the cultural norms of the organization.

The personal power that emanates from the inner self requires awareness of your risk taking patterns and how to use them to feel positive about yourself. It also requires relying upon self-management skills, managing your fears, being realistic, being strong enough to be vulnerable, and formulating a clear vision of personal goals.

On an interpersonal level, personal effectiveness involves influencing others in ways that leave both parties feeling more competent and self-confident. Unlike oppression and acting aggressively to dominate others which undermines power at all levels, interpersonal power allows an exchange of information, resources, and support to reach mutual goals and reinforce power at all levels.

You can acquire organizational power by tapping the small power bases within the organization, using teams to share information, problem solve, and achieve results. Also, being aware of the cultural norms of the organization enables you to create new channels of communication.

Since personal effectiveness demands playing multiple roles and employing several types of skills, an analysis of your skills becomes the first step in formulating a Personal Effectiveness Plan.

ANSWERS AND FOLLOW-UP TO EXERCISE 3-1. Assessing Your Power Assumptions

The correct answers to Exercise 3-1 are listed below. To determine the reasoning behind each correct statement, in Part B write down the prevailing viewpoint that underlies each statement.

Part A

1. b
2. a
3. c
4. b
5. a

ANSWERS AND FOLLOW-UP TO EXERCISE 3-1. *(Continued)*

Part B

Prevailing Viewpoint

1.
2.
3.
4.
5.

ANSWERS TO EXERCISE 3-2. Identification of Mini-Entrepreneurial Roles

Role	Skills Used
I. Communicator	Communicating effectively with people within various departments and at different organizational levels. Pinpointing the needs and objectives of others.
II. Collaborator	Working jointly with others inside and outside my work unit to accomplish a task. Negotiating agreements within a group.
III. Realist	Adapting to changing priorities and circumstances beyond my control.
IV. Initiator	Anticipating problems before they occur. Initiating corrective action as problems arise.
V. Collaborator	Explaining another person's viewpoint to others. Working jointly with others inside and outside my work unit to accomplish a task.

CAREER VALUES AND THE CORPORATE CULTURE

Capitalizing on YOU, Inc.

HOW TO GET THINGS DONE

Louise Meyer, a former marketing communications manager of a high-tech company, recently accepted an account manager position with a public relations agency, where she has worked for six weeks. While a senior account executive and marketing communications manager at CBX company, she produced technical and promotional literature and implemented advertising and marketing support programs for the various product lines.

Louise's long-term career goal is to return to a corporation as a manager of corporate communications. Her desire to acquire more public relations experience prompted this job change.

Allison Wang, a former coworker in marketing communications, has assumed Louise's previous job and is meeting her for lunch:

ALLISON: So how are you finding working for an agency as opposed to CBX?

LOUISE: Well I'm still going through culture shock.

ALLISON: How so?

LOUISE: As one person dealing with several clients, it's very difficult not to be selfish. Because if you lose a couple of clients, you may not be there. So you have to "box it out" to get support internally to make sure you are delivering your goods on time. You are competing with all the other people in the agency. So it becomes a very egocentric environment.

ALLISON: Now Louise, I think you are forgetting about some of the managers we worked with who weren't exactly egoless.

LOUISE: Yes, you're right. But what I don't see here that we had at CBX is the sharing of resources and information. Now I admit that it was sometimes difficult to exchange information, but the environment, the culture, supported working things out so that we could reach common goals.

ALLISON: Speaking of reaching common goals, can you give me some tips on how I can work with Jim Houston? He takes everything so literally that I feel like I need to draw a picture, an engineering specification.

LOUISE: That's exactly what you need to do. I remember when we planned the marketing seminars for 16 cities. I had difficulty getting him to think about the marketing objective and the planning process. So I started drawing some boxes for a flowchart. I said, "Here's where we are and here's where we want to be." We divided them into time blocks and functions. I used the jargon that I had heard him use, in playing back what my need was. Then he said, "Oh well that's easy." He got out some chalk and started drawing on the board and pretty soon we had our schedule and what resources we needed to get the job done.

ALLISON: It sounds so easy. I can see him responding to that process instead of asking him for his marketing objective. He doesn't think in those terms. Now how can I help you work out the discomfort you're feeling?

LOUISE: I'll just take it one step at a time. For now, I need to get back to the office.

As Allison left Louise, she wondered if Louise would have accepted the job at the agency if she had been aware of the cultural differences between work environments.

What major differences exist between the culture at CBX and the agency? What shifts in work style contribute to Louise's sense of job dissatisfaction?

BUILDING YOUR PEP

Now that you have begun to collect some data on yourself and also have a framework for assessing this information, you can continue to build your PEP according to your specific job situation and particular needs. Discovering what is important to you in an organization and what makes a job satisfying is part of determining your current and future job needs. This information will enable you to plot the relationship between career values (what is important to you in your career), corporate culture (what is important to the organization), and career success. Ultimately self-knowledge and knowledge about corporate culture go hand-in-hand with career success, for in reality you can be successful only to the extent that your personal values and work style blend well with the organization's. Now you can begin both integrating your personal/professional skills, values, and goals with the demands and expectations of the high-tech environment and capitalizing on your personal assets. An analysis of your career values and work style is really an investment in developing your personal effectiveness, becoming a mini-entrepreneur.

To expand your personal power, first you must uncover your strengths and career values and then compare them to the values of various corporate cultures. You have had an opportunity to assess your competencies using the Mini-Entrepreneurial Skills Inventory. Now take an indepth look at your current job needs and career values to determine what excites you about your job. Once you have done this self-assessment, you can take an objective look at the various types of cultures, including the high-tech entrepreneurial culture.

Career Values

Career values lie at the core of job satisfaction and career success. Without an awareness of what intrinsic and extrinsic rewards are important to you and what you find satisfying in a particular job, you lack the vital information and self-knowledge necessary for becoming personally effective. As a first step in determining your career values, complete Exercise 4-1.

EXERCISE 4-1. Career Choices

DIRECTIONS: Prioritize each of the job situations listed below by placing a "1" next to your first choice, a "2" next to your second choice, and so forth.

_____   You have been asked by the division manager to join a start-up team that will go to Ireland to help open a new plant. You have been selected based on demonstrated competence in your field. This offer is a promotion that represents an increase in pay and could open additional opportunities in the future.

_____   You have been asked by a former coworker who recently joined a start-up company to become a part of its top-level team. He assures you that the company, now in a high growth mode, will yield you high financial returns.

_____   You have been offered a management position within the same functional area. A change in job title and salary accompanies this offer.

_____   You have been asked by the division manager to become manager for the Participatory Management Program. You would implement the program for all the divisions. It requires a high degree of interpersonal competence. The offer affords high visibility and a pay increase.

Associated with each of these choices are values and assumptions about what is important to you. Let's examine the career values associated with each of these choices.

A career abroad:	Adventure, mobility, challenge, responsibility, creativity
A start-up:	Wealth, entrepreneurship, automony, competitiveness
A promotion:	Advancement, authority, affiliation, stability, recognition, status
A people job:	Interaction, contribution, social interest, creativity, status

Each of these career choices provides an outlet to exercise your competence and attain a sense of personal satisfaction, depending on what is important to you at this point in your career. What may be valued now in your career may not rank so highly in the future. As you grow and change so do your needs and values.

Now let's take a look at how mini-entrepreneurs make career choices. Marta Dunlap left her position of product marketing manager because of the lack of advancement opportunities available to her as a woman. She realized how much she valued developing her career, became aware of built-in occupational biases in her work setting (a preference for individuals with military experience), and decided to transfer.

She explains:

> *I realized that I wasn't going anywhere in the division. It was frankly admitted to me that women were going to be held back, that being female was going to be held against me in this business. I wasn't going to be a salesperson, because I wasn't a male and a hardware engineer. There is a very heavy bias against anyone without an engineering background. The customers are the different branches of the military who have trouble dealing with a woman unless you have military experience.*

> *Although I got outstanding reviews, I really couldn't get the development I wanted in my career. So I decided it was time to move on. There were sales managers that didn't want to see me go to and offered to help. I really appreciated that, but I would be going against the grain. It would be a uphill struggle.*

Unless Marta could see a clear path leading to a promotion, she was not willing to "stick it out."

Unlike Marta, Robert Devore, a production manager for an international company that manufactures integrated circuits, makes his career choices for different reasons:

> *I chose the assignment overseas because I like start-up fix-it situations. I really don't like long years in a job sustaining something that's running well. It bores me. I really like to spend three or four years in a situation which is really a mess or to start something from scratch. I started up our plant in the Philippines in the test engineering and production areas. It was a highly focused, highly pressured situation. I couldn't be anything but a hero.*

For Robert, a new job must present a challenge, be somewhat risky, and offer new experiences.

To determine your current career values, complete Exercise 4-2.

EXERCISE 4-2. Career Values

I. In the column labeled "Rating," indicate the degree of importance for each value using the following letters.

VERY IMPORTANT   = V
SOMEWHAT IMPORTANT = S
NOT AT ALL IMPORTANT = N

Career Values

VALUE	DEFINITION	RATING	PRIORITY
Achievement	Personal/Professional feelings of accomplishment.		
Advancement	Opportunities for being promoted.		
Adventure	Opportunities for new experiences, risk taking.		
Affiliation	Recognition as being a member of a group or organization.		
Authority	Responsibility for directing the work of others.		

EXERCISE 4-2. *(Continued)*

VALUE	DEFINITION	RATING	PRIORITY
Autonomy	Freedom to develop own approach to do the job. Work independently.		
Challenge	Work that demands the resourcefulness to meet new situations.		
Comfort	Low pressure, few variations.		
Competitiveness	Desire to win, demonstrate competence.		
Conformity	Opportunity to let others set expectations and directions.		
Contribution	Opportunity to have an impact on the company.		
Cooperation	Work in a friendly and open atmosphere.		

EXERCISE 4-2. *(Continued)*

VALUE	DEFINITION	RATING	PRIORITY
Creativity	Opportunity to innovate and solve new problems.		
Entrepreneurship	Work as if self-employed, develop new ideas.		
Environment	Workplace is attractive and well designed.		
Interaction	Frequent inter-personal contact.		
Knowledge	Opportunity for new learning.		
Mobility	Travel and frequent relocation options.		
Personal Time	Opportunity for time for pursuits outside of work.		
Pleasure	Opportunity to join in celebrations and social activities.		

EXERCISE 4-2. *(Continued)*

VALUE	DEFINITION	RATING	PRIORITY
Recognition	Receive credit, positive feedback.		
Responsibility	Held accountable for important tasks.		
Security	Job not likely to be eliminated.		
Social Interest	Helping people either individually or in groups.		
Stability	Job situation fairly unchanging.		
Status	Job viewed as important in the company.		
Wealth	Making a lot of money.		

II. *After you have rated each value, in the "Priority" column next to every value with a "V" rating, identify your first priority by placing a "1" in the column, your second highest priority, place a "2", and your third highest priority, place a "3".*

EXERCISE 4-2. *(Continued)*

III. List your top three career values.

1. _____

2. _____

3. _____

Now that you are aware of your career values, you can begin to understand what points you in a certain career direction and what is important as you strive to achieve job satisfaction and career success and optimize your personal effectiveness. How, then, do your career values relate to personal effectiveness in high-tech environments? An understanding of corporate culture and individual excellence go hand-in-glove. Increasing your personal effectiveness requires understanding how your own career values mix or don't mix with corporate values. The crucial question then becomes: Can I thrive and succeed in this corporate culture? This is the question that Louise Meyer needs to ask herself. You will be wasting a lot of time and energy striving to be personally effective if you are unable to adapt to the demands of a new work environment, feel uncomfortable, and feel that you are compromising what is important to you. Internal conflicts create stress and stress diminishes personal effectiveness. For Marta, facing her career roadblock head-on freed her to find real career satisfaction. She will not only be more satisfied but more effective while free from the feeling that she is "fighting an uphill battle."

Minimize stress by paying attention to your needs and understanding what motivates you, what gets you going.

Motivation

David McClelland, a Harvard University psychologist, has proposed one approach to understanding motivation. He contends that needs are socially acquired and differ among societies. According to McClelland, our needs for affiliation, achievement, and power are prime motivators. The high-tech entrepreneurial culture creates an environment to fulfill these needs: job excellence is rewarded, informal exchanges occur, lower-level employees are involved in decision making. Personal standards for success satisfy our achievement need, and the high-tech entrepreneurial culture glorifies achievement by placing a high value on individual expertise and brainpower regardless of position. A team feeling, relationships with others, and a sense of identification with a group with similar goals satisfy our affiliation needs through warmth, support, and joint problem solving. The need to influence others, to have an impact on others in a positive way as opposed to dominating others, gives birth to power. This positive power can be found in the high-tech entrepreneurial culture which emphasizes decision making at the lowest levels. Each person has different degrees of need in each area.

Tom Atwater's experiences give us a taste for how these needs are expressed within the entrepreneurial culture. As a product consultant for an international software company, Tom enjoys and appreciates the team approach to problem solving and reaching goals. As a certified public accountant, Tom entered the company through the Research and Development door, first working on a software package for financial accounting. He eventually transferred to the Product Support area. He explains his reasons for making the change:

> *In Research and Development I didn't get the personal contact with customers that I now get. In that deparment I just got one viewpoint of the product, but in Product Support I can find out what people really think about it. I am better suited for a product support or marketing role, because I enjoy listening to what the customer has to say.*

Here he also points out what is satisfying to him in working with others and in so doing reveals his needs for affiliation, achievement, and power.

AFFILIATION
We are very excited about our product, and we want to give a little extra to the customer. We have a sense of ownership. We want to feel good about it. No single individual takes all the credit or the knocks. We do it as a team.

ACHIEVEMENT
We are less in a reaction mode now. Before I would just be able to answer phone calls from customers and respond to their questions. Now we can do more planning and analyze the documentation to see where the problems are. I talk to people in Research and Development and Marketing to see where we need to go and what we need to do to improve, to succeed.

POWER
On a regular basis I work with people from the various departments. I interact with people in Accounting, Corporate Office Services, Research and Development, and Marketing. I am able to wear different hats depending on what kind of problem I have. I may express my views more strongly if I am representing a customer's problem. I'm acting as an advocate for the customer. If I am dealing with the controller, my style is more formal, professional and less cordial than if I am talking to a programmer. Other times I am more informal. I might go out for a beer with the Marketing and R and D people to talk over a problem. I like having that kind of influence in moving the organization.

Tom's style blends well with the style of his organization. He is keenly aware of his needs and how they can take root and grow within his work environment.

Your needs push you toward certain job activities and mold your career values. Job satisfaction, then, asks that you match your career values with those of the high-tech entrepreneurial culture. In the process you come closer to reaching personal effectiveness. Let's now examine various corporate cultures.

Corporate Cultures

Corporate cultures consists of shared values and beliefs sometimes unstated and communicated symbolically through the corporation. The high-tech entrepreneurial culture reinforces, promotes, and perpetuates a specific set of shared values. Company founders have been known to stress certain humanistic values, people values such as respect for the individual, open communication, and team work. These values serve as guiding principles for individual action.

Lisa Ishimoto, a systems engineering manager for a high-tech entrepreneurial company, describes just how powerful these values are in affecting job satisfaction. What one person loves and thrives in, another person may find suffocating:

> *A person who came from the same company which I did hated it here. It was just way too unstructured for him. He finally quit.*
>
> *Some people go through a real culture shock when they come here. It's a culture that I thrive in and others absolutely die in.*

So you can see just how powerful a part corporate culture plays in shaping job effectiveness and career decision making.

Two different perspectives exist from which to view corporate culture: individual's viewpoint and the organization's viewpoint. So in effect, you can look at building a culture from the top down and bottom up. From an organizational perspective (top down), shared values define and mold the culture. The organization as a whole attempts to present itself as a small homogenous society, striving for integration of common beliefs, assumptions of "how things are done around here," or norms.

You, therefore, have two affiliations within the corporate culture: a member of the corporate culture at large (the entire company) and a member of a work group existing within the pervasive corporate culture. Using the corporate culture analogy enables you to picture these work units as subcultures, distinct and separate from, yet a part of, the larger culture. Each of these subcultures has its language, jargon, frame of reference, and preferred work style. Then how can you best operate within these two sets of rules? How does the corporate culture strive to create an organizational melting pot?

As discussed in Chapter 1, the high-tech entrepreneurial culture attempts to pull together and assimilate these differences by using teams, open and informal communication, and a physical environment designed to break down communication barriers. Figure 4-1 gives a framework for examining the elements of corporate culture. You cannot really succeed or come close to reaching personal effectiveness unless you are aware of your own career values, the corporate culture, and know how to get things done within a cross-cultural environment.

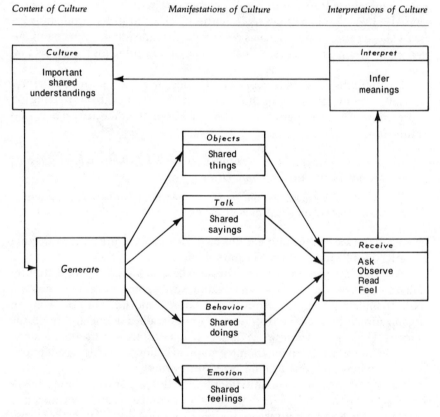

FIGURE 4-1. Framework for Diagnosing Culture. Reprinted from Vijay Sathe. "Implications of Corporate Culture: A Manageer's Guide to Action." *Organizational Dynamics*, Autumn 1983, pg. 8. Reprinted with permission.

Understanding the dynamics of corporate culture enables you to:

- Identify the appropriate relationship between you and the organization (the "social contract" that legislates what is expected);
- Specify the goals and values upon which the success and worth of the corporation is based;
- Determine which of your career values will be supported and positively reinforced through recognition and rewards;
- Recognize how you can expect to be treated by coworkers and vice versa, collaboratively or competitively, formally or informally;
- Determine how to interact with individuals and groups outside of the corporation (customers, vendors, community groups).

What is shared in the minds of organization members is as important and often more important than what is openly stated. So much so that the objects (shared thing, shared sayings, shared doings, shared feelings) become the "laundry list" for understanding the culture; they are the clues to the culture.

To interpret the culture, you need to ask how things are done, observe the actions and behavior of others to pick up important cues; read literature ranging from the corporate philosophy to an interoffice memo to find out what's really going on; determine how others feel about the way things are done around the organization and how they feel in general about the company.

Table 4-1 provides examples of the contents listed in Figure 4-1.

MESHING CAREER AND CORPORATE VALUES

Shared values define the fundamental corporate character and help shape your behavior and attitudes as you enter the corporate ranks. Exercise 4-2 gave you a chance to identify your career values. You can now take this information and compare it to the values of the corporate culture. Although not all corporate cultures fall within four distinct categories, you can use these categories as a way of differentiating and recognizing types of cultures or corporate character.

Types of Corporate Cultures

The following types of corporate culture include descriptions of how decisions are made, how human resources are used, and how the external environment is viewed. Although most companies will overlap between categories, they do tend to fall within one category as opposed to another.

TABLE 4-1

Important Shared Understanding from Shared Things, Shared Sayings, Shared Doings and Shared Feelings, Company X

Important Shared Understandings	*Shared Doings*
1. Provide highly responsive, quality customer service (SS1, SS2, SD2, SD5).	SD1. Participate in lots of meetings.
	SD2. Make sure organization is detail-oriented to provide quality customer service.
2. Get things done well and quickly ("expediting") (SS1, SD1, SD4, SD5).	
	SD3. Engage in personal relationships and communications.
3. Operate informally (ST1, SS3, SD3, SD6).	SD4. Rally to meet customer needs in a crisis.
4. Perceive company as part of the family (ST2, SD6, SF1, SF2, SF3).	SD5. Expedite jobs to deliver highly responsive service.
5. Encourage constructive disagreement (ST3, SD1).	SD6. Maintain close relationship with union.
Shared Things	*Shared Feelings*
ST1. Shirt sleeves.	SF1. The company is good to me.
ST2. One-company town.	SF2. We like this place.
ST3. Open offices.	SF3. We care about this company because it cares about us as as individuals.
Shared Savings	
SS1. "Get out there" to understand the customer. (Belief in travel)	
SS2. "We cannot rely on systems" to meet customer needs. (Highly responsive customer service)	
SS3. "We don't stand on rank." (No parking privileges)	

Reprinted with permission from Vijay Sathe, "Implications of Corporate Culture: A Manager's Guide to Action," *Organizational Dynamics*, Autumn 1983.

Authoritarian: Might Makes Right

The authoritarian culture reacts to the external environment and, in particular, competition as if they were enemies. Within the company those in positions of power strive to maintain absolute control over subordinates. The attitude of "might makes right" pervades and colors interactions between employees. The law of the jungle seems to dictate relationships particularly among executives as they compete for personal advantages. A training manager of an authoritarian company explains how management style affected his work unit:

> *There was a lot of backbiting among executives, particularly my boss, the V.P. of Human Resources, and the V.P. of Marketing. Since the training function was new to the company, it took a backseat to marketing. The perception was that marketing brought in the "bucks" for the company. The same conference room was used for both training workshops and customer sales demonstrations. We both also shared a storage room.*

> *After suggesting that training materials should be stored elsewhere, they chose to solve the real estate problem by changing the lock and not giving me a key. I felt like a schoolboy being slapped on the wrist.*

In this culture, top management, undoubtedly, makes the decisions; and information, by passing through many levels, often becomes distorted. Aggression is accepted as part of the cultural dynamics. When a quick response is needed, the time lag creates delays. Because power and control is associated with position or formal authority, the culture is not likely to easily accommodate change.

While the authoritarian culture provides channels for aggressive individuals to fight their way to the top, it offers little incentive to the loyal and steadfast individual. The concern for control dictates the policing of employees. As a result, the individual worker conforms out of compliance rather than a sense of culture identification.

Bureaucratic: Document It

The bureaucratic culture strives to be as rational and orderly as possible with a preoccupation with legality, legitimacy, and responsibility. Contrasting the authoritarian culture, this culture carefully defines and documents rights and privileges. Emphasizing hierarchy and status, the bureaucratic culture dilutes absolute power with legality and legitimacy.

Since stability and respectability are valued as much as competence, a correct or appropriate response is given more weight than the effective one. Cumbersome procedures slow down decisions and information flow and sabotage change. Those businesses that either control their market or operate in areas that are highly regulated by law develop a bureaucratic culture. Banks, insurance companies, and public utilities fall within this category.

The bureaucratic culture approaches the tasks of dealing with decision making and problem solving by work simplification. Each job is broken down into smaller units. When innovative change is required, individuals are likely to continue the same procedures.

Authoritarian and bureaucratic cultures do not provide opportunities for individual initiative, independent judgment, or commitment. Incompetence is more likely to slip through the cracks in these kinds of environments, while indifference hides behind the facade of caution.

An attitude survey conducted by a large insurance company revealed that the employee development needs of a department were being ignored and were critical to retaining competent personnel. To deal with the employee dissatisfaction, the department hired a human resources specialist. She describes the bureaucratic roadblocks she encountered:

> *We implemented a career development program consisting of a number of career planning workshops for interested employees. They were given during company hours. Although I was not hired by the Training department, I received assistance from other trainers from other departments such as claims and sales. The program was well-received, and other departments within the company wanted similar workshops. I wanted to publish an article on the program in the company newsletter. However the Training executive "panned the idea" because his staff wouldn't be able to respond to the requests which might develop. My boss, his peer, supported him out of a sense of protocol.*
>
> *Although I left the company to accept a higher level position, I later heard that the Training Department had reorganized and was starting from scratch in designing a career development program for managers. They were reinventing the wheel at a tremendous cost to the company.*

In this situation what was appropriate is based on protocol, caution, and respectability as opposed to effectiveness. Culture can be a liability when shared values are not "in sync" with its members' needs.

Supportive: You Scratch My Back, I'll Scratch Yours

Unlike the previous two cultures, the supportive culture exists primarily to serve the needs of its members. The organization enables members to share resources, material, and information.

Authority is deemphasized and, when necessary, assigned on the basis of task completion. Individuals, expected to interact with each other through caring and helpfulness, use consensus in decision making and act according to their personal goals and values.

Examples of supportive cultures include groups of professionals joined together in research and development and some consulting companies designed to meet the needs of its members.

Capable of adapting to complexity and change, the supportive culture contains fluid structures and open communications. Individuals who are independent and self-directed are served well by this structure.

Entrepreneurial/Innovative: Let's Play to Succeed

Unlike the authoritarian culture, authority in the entrepreneurial/innovative culture is not based solely on power or position but rather on knowledge or competence. Risk taking and achievement are valued highly. If outmoded roles, rules, and regulations impede problem solving, they are modified. Collaboration is crucial for problem solving and decision making and in meeting changing marketplace conditions and demands. Team and task forces create an atmosphere of "playing to succeed."

With a superordinate goal of achievement, the entrepreneurial/innovative culture creates opportunities for the individual to take initiative, assert independent judgment, and identify with company goals. This culture treats people who act as if their job is their own small business like inhouse entrepreneurs and rewards them for success. Because they have a sense of identification with group goals, they take on a sense of commitment to the company.

Self-Evaluation

Although these categories of corporate culture provide a rather simplistic view of cultural types, they can be useful tools to determine which environment will least conflict with your needs and career values. A perfect match is unrealistic since both individual values and corporate culture are transitory. Furthermore, not all high-tech environments can be considered entrepreneurial or innovative. Those high-tech companies which rely heavily on outside funding, such as the military, tend to be constrained by federal rules and regulations. In this case, they may be more authoritarian or bureaucratic.

Depending on your current needs and career values, you may prefer working in an environment that provides clear lines of authority and a hierarchical structure. Another factor to consider is the relative strength of the culture. Not all cultures equally influence individual behavior. Cultures with openly stated, shared beliefs and values make a stronger impact on behavior because more shared assumptions guide behavior.

To determine which type of corporate culture may be best suited for accommodating your career values, review Table 4-2.

You are investing in a career, capitalizing on your personal style, and optimizing your personal effectiveness by identifying the type of corporate culture you find attractive. You should now have a good idea of your preferred career values and the type of culture which complements these values.

TABLE 4-2

Corporate Cultures and Opportunities for Involvement

Cultural Types/ Motto	Decision Making	Communication	Cooperation	Commitment
Authoritarian/ Might makes right	Direction from authority.	Through lines of authority or "grapevine."	Competition for a place at the top.	Based on compliance to authority.
Bureaucratic/ Document it	Results from legalistic methods or process.	Formal, through hierarchy or "grapevine."	Based on letter of the law.	Based on compliance to letter of the law.
Supportive/You scratch my back, I'll scratch yours	Through discussion and agreement.	Open and informal.	Based on mutual interests. Cooperation outweighs competition.	Toward personal goals primarily; secondarily to organizational goals.
Entrepreneurial/ innovative/ Let's play to succeed	Through constructive dissent, consensus	Open and informal communication.	Based on gamespersonship and shared values.	Interpersonal group commitment based on identification with shared values.

Working with Subcultures

Each company, regardless of its corporate culture, contains functional areas such as finance, human resources, engineering, etc. Each of these professional work groups has a conceptual framework, technical language, or jargon and a preferred work style. They comprise a subculture with its own particular communication style. You can detect subcultural norms or ways of doing things by noticing how people relate to one another, communicate verbally and nonverbally through cues.

Determine whether you can operate comfortably and effectively within the high-tech entrepreneurial culture by pinpointing its expectations, beliefs, and assumptions. The information that you have accumulated so far on career values, corporate culture, and cultural norms should enable you to do this. To strengthen your personal effectiveness, you must enlarge your understanding of the corporate culture by examining subcultures or work groups.

Cross-Cultural Work Styles

How do personally effective mini-entrepreneurs operate in such a cross-cultural environment? They improve intergroup communications by taking on roles as interpreters, mediators, and facilitators, while being sensitive to the needs and objectives of coworkers. Let's review the actions of a mini-entrepreneur, Tim Allen.

In his role as product marketing engineer for a integrated circuits company, Tim explains that the "bottom line" is to keep the customer satisfied. He often finds himself acting as an interpreter when interacting with individuals from various work groups: engineering, quality assurance, purchasing, and marketing. He switches between interpreting highly technical information to nontechnical people and vice versa. Part of his job is to transmit messages from the division to the customer. He explains the cultural dynamics involved:

Taking what our engineers are saying and translating it for the customer becomes difficult. I can easily take the terminology of the customer such as "an access time of 450 nanoseconds" and feed it back to our engineers. It's like taking English and translating it into Spanish. But changing Spanish into English is more difficult. I was thrown into a fire when I was responsible for making a presentation to a customer. I was really concerned about how I would deliver the information to nontechnical people. I knew there would be design engineers present representing the customer and some Purchasing people. But I knew that they probably wouldn't understand the same type of information as our people here at the division.

So I watched eyes to see who was falling asleep and who was completely lost. I made a general statement and then got more specific. I looked over at the technical person from their (the customer's) company. Then he picked up the information and said, "And Joe what that means to us is. . . ." So it becomes a team effort when you can get their technical person talking for you. What it means to me is that now he (the technical person) understands. He is getting two versions of the same story.

Wearing the hat of interpreter, Tim picks up on the sensitivities and subtleties involved in communicating with subcultures or work groups who have different outlooks, jargon, and work styles. His ability to bridge gaps between work groups facilitates communication, for differences in work groups can also create distances and frustration unless approached objectively.

Step for Communicating

To fine tune your interpersonal skills in communicating with subcultures, refer to the following checklist. In following these steps, you are simply applying general principles of clear communication to a specific situation.

A. Identify Patterns

1. List norms of behavior, words, jargon, and their implied meanings.
2. Verify your interpretation with a group member you can trust.

B. Acknowledge Differences

1. List the difference in the way things are done between your work group and the other being observed.

C. Make Contact

1. Attempt to use the same language to build communication bridges.
2. Acknowledge feelings expressed by the other group members.
3. Explain your perception in terms of their concepts and language.

Without an understanding of intergroup relations, you will be lost when caught in the middle of group conflicts. Remember, perception of differences in viewpoint, language, priorities, and overall work style form the basis of any conflict.

EXAMINING YOUR WORK STYLE

To fully understand differences in work styles, you first must be aware of your own. In doing so you will learn to distinguish between various work styles and the cultures which are conducive to those styles. Let's examine differences in work styles along the lines of building trust and communicating openly and informally. As pointed out earlier, corporate cultures, their values in particular, influence the behavior of individuals at all levels of the organization and so mold the work behavior of their people by giving direction to specific action. Peter Applebee's actions demonstrate his belief in and commitment to nurturing his corporate culture. As the manager of the Education

Center for an international software company, he and his staff are responsible for providing a four-week orientation and training program to newly hired product consultants. He explains how the organization stresses open communication and mutual support building:

> The real objective of orientation is to make new product consultants understand the company and make them have a sense of belonging in our culture so that they can identify with the culture. My mandate is, however, to train them technically in our software products. By asking the vice presidents and managers from the departments to speak with them, they get a chance to do some networking and to build some support for themselves so that when they are 3000 miles away, they can feel comfortable about calling them up for some advice. They'll be able to match names with faces.
>
> Here you can really call up anyone you want. I suppose that the organization structure is in place, because there needs to be one. Our president even answers his own phone and is very accessible to all employees. This attitude carries over into the rest of the company with people being available to answer questions and give feedback.

In contrast Penny Sumner, a training and development manager of a financial services company, describes how people communicate with more formality and distance:

> I was rather shocked when I first came to the company and glanced at a few interoffice memos. Everyone addressed each other with Mr. or Ms. If there were several people they would use 'messieurs.' I was accustomed to addressing people with their first and last names.
>
> Our department was housed on the same floor. I was surprised how frequently people used the telephone when I could actually see the person calling me across the room. In fact one day I received a phone call from the assistant controller. His voice sounded as if he were speaking through a tunnel. Well I realized that he was having a meeting with his managers and was talking into the speaker designed for conference calls. After he told me what was going on, I suggested that I attend the meeting (a few yards away) to answer their questions. I couldn't believe that such formality prevailed. From that point on, I made sure that I met face-to-face with people to talk about problems. It did make a difference in how well we communicated.

Having gained insight into contrasting cultures and work styles, you can begin focusing on your own style. To determine how you work best and which cultural norms you find most conducive to your work style, complete Exercise 4-3.

EXERCISE 4-3. Work Style Assessment

DIRECTIONS: Review the work style descriptions listed on both the right and the left. Then place a check above the number that best describes the relative strength of your work style. The ratings below correspond to the numbers in each description.

1 = Sometimes   2 = Often   3 = Always

Initiate action on my own.	3 2 1 0 1 2 3	Wait for general direction from others.

Make time to communicate often with others.	3 2 1 0 1 2 3	Unable to communicate with others due to deadlines and location.

Work as part of a team even if not formally assigned.	3 2 1 0 1 2 3	Work independently due to work assignment.

Able to pursue both personal and job goals.	3 2 1 0 1 2 3	Follow goals established by management.

Able to express myself openly and informally.	3 2 1 0 1 2 3	Value more professional and formal interactions.

Take charge of coordinating activities and share the responsibility.	3 2 1 0 1 2 3	Allow others to take over to avoid any disagreeing.

Build trust through mutual support regardless of function.	3 2 1 0 1 2 3	Maintain allegiance to own functional group.

EXERCISE 4-3. *(Continued)*

Innovate and work creatively at all times.							Tend to follow predictable course of action.
	3	2	1	0	1	2	3

Make effective decisions with peers.							Expect management to make decisions.
	3	2	1	0	1	2	3

Innovate and
work creatively   Tend to follow
at all times.   3   2   1   0   1   2   3   predictable
                                                      course of action.

Make effective
decisions with   Expect
peers.   3   2   1   0   1   2   3   management to
                                                      make decisions.

Being rewarded
for risk taking.   Being rewarded
                   3   2   1   0   1   2   3   for maintaining
                                                      the status quo.

Stay involved
until the job   Let others
is completed.   3   2   1   0   1   2   3   take the
                                                      responsibility
                                                      for job
                                                      completion.

Plan ahead
to reach goals.   3   2   1   0   1   2   3   Take things
                                                      as they come.

   See directions at end of this chapter for an interpretation of your scores and directions for further completing your PEP.

EXPANDING YOUR PEP

You now have had the opportunity to assess yourself in relationship to your values, attitudes toward the high-tech entrepreneurial environment, and work style. This information is valuable as you continue to build your PEP. So far you have collected data on your skills in Chapter 2. With the analysis you have done in this chapter, you can now pinpoint discrepancies between your current work style and those strategies stressed by the high-tech entrepreneurial culture. Let's use Marta Dunlap's situation to determine how skills and work styles differ and what steps to take to eliminate the temporary gap between the ideal and your current work style. Moving from a product marketing position to a customer marketing position, and from one division to another, she explains her adjustment, her current work style, and how she hopes to change it once she gets familiar with her job, her role, and the cultural norms of the division.

In terms of professional/technical skills, being able to write and manage a large project, I am using the same skills that I've used previously. In terms of people skills, which I think are sometimes more important, they weren't really tested until last week. Because during the first month and a half of doing this document, I was writing in isolation. I hated that period. It was a very painful, frustrating process. I didn't really have all that much access to people who could help me or give me the information upfront. I just needed to meet my deadline.

It wasn't until I got out my rough draft and got their comments that I started talking to people. The skills of working with people in a group will become more important over the next few weeks, as I take the time to get to know people and work with them.

Marta was relying entirely upon her writing skills to get her job done because of the time pressure involved in meeting her deadline, the nature of the project, and her newness in the job. Her work style, working independently, conflicted with her natural style of working as part of a team. For Marta then, her work style gap would include:

Work Style Gap

Ideal	Actual
Work as part of a team	Work independently

Marta's writing project could have been more of a team effort if she had been familiar with coworkers and developed a rapport. Now aware of how her work style affects how to get things done, she can take steps to work less independently. The demands of her first assignment dictated that she work more independently.

In contrast to Marta's situation, Penny Sumner feels pressure, stemming from cultural norms, to change her work style as it relates to communicating informally. She encountered cultural differences when moving from a financial services company to a high-tech company. She explains:

Working within a high-tech environment I find that I am changing the way I communicate with people. In my former company, people were more formal in the way they communicated and their speech. I used more abstract words to describe methods and concepts. But when I use the same language here in this high-tech, manufacturing environment, I find that people responded with a puzzled look on their faces. So I am starting to listen to their language and beginning to use it better. For example, when describing the process of follow-

ing up on an assignment, we use the term 'close the loop,' while my former coworkers would use the phrase, 'get your feedback.'

Here everyone communicates face to face so that I constantly have managers coming in and out of my office. I make sure that I get out of my office to conduct business on an informal basis, over coffee, over lunch, at company sponsored social events such as dinner meetings and even baseball games.

The change in corporate culture necessitates a change in work style. Penny's Personal Effectiveness Plan would include a work style gap as follows:

Work Style Gap

Ideal	Actual
Able to express myself openly and informally	Stress restrained, formal interactions

With an idea and some feeling for how work styles affect personal effectiveness, begin assessing your own. Review the Work Style Assessment (Exercise 4-3) and determine your gaps or areas where realignment is needed between the ideal and the actual. Now complete the "Work Style Discrepancies" section of your PEP by listing the two areas from Exercise 4-3 in which you scored the lowest or in which you need the most improvement.

EXERCISE 4-4. Work Style Discrepancies for Personal Effectiveness Plan

Work Style Discrepancies

Ideal	Actual
1. _____	_____
_____	_____
2. _____	_____
_____	_____

To provide you with a preview of your PEP refer to Figure 4-2. Marta Dunlap and Penny Sumner provide examples of specific action steps to take in closing the gap between your ideal and actual work style. If we were

SKILLS

   Strengths

   1. _____

   2. _____

AREAS FOR IMPROVEMENT   ACTION STEPS

SKILLS

   1. _____   _____

   2. _____   _____

WORK STYLE GAPS

     Ideal   Actual

1. _____   _____

   _____   _____

ROLES   ACTION STEPS

   PARTICIPATION

     1. _____   _____

   COMMITMENT

     1. _____   _____

   CREATIVITY

     1. _____   _____

WORK GOALS

   Job Goals

   1. _____   1. _____

     _____   _____

   Innovative Goals

   1. _____   1. _____

     _____   _____

CAREER GOAL

   _____   _____

   _____   _____

FIGURE 4-2. Personal Effectiveness Plan.

to complete the "Work Style Gaps" section of the PEP for each of them, it would include:

Work Style Gaps		Action Steps
Ideal	Actual	
(Marta)		
1. Work as part of a team	Work independently	1. Make contact with others
		2. Discover their job role, skills, and work style
		3. Build mutual support
(Penny)		
1. Express myself openly and informally	Stress restrained formal interactions	1. Use similar language
		2. Follow work style patterns of other top performers

You will complete a PEP by the end of this book after you will have accumulated additional information on how to perform other roles.

Now that you have a concept of the format and contents, you can focus on more specific steps to follow for outlining actions to strengthen your roles and become personally effective.

CONCLUSION

Pinpointing your career values becomes an investment in your career as does identifying your areas of strength and skill improvement needs. By recognizing the connection between career values, types of corporate culture, cultural norms, and work styles, you begin to capitalize on your personal assets, and ultimately, optimize your personal effectiveness. As you begin to see the chain reaction between needs, job satisfaction, and career values, you will also see the relationship between career values and personal choice. You gain greater control over your career by consciously choosing the most suitable type of work environment or corporate culture for you.

The high-tech entrepreneurial culture fosters certain values and cultural norms. Although many variations of corporate culture exist, a conceptual framework for assessing them provides vital information for identifying expectations, both your own and those of the company. With this framework, you can expand your understanding of the dynamics of culture on a company-wide scale and also on a work group scale. This is necessary for optimizing your personal effectiveness that requires learning how to operate, "how to get things done," within the corporate culture and the subcultures. The first step toward understanding subcultures is to examine your own work style.

With this additional self knowledge of career values and work styles, as well as a conceptual framework for diagnosing corporate cultures, you can expand your Personal Effectiveness Plan.

ANSWERS TO EXERCISE 4-3. Work Style Assessment

   I. To *calculate your score, total ONLY the numbers to the left of the zero. If you scored:*

   A. 24—36 points, your work style is conducive to the high-tech entrepreneurial culture. You will most likely be productive and job satisfied in this culture.

   B. 12—23 points, with time, skill development and work style awareness, you can develop a work style conducive to the high-tech entrepreneurial culture.

   C. 11 points or below, you will probably find that your work style conflicts with the high-tech entrepreneurial culture.

  II. *Total only the numbers to the right of the zero. If you scored:*

   A. 12 points or less, with time and skill development you can develop a work style conducive to the high-tech entrepreneurial culture.

   B. 13 points or more, you will probably find that your work style conflicts with the high-tech entrepreneurial culture.

 III. *To determine action steps to list in your PEP for developing an entrepreneurial work style, see descriptions listed on the left-hand side of the Work Style Assessment. Through understanding the roles of the mini-entrepreneur and developing skills, you can adjust your work style by following these steps:*

   A. Identify the work style description(s) in which you scored the lowest. (The score farthest from the description listed on the left-hand side.)

   B. List this work style description in the "Work Style Gaps" section of the PEP. These gaps pinpoint the difference between the ideal and the actual behavior.

IV. *Make the connection between work style, skills, and specific actions by using the following steps:*

A. Identify the role connected to the work style descriptions. Use the following listings.

Work Style Descriptions	Role
Initiate action on my own.	Initiator
Communicate often with others.	Communicator
Work as part of a team.	Team Member
Pursue both personal and job goals.	Self-Developer
Express myself openly and informally.	Communicator
Take charge of coordinating activities.	Organizer
Build trust through mutual support.	Collaborator
Innovate and work creatively.	Innovator
Make effective decisions with peers.	Collaborator
Be rewarded for risk taking.	Innovator
Stay involved until the job is completed.	Realist
Plan ahead to reach goals.	Organizer

B. Using the role category from A, select the skill(s) from the Mini-Entrepreneurial Skills Inventory that need development and list under "action steps" of your PEP. See the following example taken from Penny Sumner's example.

Work Style Gaps		Action Steps
Ideal	Actual	
Able to express myself openly and informally.	Stress restrained formal interactions.	Use language (metaphors, stories & examples) familiar to the listener.

Part II

FINE TUNING YOUR POWER SKILLS

5

COMMUNICATING WELL

The Process Essential to All Success

BEING "IN TUNE"

Lisa Ishimoto, a systems engineering manager who has been recently promoted to a management position, and Jerry Jenson, a sales manager, are both members of a team organized to gather information for the Division Long-Range Plan (DRLP) for a high-tech company. The objective of this division-wide planning session is to develop strategies for reaching long-term company goals over the next 5 to 10 years. Lisa and Jerry have arranged meetings with their customers to determine future needs. Although Lisa and Jerry have, in the past, agreed on strategies before sales meetings, for this type of meeting neither one knows exactly what to expect, nor what the outcome may be.

After one of the "query" meetings, which was similar to a round-table discussion, Lisa and Jerry discuss the communication process they experienced:

JERRY: I had no idea that Chad was going to call in so many people from various projects to give us feedback.

LISA: Yes, and I couldn't tell from their titles if they were above him or below him in rank or if they were going to be able to answer our questions.

JERRY: You did a great job of picking up on my cues.

LISA: Going in, I didn't know what to expect, but I wanted to be sure that I wasn't going to step on your toes. After all I didn't want to ruin a potential sales opportunity. Besides, you have worked with Chad for a long time, and you know what to watch out for while I don't.

JERRY: Well, I appreciate your being "in tune" with my agenda.

LISA: It was a bit like walking a tightrope. I wanted to get as much feedback as possible so we would be prepared for the DRLP. Yet I didn't want to go off on any tangents either. We were dealing with so many levels of technical expertise.

JERRY: Yes, it was difficult trying to sift through all the information we got, but we were successful in getting what we needed for the DRLP. For a systems person you're not a bad salesman.

LISA: You mean a salesperson, Jerry, don't you?

Jerry smiled and nodded in agreement. As he walked away from Lisa's office, he wished that the other systems engineers were as proficient in communicating, and in particular, in listening as Lisa.

Which specific listening skills was Jerry thinking of? How did the effective use of communication skills affect the results of the meeting? Had Jerry and Lisa not been "in tune" with one another, what would have been the results?

Communication requires you to step outside your work world, look beyond your own perceptions, and be conscious of both the words and language used to express your own point of view. It asks that you transcend your ego and look beyond what works for you to what other people need and desire. It demands that you take off your occupational blinders, place your personal values in the back seat, and see the world through another person's eyes. Most of all, communication begs you to use skillful, empathetic listening.

So far you have been building your personal power by assessing your skills relative to those used by mini-entrepreneurs and matching your career values and work style to those of the high-tech entrepreneurial culture. Now let's focus on communication skill building, which is the first step to becoming personally effective. In Chapter 4 you saw how career values and corporate culture interlock and how values shape the behavior of subcultures or work groups. You were also given techniques for overcoming differences and finding common ground. You can go one step further to bridge differences between work groups by studying communication on a one-to-one basis.

This chapter will present tools for enhancing communication skills that are basic to and essential for establishing interpersonal competence. To effectively communicate, first you need to be aware of the nature of corporate culture and, second, notice how the culture influences how people communicate with one another both in language use and interaction style. In other words, you need to observe whether executives freely walk in and out of work areas and mingle comfortably with the rank and file. Because the high-tech entrepreneurial culture stresses open and informal communication, you must be sensitive and receptive to individuals at all levels and with varied occupational interests and diverse career values. Be fluid as opposed to following rigid protocol or standard operating procedures; be open to new and innovative ideas which initially may appear unworkable and impractical. Most of all, you need to take a vested interest in solving others' problems even if they are not a part of your work group or designated team, and listen with an open mind.

SHARPENING YOUR COMMUNICATION SKILLS

To enhance your communication competence, first you need to know when and how to use language in the appropriate social context or corporate cultural context. As a competent communicator you can achieve what you want in socially acceptable ways, which involves affirming your individual needs and regard for self, as well as the needs of others such as self-esteem and respect. The premium placed on both production and people needs, within the high-tech entrepreneurial culture, upgrades the quality of people interactions, and in effect, raises the interpersonal competency level required of you.

Mini-entrepreneurs communicate responsibly and effectively with others to solve problems. It isn't enough to bluntly make demands and expect people to jump. It isn't enough to point your finger at the culprit while the existing problem lies untouched. Mini-entrepreneurs "feel out" situations, go to the source, and communicate with a style that does not shatter the other person's ego. On the other hand, they communicate honestly by "leveling" (speaking honestly). Real communication through leveling is so important that it is included as a guideline for behavior in the written corporate philosophy of an entrepreneurial company. In addition to clear and honest expression, mini-entrepreneurs listen as if they have antennae atop their heads, detecting early warning signs that signal something is off-target.

To determine your communication competency level at this point in your career, complete Exercise 5-1.

EXERCISE 5-1. Assessing Your Communication Skills

Rate yourself by circling the number that best describes your ability to use the skill listed.

Skill	Rating			
	Least Skilled Area	Below Average	Average	Strength
1. Use words, pronunciation, and grammar that do not alienate others.	1	2	3	4
2. Use words understood by others.	1	2	3	4
3. Use appropriate rate, volume, and clarify in face-to-face situations.	1	2	3	4
4. Use language appropriate to different listeners.	1	2	3	4
5. Understand directions.	1	2	3	4
6. Understand complaints & needs of others.	1	2	3	4
7. Understand expectations of others.	1	2	3	4
8. Recognize key ideas in conversations with others.	1	2	3	4
9. Recognize intent of others: threats, commands, promises.	1	2	3	4

EXERCISE 5-1. *(Continued)*

Skill	Rating			
	Least Skilled Area	Below Average	Average	Strength
10. Distinguish between informative and persuasive messages.	1	2	3	4
11. Recognize when another does not understand a message.	1	2	3	4
12. Restate information given by others.	1	2	3	4
13. Ask questions in a manner that results in cooperation.	1	2	3	4
14. Recognize feelings of others.	1	2	3	4
15. Describe accurately differences in opinion between self and others.	1	2	3	4
16. Express satisfaction to coworkers about their work.	1	2	3	4
17. Express feelings of satisfaction/dissatisfaction to the appropriate person.	1	2	3	4
18. Phrase questions properly to get accurate information.	1	2	3	4
Total	____	____	____	____

First compute the totals for each column. Now calculate the final score by totalling the scores from each column.

Final Score_____

Refer to the end of this chapter for an interpretation of your scores.

THE COMMUNICATION PROCESS

By completing Exercise 5-1, undoubtedly you have pinpointed those communication skills that are your strengths. Types of communication skills include active listening, speaking, and interpersonal skills. If you don't use the appropriate skills, particularly active listening, you risk misinterpreting messages. Active listening requires you to verbalize your understanding of the speaker's message as a way of keeping pace. Misunderstandings and conflicts that appear to be personality clashes result when you communicate ineffectively either by not conveying your message or not actively listening. The communication process too easily becomes counterproductive if patience and sensitivity are ignored and skills are used clumsily.

Defining Communication

Technically, communication is the exchange or imparting of thoughts, opinions, or information through speech, writing, or signs. Communicating for results is both an art and a science. It requires intuition to focus on the real issues despite the words spoken, and at the same time, be aware of your choice of words. This chapter focuses on interpersonal communication. When you effectively communicate with another person, shared meanings and shared understandings will result. The basic components of communication include: a message, a sender, a bridge of meaning, a receiver, and interference. Figure 5-1 illustrates this process.

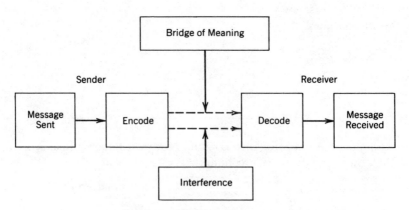

FIGURE 5-1. The Communication Process.

According to this model, you send a message that is encoded into words and nonverbal expressions such as tone of voice, facial expressions, and gestures. Your listener decodes the message according to his or her understanding and past experiences. Interference or communication barriers that you confront may be physical, such as impaired vision or hearing, or environmental distractions, such as other people talking or noises in the environment. Other types of interference, however, can be psychological and arise from differences in frame of reference, values, and experiences. The listener's interpretation of your message may be markedly different from what you had intended. Something is always communicated in an interaction between two or more people. The crucial questions are: How can I make sure that the listener interprets my message in the way I wanted?; What can I do to build a bridge of meaning to minimize the interference? To answer this question, first you must be aware of the needs of the listener. The portion of the message that the listener finds important depends on the person's motivation for participating in the interaction. What, then, does each person have to gain or lose in the interaction?

Goals

There are four primary goals of verbal exchange:

Pleasure Seeking

This interaction strengthens bonds of friendship or reduces feelings of loneliness and isolation. It expresses a basic human need and accounts for many types of conversations including "small talk" or "rap sessions."

Talking It Out

In this exchange, people attempt to alleviate emotional upset or tension by "talking things out." As the listener, your presence and acknowledgment of feelings through empathy is more important than giving advice.

Prescribing

In this type of interaction, you will dictate or order your listener to take some course of action or behave in a certain fashion. For example, a medical doctor tells a patient what to do to become healthy. Within the work setting, a supervisor interacts with an employee by setting expectations around job behavior and giving directions on tasks to be accomplished. The goal of these interactions is to direct the behavior of others by specifying actions to be taken.

Persuading

When you enter into a conversation with this objective in mind, you seek a specific response from the listener and, unlike prescribing, nudge or lead your listener to a desired response. For example, you may ask another person if he or she is hungry with the intent of going out to lunch together. A more manipulative example is described in the courtroom as "leading the witness."

You persuade when you attempt to alter another's beliefs and attitudes in a subtle way. You may influence a person so that the decision ultimately seems to come from within that person. In some instances, this process may take place over a long period of time and sometimes you never know whether the goal has been reached. Socializing new employees to the values of the corporate culture falls within this category. It happens when you teach another person "how things are done around here."

The Effect of Corporate Culture

Chapter 4 presented some tools for understanding corporate culture in general and your work style in particular. Corporate culture and individual work style both determine which communication goals dominate relationships. In the high-tech entrepreneurial culture, opportunities for communicating informally create situations for mutual pleasure and information exchange. The physical environment, partitioned offices and recreational facilities, as well as the management style, participative management and project teams, elicit open communication. The artificial boundaries of work and play dissolve, and when combined, promote open, casual, and worthwhile exchanges. Craig McMillen, a project coordinator in the Engineering Services department, describes how he operates in the high-tech entrepreneurial environment and communicates for results:

> *Working in an engineering environment is new for me. There were some guys around here that I couldn't believe, a bit eccentric. Well I thought that I'm going to have to figure these guys out. I've got to get a lot of information from them. And I've heard from other people that some of them are very difficult to approach. I've done things like learn how to play horseshoes so that I would be able to go down to the "rec" center to play. I've mingled in that way, and it worked. The recreation center has been one of my biggest sources of information. There's all sorts of channels to communicate around here.*

Even though the working environment supports mini-entrepreneurs like Craig McMillen and is designed to facilitate communication, communication barriers or gaps are unavoidable, given the diversity and multiplicity of our work force. Let's now analyze potential communication barriers or gaps.

BRIDGING COMMUNICATION GAPS

Communication gaps really stem from real estate problems or territorial boundaries. When you first meet someone, you stake out boundaries. Edgar Schein has identified the questions that are likely to concern you when first meeting another person:

- Role or identity (What is my role or who am I to be?);
- Status relating to control and influence (Will I be able to control and influence others?);
- Territory overlap to determine needs and goals (Will the group goals include my own needs?);
- Acceptance and intimacy (Will I be liked and accepted by the group?).

Your expectations and previous experience, which you bring to a personal encounter, shape decisions involving control, influence, and intimacy.

To learn something new, you really need to overstep communication boundaries. Boundaries are neither good nor bad. A boundary can work to your advantage by self-protection and can also work to your disadvantage by avoiding conflict at all costs. On the other hand, risk taking is an essential ingredient for learning, which asks that you experiment with certain boundaries and break the habit playing it safe. Overcoming this habit means listening to new information as well as expressing feelings of anger, warmth and support, in other words, being fully human and allowing other to be fully human as well. If the risk is too great (e.g., making a fool of yourself or feeling vulnerable by going against cultural norms), the boundaries become barriers to communication. In the nonentrepreneurial culture, sharing information and giving advice out of a sense of concern and helpfulness can be risky if it conflicts with cultural norms. Craig McMillen gives an example:

> I was really sticking my neck out when in my previous job I warned a coworker of a potential problem. But because there were these border lines between his department and mine, he didn't listen to me. I said, "You're going to get hit between the eyes here real fast if you don't do this." He told me that he talked to his boss and that I shouldn't be concerned so just to drop it. I was told by his boss to leave him alone and to stay out of it.

This situation shows it was too risky for Craig's coworker to listen to information that may contradict the status quo, the powers that be. So he (Craig's coworker) opted to play it safe and close his ears to what could have been potentially helpful information.

The Rapport Matrix

Over and above communication gaps that stem from the use of language, several types of barriers or gaps arise from an individual's occupational frame of reference, personal values, and internal style of processing information. To overcome these differences and build a rapport with coworkers, the Rapport Matrix has been developed (see Table 5-1) to help pinpoint sources of communication gaps and strategies to overcoming them.

TABLE 5-1

Rapport Matrix

Source of Barrier	Description	How to Build Rapport
Occupational blinders	Characteristic personality traits revealed through: perception of environment, values, and language (e.g., a person who likes to teach, develop, enlighten people is "people oriented").	1. Acknowledge valued competencies. 2. Recognize self-perception. 3. Identify with outlook of other person. 4. Pinpoint technical language, jargon, buzzwords. 5. Recognize interpersonal style of other person. 6. Phrase message of question in words familiar to the other person.
Gut-level values	Attitudes, beliefs, behaviors arising from values shaped by generational clusters (e.g., baby-boom or Depression generation).	1. Recognize clash in values. 2. Acknowledge your uneasiness. 3. See clash as a communication barrier. 4. Is it worth reacting to it? 5. If not, ignore. 6. If yes, provide an alternative point of view, keeping focus on job performance.

TABLE 5-1 (*Continued*)

Source of Barrier	Description	How to Build Rapport
Internal processing	How we make sense of the world and process information is through representational systems or sensory experiences: visual (mental pictures), auditory (internal dialogue), kinesthetic (feeling and sensations) (e.g., an artist experiences the world visually).	1. Listen to words for clues of type of system. 2. Identify the representational system. 3. Couch your message in other person's dominant representational system.

There are three dimensions of the Rapport Matrix: sources of communication barriers, descriptions of these sources, and techniques for building rapport. You can become more versatile as a communicator and flex your interpersonal muscles if you use the matrix as a reference tool for unraveling the communication process and identifying personal experiences affecting it. In short, it helps you "read" others. Similar to an engineer's specifications, this matrix identifies gaps and barriers and outlines paths for overcoming them. Regardless of your occupation, values, and way of processing information, you can use the Rapport Matrix to heighten your awareness of communication styles.

The Rapport Matrix can help you fine-tune your communication skills by clarifying the communication process, pinpointing potential pitfalls, and identifying techniques for avoiding pitfalls. The communication process can be confusing and unproductive, unless you are clear about your objective and the perspective of the person or persons being addressed. Understanding the process can help you: reorient your perspective and strengthen the impact of your message; get in touch with the needs and sensitivities of the person with whom you are communicating; and seek feedback through verbal and nonverbal messages to see if both are on the same track.

Potential pitfalls include overuse of technical language and jargon which is unfamiliar to the listener, listening blocks arising from a values clash, and preconceived notions or stereotypical thinking that results in negative attitudes. For in reality, if you tell someone something and that person does not understand, it is not that person's fault but yours. You must communicate using words and images that will allow your message to be interpreted as you desire.

Work Environments as Barriers

Your personal attitudes, attributes, and experiences create communication barriers. Each person is unique and has established a pattern of thinking and behaving. By understanding that barriers stem from your unique way of processing information, you may increase your repertoire of communication skills by using words that do not alienate others, understanding the expectations of others, accurately describing differences in opinion.

To surmount occupational barriers, first take off your occupational blinders. John Holland has developed a framework for classifying vocational interests and choices. His theory shows how we all get locked into our own point of view. Ironically, our education and training often becomes occupational hazards. His theory provides a focal point for comprehending interpersonal competence. When applied to the process, his categories of vocational or occupational interests are useful in recognizing occupational frames of reference that can erect communication barriers. These categories are illustrated in Figure 5-2. The work environments in which people display work behaviors and personal traits are: mechanistic or realistic, investigative, artistic, social enterprising, and conventional. Each environment produces a certain personality type:

Work Environment	Personality Type
Mechanistic (Realistic)	Tinker
Investigative	Scientist
Artistic	Creative designer
Social	People person
Enterprising	Entrepreneur
Conventional	Organizer

Various work environments form boundaries that further isolate and separate those who do not share the same set of assumptions, procedures, sources of information, and sense of what is important. People within these environments respond to situations and problems similarly. In effect, they create an interpersonal environment, their own familiar world. By describing

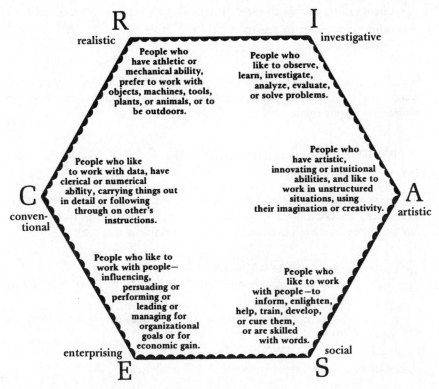

FIGURE 5-2. Occupational Boundaries and Personality Types. *Source*: Richard Bolles. *The Three Boxes of Life*. Berkeley, CA: Ten Speed Press, 1978, pg. 127. Reprinted with permission.

these environments we are really speaking of inherent traits of human beings, the things we do naturally as people. But we also can deal with these traits so they will not cause problems. Let's now examine types of interpersonal environments.

The Mechanistic or Realistic Environment: A Playground for Tinkers

Job demands and opportunities that require the systematic manipulation of objects, tools, and machines characterize the realistic environment. The atmosphere created by job demands, opportunities, and people operates in the following fashion by:

• Fostering technical competence and achievements;

- Encouraging people to see themselves as having mechanical ability;
- Influencing them to see the world in simple, tangible ways and with traditional values.

In this environment people tend to cope with others in a direct, straightforward manner. Tinkers are clever at organizing and manipulating their surroundings to suit them.

The Investigative Environment: A Laboratory for the Scientist

Job demands and opportunities that create the investigative environment include the observation and systematic, creative investigation of physical, biological, or cultural phenomena. The environment tends to:

- Value scientific competencies and achievements;
- Encourage people to see themselves as scholarly, as having mathematical or scientific ability; and
- Emphasize perceiving the world in complex, abstract, independent, and original ways.

Scientists cope with others in rational and analytical ways.

The Artistic Environment: A Workshop for the Creative Designer

The artistic environment distinguishes itself with demands and opportunities that involve ambiguous, free, unsystematized activities and competencies to create art forms or products. The interaction of artistic types within the environment:

- Fosters artistic competencies and achievements;
- Influences people to see themselves as expressive, original, intuitive, nonconforming, and independent; and
- Encourages people to see the world in complex, interdependent, unconventional, and flexible ways.

Artistic types are more likely to cope with others in personal, emotional, and expressive ways.

The Social Environment: A Field Site for the People Person

The challenges of the social environment include influencing others to inform, train, develop, cure, or enlighten. The social environment creates an atmosphere that:

- Fosters social or interpersonal competence; and
- Encourages people to see themselves as enjoying the task of helping others, understanding others, and being cooperative and sociable.

Sociable people are more apt to cope with others by being persuasive, helpful, and cooperative.

The Enterprising Environment: A Playground for Entrepreneurs

Challenges that involve manipulating or influencing others to attain organizational or self-interest goals characterize the enterprising environment. Job demands, opportunities, and people combine to:

- Foster enterprising competencies and achievements;
- Inspire people to see themselves as assertive, self-confident, sociable, and possessing leadership and speaking abilities; and
- Encourage people to perceive the world in terms of power, status, and responsibility.

Enterprising people are more prone to cope with others by influencing, persuading, performing, or leading for personal profit, gain, or growth.

The Conventional Environment: A Data Bank for the Organizer

The conventional environment can be described as involving the systematic manipulation of data such as record keeping, filing material, organizing written and numerical data according to a prescribed plan, and operating business and data processing machines.
This environment:

- Encourages people to see themselves as conforming, orderly, organized, and possessing clerical competencies; and

- Inspires people to see themselves as adept at carrying out the details and following through on the ideas and directions of others.

People in the conventional environment are apt to cope with others in a controlling, conforming, practical fashion.

Each of these model environments reinforces a characteristic group of activities, competencies, and work style preferences. Each model environment shapes attitudes, values, and roles and gives an insight into interpreting and deciphering the person–environment relationship and helps you recognize your own occupational frame of reference. However, while most people fall into one of these general categories, often they are mixtures. How, then, can this information be applied to overcome communication barriers? Mini-entrepreneurs in high-tech environments use their knowledge and perceptions of these occupational frames of reference to their advantage. Let's take a look at a mini-entrepreneur in action.

How to Leap Occupational Barriers

In Chapter 4, Louise Meyer, a former marketing communications manager, explained how she communicated effectively with a product marketing manager and achieved the results she wanted. She elaborates further as she describes how she applied the communications skills listed in the Mini-Entrepreneurial Skill Inventory:

It is very important to understand how people communicate or don't communicate verbally. And that has to do with an intuitive sense of personality types. You use words that portray that personality type. Then it's formulating the questions that are going to be receptive to your listener to get back the information you need, not necessarily what they want to give you. So it is a sense of who they are, where they are and actually, taking on that part of their personality. If you use your own style, they translate it according to their own personality, frame of reference, and experience base and often do not answer the questions that you need to answer to.

I experience this with the product marketing managers whose background is in engineering and who have been put into the Marketing function. Many of them try to couch marketing information in engineering logic. They would try to sell their product and answer questions in a logical progression rather than from a feeling, gut level which is from a marketing base. So I use their jargon and change my words to get the information I need.

For example, getting technical literature from them was difficult. So instead of using the term "orchestrated" I talked about the "discipline" of scheduling the production of technical literature. They don't like the word "orchestrated" because it has a sense of harmony and softness about it. They can't align themselves with it. So by using the word "discipline" they were able to buy into the schedule.

Here we see the discrepancies in background, attitudes, values, and frames of reference. Louise associates and identifies with the artistic environment, while the product marketing manager identifies with the investigative and mechanistic environments. Because Louise is aware of the impact of her communication style, she selects words that the listener can understand, identify with, and support. Specifically, how did she alter her behavior? She used the following guidelines outlined in the Rapport Matrix:

1. Acknowledge your own and other's valued competencies of the model environment (Mechanistic, Investigative, Artistic, Social, Enterprising, Conventional);
2. Recognize your own and other's self-perception (how people prefer to see themselves);
3. Identify with their outlook or how they tend to see the world;
4. Pinpoint technical term, use of language, jargon;
5. Recognize their interpersonal style, how they tend to cope with other;
6. Phrase your question or message in terms or language which they understand, feel comfortable with, and use.

Naturally, not all individuals conform perfectly to these model environments. Rather, these models serve as useful tools for gauging the appropriate communication style and adapting words and phrasing with which the listener can identify.

Understanding How People Process Information

Richard Bandler and John Grinder provide a model for understanding how people translate their internal, personal experience into verbal communication. In their book, *The Structure of Magic*, they contend that we do not operate directly with the world in which we live but we create models or maps to guide our behavior. Each person's representation of the world (map or model) determines, to a large extent, what one experiences, how the world is perceived, and what choices are available. No two individuals share exactly the same experience because each individual creates a different model. Thus, we all live in a somewhat different reality. So we must work that much harder to communicate effectively. How then can this information be applied to the fast pace of the high-tech working environment?

You can use their neurolinguistic model to reach a common understanding of the task at hand and how to effectively accomplish it as a group. By doing so, your efforts will be "in sync" with the goals of high tech—to produce equipment and material of information needed for processing information and communicating more efficiently. You will be operating like an effective processor of information, a computer perhaps, by taking data (what others say) and mentally converting it into something more easily understood. What, then, are some of the constraints or limitations you need to recognize in order to leap communication barriers?

Focus on Actions

Neurolinguistic programming focuses not so much on what people say but rather on what people do. In other words, what they do is what gives meaning to what they say. Different people manifest their thinking in different ways, and these differences correspond to the three principal senses: vision, hearing, and feeling or kinesthetics. These sensing systems are called representational systems. Internally, individuals will be generating visual images, having feelings, or talking to themselves and hearing sounds. You can tell which representational system is being used by listening to another person's verbs, adverbs, or adjectives. For example, a person whose primary representational system is visual would respond with, "I see what you are saying," while a person with an auditory primary representational system might say, "I hear what you are saying," or "That's as clear as a bell." The kinesthetic person might comment, "I feel comfortable with that decision." To establish a rapport with a person, you should speak using the same kinds of verbs the person uses.

Access Meanings

More specifically, you need to take your words (labels for parts of your personal history) and access the meaning as some set of images, some set of feelings, or some set of sounds that is comfortable for you. So in this sense, words are really "triggers" that make you conscious of certain parts of your experience. For example, people in high-tech environments know the meaning of "real time" work. Derived from computer terminology, this term triggers a vision of people making decisions when they are meeting together as opposed to doing research separately and reconvening later to make a joint decision. This procedure, like real time feedback on the computer, saves time. This term conjures up an image of people working as efficiently as a computer and reinforces the value placed on a fast-paced entrepreneurial culture.

Match Processing

Your experiences will overlap with another person's to the degree you share a culture, certain common experiences, and values. There's a slippage between the word and the experience caused by a discrepancy between your corresponding experience for a word and another person's. To establish rapport, you need to match your way of processing information (your representational system) with the other person's by using the same verbs, asking for examples, and rephrasing what you hear. You are, essentially "tracking" or keeping pace with the other person and stepping in another's footsteps. In this way you can reach a deeper understanding and a greater trust.

Now let's apply these techniques of processing information to determine the sensory system of Lisa Ishimoto. She describes how she communicates with others:

> I've taken people to lunch so we can discuss a situation. It helps to get away from the work environment so that you are not in a potential confrontation mode. A lot of times we are on opposite ends of the situation. To understand the other person's perspective, I try to have a better feel for where the other person is coming from. I try to figure out where a person's comfort zone is so that I can effectively present things to them in a way they can comprehend.

From Lisa's choice of words such as "feel" and "comfort zone," she is a kinesthetic processor. By being "in tune" with her system, her way of expressing herself, you can begin building a rapport.

The following dialogue will give you an idea of how Lisa, as a kinesthetic processor, expresses herself. In planning a presales meeting with a sales representative, she uses phrases that reflect how she deals with this situation:

LISA: I need to get a feeling for what approach you want to take.

BOB: I want to hear from each person on what their needs are and how they see using our product.

LISA: Yes, that's a good way of feeling out the "vibes" in the room and to detect any resistance on their part.

BOB: What we can do is list their needs on the flipchart.

LISA: OK That way we can create a mood of give-and-take as opposed to our giving them a dog and pony show on our product. This way we can break the ice and get a real feeling for their needs.

Penny Sumner, our training and development manager, relies on visual processing. In discussing how to organize a workshop on BASIC programming with a computer systems analyst, Penny uses phrases that refer to foreseeing or visualizing what will happen. Notice her choice of words:

PENNY: What do you envision happening in this workshop?

BOB: I would like them to have some time outside of class time to spend working on the terminals.

PENNY: So you don't see having lengthy workshops.

BOB: No, they should be an hour at the most.

PENNY: OK I see myself doing the scheduling and followup evaluations.

BOB: That's fine with me.

Now that you have been exposed to how people use different representational systems, you can begin applying this knowledge, as well as other information we've covered in the Rapport Matrix, to your PEP.

THE ROLE OF VALUES

In Chapter 4, you became aware of your career values and their relationship to your preferred work style. Now you will be able to examine your personal values which differ from career values but shape your lifestyle and attitude toward others. Your values play a significant role in building interpersonal relationships. You will probably find that you tend to attract and be attracted to those individuals who have outlooks, lifestyles, and values similar to your own. For people who hold different values, you may tolerate, show indifference, or reject depending upon the circumstances and situations. In the workplace, however, you are expected to interact with individuals from various backgrounds, with unique experiences, and dissimilar values to reach common goals.

INTERGENERATIONAL DIFFERENCES

Morris Massey provides a framework for comprehending the tremendous impact our values have on our attitudes, behavior, and ways of communicating. The recent acceleration in the rate of change of technology, legal dimensions, social behavior, education, and economic systems has created vastly different "programming" experiences between generations. Programming focuses on the impact of outside forces because these forces shape and mold everyone. The differences in these experiences have created a spectrum of varying value systems within our society. In broad categories, the major sources of programming experiences are family, educational experiences, religious inputs, media, friends, where you grew up geographically, and the amount of money that provided a base for these factors. "Gut-level" values are ingrained in you at around age 10. Unless a significant emotional event such as a divorce or death of a loved one jolts you, you are not apt to alter these values.

You can interact with people more effectively if you understand and respect their values. For example, if you are a manger dealing with a 55-year old employee and a 22-year old employee, it is extremely useful to know that the 55-year old is a member of a generational cluster that is different from that of the 22-year old.

Massey divides generations into clusters, as shown in Figure 5-3. To determine your generational cluster, determine the year when you were age 10. Then find that year on the chart and see where you fall. Keep in mind that we are talking about general categories that can help you understand from where others are coming. Most importantly, you and others do not always come to a problem from the same perspective, and to effectively communicate, you must acknowledge this and deal with it.

The synthesizers are still forming their values so we cannot completely define their values. The in-betweeners are a composite of traditional and challenger orientations. The traditionalist and the challengers both have clearly defined values which are listed as follows. Remember, values differ to the degree that real conflicts are generated. By understanding these two sets of values, you can attempt to eliminate communication barriers and begin building rapport.

Traditionalists	Challengers
Group team	Individualism
Authority	Participation
Institutional leadership	Questioning
Formality/structure	Informal/unconventionality
Puritanism	Sensuality
Social order	Equality/ability
Work for work's sake	Work for self-fulfillment
Problems	Causes
Stability	Change/experiment
Materialism	Experiences

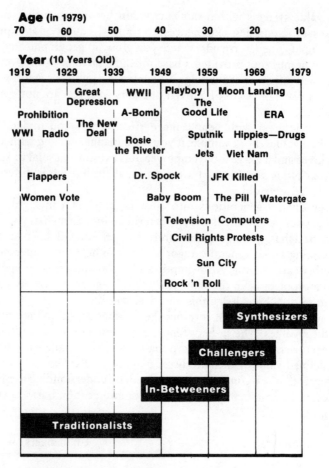

FIGURE 5-3. Generational Clusters. Reprinted from Morris Massey. *The People Puzzle.* Reston, VA: Reston Publishing Co., 1979.

As discussed in Chapter 2, the high-tech entrepreneurial culture has integrated the values of the challengers into the corporate culture. They make up the bulk of the baby-boom generation.

Avoiding Value Clashes

Similar to overcoming occupational barriers, your attempts to avoid value clashes will ease communication with those people who do not share your values because values influence your life style, work style, and attitudes. This holds true for coworkers regardless of job title, rank, and career interests. To avoid value clashes with others, you need to:

1. Recognize the values of others that may clash with your own;
2. Acknowledge the uneasiness you may feel when the other person makes statements or judgments with which you may disagree;
3. Accept the difference in point of view that may be creating a potential communication barrier;
4. Ask yourself if it is worth reacting to this difference, to accomplish the task at hand;
5. If the answer is no, ignore the statements; and
6. If the answer is yes, provide an alternate point of view; point out the relationship between the perception or assumption and the job task at hand. Focusing on job performance diminishes miscommunication and hurt feelings.

Let's examine a mini-entrepreneur in action, as he strives to build bridges of communication between engineers and machine operators. As a technical trainer, Phillip Holmes prepares training documents for operators within the fabrication area of a manufacturer of integrated circuits. He explains how, in the process of deciphering and translating engineering specifications, he enriches the operators' jobs by broadening their understanding of the fabrication process:

I think I have been able to take an instructional document prepared by engineers and make it more palatable for the operators. There are some people in management who feel that the operators don't need to know, and you should just tell them which button to push.

I always gritted my teeth at that because I figure that insults the operators' intelligence. If they are in fact human beings, and we have hired them, then let's not insult their intelligence. Let's compliment it by trying to explain as many things as we can to them.

When I taught my class, I was extremely tickled by their responses. They told me that they had been in the 'fab' area for X number of years, and they never knew how the whole picture went together. They were stuck with one or two processes, and they had no idea of how they related with each other at all. So I was able to take my verbal communication and make it interesting to them. And they would go into the 'fab' area with enthusiasm, having an overall picture of the area. About 84 percent scored highly on the tests. At least now they can hold a conversation with an engineer. The thought of, "Just push the button and don't worry about it," should have gone out 20 years ago. People are not machines.

Areas for Improvement	Action Steps
Skill	
Listening to and understanding what others say.	Use steps for diminishing occupational barriers.
Role	
Communicator	Use steps for understanding representational systems and/ or gut-level values.

FIGURE 5-4. Combining the Rapport Matrix with your PEP.

This mini-entrepreneur intervened in the communication process between engineer and operator, threw out obsolete values, and achieved results. He helps us recognize that human beings have an inborn desire to know why they are doing something. And when they do understand, they will be more effective, efficient, and better able to solve problems that they will inevitably encounter.

COMBINING THE RAPPORT MATRIX AND YOUR PEP

If communication is an area in which you would like to improve, you can incorporate specific action steps listed in the Rapport Matrix into your PEP, as done in the example in Figure 5-4.

Depending on your specific situation and predicament, draw upon the action steps listed in the Rapport Matrix and include them in your PEP.

CONCLUSION

Communicating for results requires being "in tune" with other people, their needs and expectations, and being "in touch" with the corporate culture.

Communication on a one-to-one basis, getting your message across, and understanding the messages of others involves looking beyond your own perceptions and being sensitive to the words used to express your point of view. To do so, you can use the Rapport Matrix as a tool for identifying barriers to effective communication. These barriers include occupational blinders, stemming from your educational background and professional training, generational differences, and internal styles of processing information or perceiving the world. Enhance your communication skills by applying the steps listed in the Rapport Matrix.

To be "in touch" with the corporate culture, you must take advantage of the open and causal work environment that promotes informal communication. Examples of mini-entrepreneurs communicating informally include building rapport within a recreational setting and "levelling" outside the company walls during a relaxed lunch hour.

Overall communicating for results involves balancing your needs and self-regard against the needs of others. It requires being fluid, extending artificial boundaries between you and others and between work and play and work and leisure.

ANSWERS TO EXERCISE 5-1. Assessing Your Communication Skills

If your Final Score is:

A. 66–72 points: You are a skillful communicator, you make yourself clear, understand the needs and expectations of others, and are sensitive to their viewponts.

B. 54–65 points: You generally get your message across and understand others. To enhance your communication skills identify those skills that are most important to you in your job. Use the steps outlined in the Rapport Matrix to increase your competence in the areas for improvement.

C. 18–53 points: You need to take an honest look at the relative importance of these communication skills to your current job. You also should have your supervisor assess your skills using this exercise. Together you can prioritize skills to be improved.

6

BUILDING YOUR INFLUENCE

How to Get What You Want When You Want It

TAPPING THE NETWORK

Joanne Navarro, a software production engineer, has asked Lisa Ishimota for advice on how best to solve a problem and disseminate information. Knowing that Lisa, now a systems engineering manager, began as a software production engineer and having watched her rise within the company, Joanne feels confident about Lisa's professional judgment and seeks her guidance:

JOANNE: I've found a bug in our system, and I've traced it back to the microcoded firmware. So the problem really lies within the Configuration Management area.

LISA: How are you going to let them know about it?

JOANNE: Well I suppose I can rewrite the PPG (Policy and Procedure Guidelines) and have Mark approve it. That would be one way of circulating the information, but I want to let folks know how important this is and to also get some direction from the team.

LISA: Why not call a meeting. That way you can kill two birds with one stone.

JOANNE: That sounds like a way to go. I'll schedule it for early next week. I have another question. I remember that when you worked in my area you were able to convince Mark to buy a computer. How did you go about accomplishing that?

LISA: Basically what I did was use my influence management skills in a roundabout way. First I found an ally, Chuck, who believed in the same things I did. Because he spoke better hardware language than I did, I asked him to sell the idea to Mark. I used him as my mouthpiece. Then I went to the software group in Engineering and convinced Joe who helped in the implementation. The two of them persuaded Mark to buy the computer. I had done so much leg work beforehand that we encountered very little resistance. I also wanted to make sure that I was touching base with others so that I could be sure that the ball was in the right court.

JOANNE: Why did you need the help of Chuck and Joe?

LISA: At that time I was an unknown quantity. I was new to the company and to the department. Also I was the only woman in that area. I felt that Mark didn't really know how to deal with me. I know that he felt uncomfortable in our interactions. So instead of confronting an obstacle, I went around it. There are many ways to get what you need.

As Joanne returns to her work area, she realizes that in the past, she kept to herself believing she could accomplish work goals with the help of a few team members. Now she realizes that she needs to work more closely with others and that her next step is to discover how to influence people.

So far you have assessed your personal power by identifying skill strengths and areas for improvement as they relate to your current job and professional history. You also have examined career values and their relationship to various corporate cultures, work style in relation to the norms of the entrepreneurial culture of excellence, and communication skills in relation to building rapport. Chapter 6 helped you examine communication skills that are fundamental for expanding your interpersonal power bases. The Rapport Matrix allows you to stretch your interpersonal muscles by building bridges of communication to span gaps in frames of reference, values, and ways of experiencing the world. Now you need to go one step further by using influence management skills that help you get what you need or want from others through mutual trust. Mutual trust requires that you act like a telecommunications satellite, helping others to relay their messages. The roles

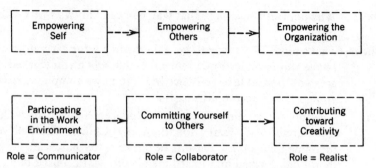

FIGURE 6-1. From Personal Power to Interpersonal Power.

you must assume to influence others (communicator, collaborator, and realist) demand skills in empathetic listening, rapport building, asserting yourself, developing an internal network, and inspiring others with a common vision.

Similar to the building blocks for personal effectiveness in Figure 3-2, Figure 6-1 points out the roles that are needed to shift gears from personal to interpersonal power.

As stated earlier, personal and interpersonal power, in reality, are not all that different. Personal power involves knowing yourself, skills, and values, while interpersonal power involves using influence skills in a mutually beneficial way. When attempting to understand interpersonal competence, it is convenient and practical to think in these terms. In essence, power means helping others within the organization to succeed because power is granted by others when it best suits them.

Within the entrepreneurial culture of excellence, power and influence flow into the hands of mini-entrepreneurs who share brainpower. Their cooperation and coordination keep the wheels of productivity moving. Their interdependence becomes the key to survival. Lisa Ishimoto recognizes this by asking her people to express their views: "I tend to be a very strong personality. So I give my people permission to contradict me. I tell them that I want them to tell me if I am wrong."

Mini-entrepreneurs, then, in helping to carry the ball become quasi-managers learning to manage self and influence others in an informal yet highly effective manner. As a project coordinator, Craig McMillen depends greatly on his influence skills to get his job done:

I have to go into different areas and dip into the various cultures and find out what their sensitive points are to get them to be productive. You have to recognize what their needs are. Right away, you have to see if this guy is "on" or "off" today. You're basing millions of dollars of schedules based on peoples' emotions. But you have to go out and deal with these emotions.

If you don't handle it right and you're looking for that input, some people will turn the other way. You're expected to go out and get that information.

Mini-entrepreneurs become skilled in managerial tasks, such as getting things done through people, using influence strategies, and skills. They impact without total control or manipulation. They get involved without wanting to run the show; and they exercise their interpersonal power without dominating others. Power and influence, in reality, flow in all directions, vertically, laterally, and diagonally. To perform effectively in this culture, mini-entrepreneurs tap networks or clusters of people who share information, resources, and good times by using influence strategies. To contribute to the successful management of their work unit or team, they warn others of potential pitfalls, voice their concerns, and disagree openly and honestly.

THE NATURE OF INFLUENCE

Influence is making an impact on others so you get what you want without being coercive or hurtful. It requires the ability to pinpoint other peoples' needs and develop a strategy to gain their cooperation. It is not creating a situation in which someone wins and someone loses. Practical joking and playfulness do exist in the entrepreneurial culture. It's just that win/lose situations are avoided in favor of collaborative problem solving. Influencing others means putting your cards on the table, negotiating, and bargaining as opposed to "out-smarting" the other person for personal gain.

Marta Dunlap succinctly defines influence:

It's being able to figure out what you want, who can help you, and how to do things within the organization. It means knowing how to move people and how to move the organization. It means knowing how to sell yourself in the organization.

The Role of Relationships

Your goal in influencing others is to build successful relationships to get what you need to satisfy organizational goals. Getting what you need may include information or equipment to meet group goals and ultimately effect change. You really manage strategies for change by managing your relationships.

Dependence on others to get your job done makes relationships an essential ingredient for influencing others.

Craig McMillen shares his secret for developing productive working relationships:

> *When I have to mingle with a group of people, the first thing I do is to try to find out what their social interests are. I'll build on that common ground. I've done a lot of things in sports.*
>
> *I think of myself as a pretty good judge of people, what their needs are and what they don't want to hear. So I'll try to find out what their special interests are. I'll say, 'I'm Craig McMillen from Building 1. I saw you on the courts playing tennis the other day.' We'll strike up a conversation. A feeling of 'you're OK' develops between us. It's that simple.*

Relationships anchor your opinions, attitudes, habits, and values. When you interact with someone on a regular basis, you become familiar and feel secure with each other because you generate and share common ideas and attitudes. Differences dissolve and trust strengthens the bonds of your relationship. Like a chain reaction, networks of people pass on what they see, hear, or read to others. You are able to influence others because they trust that you will let them know what is really happening.

Power relationships of a situation determine the nature of resulting trade-offs. You gain power through either control, influence, or trust. In reality, goals that meet the needs and interests of all the groups affected by a proposed change are desirable but rarely attainable. Each functional area has its own perspective and way of operating. The gap between marketing and engineering functions exemplifies this. Typically, marketing people, according to engineers, will always want a product even before the engineers have time to develop it. And engineers think that marketing people don't understand the complexities involved in the product design. Marketing people believe that engineers, by wanting more time to design the perfect product, are oblivious to timing in the marketplace. To reach group goals, then, you need to negotiate by making trade-offs to meet the needs and demands of other groups. Then, real power in relationships stems from a trust and willingness to negotiate.

Beyond building trusting relationships, be both selective in whom you choose and perceptive in knowing what another person can do for you. To get the most mileage from influence skills, you must first determine who the powerwielders are before asking for needed information and resources. Lisa Ishimoto describes how she determines the powerwielders:

> *You can get the support that you need by finding those people in power. Organization charts don't tell you who really has the power. They just tell you*

where you need to go to get information. You can go into an organization, and you can see who has the power by watching who people go to. Also you notice who is quoted or whose names are mentioned in conversations. You pick up on the name dropping. Most of all, you notice who gets what when they need it.

To influence others you need to make contact with others, maintain and nurture these relationships, and build a network of powerwielders.

Interdependence and Influence

Given the opportunity to share in core decisions, mini-entrepreneurs have a stake in team performance, for team results reflect both individual and team effort and capability. The team is only as strong as its weakest link. Not possessing formal authority, mini-entrepreneurs use the nonlethal tool of influence to achieve adequate control and coordination. In Lisa Ishimoto's words: "Here you can be very effective and get things done without having the positional authority. You don't have to have the title."

Mini-entrepreneurs nurture their relationships with others, various managers, peers with whom they interface, and even top executives. Beyond nurturing relationships, they manage their relationships by balancing competing interests, seeing issues in a wider, multicultural context (from several subcultural vantage points), and working collaboratively. They sustain good working relationships with those people who do not always agree and who are willing to fight for their interests.

Results with TIPs

An action plan with TIPs—Teamwork, Informality and Performance—is a plan for successfully influencing others. Opportunities to use all three are abundant, depending upon immediate goals. Mini-entrepreneurs may be assigned to several project areas that require TIPs. For example, both Craig McMillen and Tim Allen are part of four different project teams. Collaborative problem solving has a ripple effect when shared solutions arising from one team also benefits another team. A "piggy back" effect actually occurs as one person borrows from one idea slightly altering it to fit a different problem and influencing others to accept. Craig McMillen explains how this happens:

When we have our Monday morning meetings, we all get a copy of the status reports and follow along. We also exchange reports on our different programs. The ideas behind this is to share information and to learn. I've been able to take information from one meeting and share it with another team I'm on, and I end up being the hero. They're amazed that I even thought of it when it was something that was brought up in my other meeting.

Teamwork reinforces the old adage, "Two heads are better than one." Informal networks for communicating are abundant and thrive in this culture. Beer busts, dinner meetings, and the company recreation facilities provide ample opportunity to mix with coworkers while eliminating occupational, generational, and status barriers.

When mini-entrepreneurs use their energy, and informally manage the energy of others toward common goals, performance takes the lead. Whether it is solving problems, motivating and inspiring others, stimulating cooperation and trust, bargaining or negotiating, a key to effective performance is successfully influencing others.

Your Influence Pattern

Now you can gain a perspective on your own influence patterns by completing Exercise 6-1.

EXERCISE 6-1. Examining Your Influence Patterns

Circle the number that represents how often you display the described behavior using the following ratings:

4 = Always	*2 = Sometimes*
3 = Often	*1 = Never*

	N	S	O	A
1. I develop work group alliances with people with whom I socialize off the job.	1	2	3	4
2. I obtain the informal support of higher ups.	1	2	3	4
3. I get important information more efficiently & effectively through informal channels (e.g., face-to-face communications) than through formal channels (e.g., written procedures, manuals, group memos).	1	2	3	4
4. I concentrate on satisfying the key person involved in an issue, the one who has the most influence over what will happen.	1	2	3	4
5. I indulge in minor violations of procedures when deadlines are pressing.	1	2	3	4

EXERCISE 6-1. (Continued)

Circle the number that represents how often you display the described behavior using the following ratings:

4 = *Always*   2 = *Sometimes*
3 = *Often*   1 = *Never*

	N	S	O	A
6. I make contact with others outside of my own work unit & with whom I interface to get needed information.	1	2	3	4
7. I make efforts to discuss important issues & problems with my boss even if he/she is not readily available.	1	2	3	4
8. I express my need for help when necessary.	1	2	3	4
9. I obtain the support of coworkers to back up my requests.	1	2	3	4
10. I explain the benefits that are wanted by the other person.	1	2	3	4
Total				

Refer to the end of this chapter for an interpretation of your score.

BUILDING INFLUENCE THROUGH INTERNAL NETWORKING

Internal networking is the process of developing and nurturing your relationships for information, advice, and moral support. You create an internal network when you build a community of contacts by cutting across work groups or subculture, teams, occupational lines, and management levels and tapping into these self-created networks. You really help yourself and others become more effective by sharing know-how and resources. After all, you should ask for help when you need it as well as provide assistance to others. It means building a network of allies who can also represent you and speak on your behalf.

The entrepreneurial culture, in granting individuals the freedom and leeway to get their jobs done, encourages a networking process that gets the job done with the help of others outside the team. It gives legitimacy to the "grapevine." Shared information is more than idle gossip; it is valued information for reaching personal and organizational goals. For mini-entrepreneurs, Management By Wandering Around (MBWA) increases the odds for networking. Craig McMillen gives an example of how the networking process works:

> *There is a group of 10 people who are not a part of my immediate work group. I am not formally assigned to this group. They are all new to the company. The people on my teams are very experienced. My team members were able to 'clue me in' on things that the "10" might get burned on. So I warned them about what to look out for even though I'm not on their team. That has to be done, or they will fall down and slip schedule.*

In this situation a networker who cared about a group's performance increased its chance for success.

Craig spends about three-fourths of his time away from his teams to problem solve collaboratively. His actions result in a network of people who are at his fingertips when needed. Craig describes the two-way networking process that involves give and take:

> *We are installing a new accounting system, and it is taking a lot of effort on everyone's part. There are a few bugs in the system. For some reason I'm known as the guy who knows the system. I guess it's because I work with it so much. In fact the accounting people are starting to come to me for help. What I will do is contact the programmer at the division to get information to solve the problem. When it's fixed I'll let the accounting people know about it.*

In these examples, Craig relied upon skills of collaborative problem solving and being a realist while building a network. These skills, which are included in the Mini-Entrepreneurial Skills Inventory, are outlined in the following list:

ROLE	SKILL
Collaborator	10 Explaining another person's viewpoint to others.
	20 Working jointly with others inside and outside my work unit to accomplish a task.
Realist	34 Envisioning the end product/result before the project begins and communicating the vision to others.

While networking internally, Marta Dunlap ensures that she has something to give in the process. Internal networking for her is a give-and-take process, as she explains:

> *After having just completed writing a document on a product line, a friend, whom I worked with at the other division, asked me for a copy. Initially, I told her that she could have one in two weeks, after it comes back from the printer. But I like Ann. So I wanted to bend over backward for her. I suggested that she take a copy from the office of someone who recently left the company. She made sure that she got it. Then I noticed that she didn't have the final diagrams. So I went to the copy machine, copied them for her and delivered them to her.*
>
> *She really appreciated that. This is a case in which she is networking and I'm responding. I know that it will pay off. It was far more effective to do that and deliver it to her than having the secretary do it a day later. It doesn't have the same impact. These are minor "gives and takes" that are really important.*

Now that you have a few examples of how the networking process operates, you can begin to examine your own networking patterns by completing Exercise 6-2.

EXERCISE 6-2. Examining Your Networking Patterns

1. List the number of new contacts you have made outside your immediate work group over the last few months. These contacts should be beyond your routine contacts needed to accomplish work goals. You may want to check your appointment book to trigger your memory.
2. What were the outcomes of each? (information gained, future referrals made)?
3. What common ground was established between you and other contacts?
4. What possible follow-up activity can you pursue? (luncheon meeting, tennis match after work, trade association meeting)?

Building a community of interpersonal relationships is one way of expanding your power and influence, but you must also broaden your skill base of interpersonal competence.

BEING INFLUENTIALLY AGILE

Mini-entrepreneurs are fast on their feet and influentially agile. They take an open stance by remaining flexible and adaptable to whatever situation they face. They meet the challenge of influencing others by adjusting to cultural norms while simultaneously striving to change for the better. This balancing act requires enough sensitivity to know when and how to adapt your influence style to the demands of the situation. What then are the separate pieces that must be recognized and assembled to make up the big picture?

Mini-entrepreneurs apply influence strategies to change the behavior of others, such as managers, team members, and other coworkers. Like these top performers, you really cannot make a difference in anyone's life without first making an impact. Your influence strategy selection will vary according to your work goal and the other person's power, attitudes, and values. As you strive to be influential, you must also be resourceful and flexible. Your selling skills really depend on, not only meeting a need, but thinking through the other person's values and openness to change.

To determine how to adjust your influence strategy to the person and situation, you must first be "in touch" with the other person's perceptions and needs. This requires a certain degree of involvement.

Measuring Your Involvement with Others

Your involvement with others can range from noninvolvement to indifference to mutual respect and trust. Figure 6-2 illustrates the relative closeness you share with other people in your life. The degree of closeness and distance in a relationship determines your choice of an influence strategy. The concentric circles in Figure 6-2 show that a relationship that combines the characteristics included in circles B and C, between a friendship and a purely functional relationship, builds trust and increases your sphere of influence. Marta Dunlap tells how she relies on these relationships: "I feel perfectly comfortable when I'm determining how to go about getting an answer to my question to call upon my friends around here, friends in the business sense not in the personal sense."

Undoubtedly, you are beginning to see that you need to be responsive to others to influence them. You become responsive by appealing to the other person's wants and needs. You can't really influence anyone until you know they're stance. Use both influential self-expression and responsiveness, one is of very little use without the other. Your argument may be persuasive and

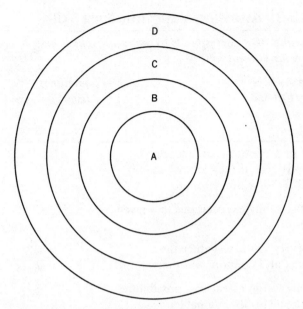

Circle A includes intimate relationships with individuals who you trust, care about, and can share confidential information (spouse, close friend, relative, or children).

Circle B includes individuals who you interact with on a regular basis for the purpose of mutual exchange or for the pleasure of their company. The relationship fulfills certain emotional or social needs. The degree of closeness depends on your needs and your dependence on the person for fulfilling these needs.

Circle C includes functional relationships that serve specific needs. These relationships may be with your doctor, lawyer, boss, customer, coworker, or colleague.

Circle D includes relationships with casual acquaintances.

FIGURE 6-2. Closeness and Distance in Relationships.

convincing, but you will not make an impact unless you are responsive and can totally tune into the other person.

Now that you have a brief overview of influence and how to build it, acquaint yourself with types of influence strategies and their supporting skills by completing Exercise 6-3.

EXERCISE 6-3. Assessing Your Influence Skills

Circle the number that corresponds to the rating which best describes your behavior on your current job.

> 4 = *Always*   2 = *Sometimes*
> 3 = *Often*   1 = *Never*

	N	S	O	A
1. I persist in presenting new ideas and suggestions even if they are not readily accepted the first time around.	1	2	3	4
2. I clearly state my expectations in a given situation.	1	2	3	4
3. I make every effort to gather the viewpoints and opinions of others.	1	2	3	4
4. I share my vision of exciting possibilities that are realistically attainable.	1	2	3	4
5. In emotionally tense situations, I am able to step back and recognize what is really happening.	1	2	3	4
6. I support my proposal with facts, figures, and other data.	1	2	3	4
7. I give feedback to others in an objective and helpful manner.	1	2	3	4
8. When others run into problems, I can empathize with them.	1	2	3	4
9. I show my excitement and enthusiasm for new ideas and suggestions.	1	2	3	4
10. When interacting with others I am able to look beyond the spoken words and can recognize hidden agendas.	1	2	3	4
11. I sell my proposals by stressing the advantages and positive outcomes.	1	2	3	4
12. I openly state my feelings without abusing others.	1	2	3	4

EXERCISE 6-3. (Continued)

Circle the number that corresponds to the rating which best describes your behavior on your current job.

    4 = Always   *2 = Sometimes*
    3 = Often   *1 = Never*

	N	S	O	A
13. I accurately describe differences in opinion between self and others.	1	2	3	4
14. I point out company goals as a way of getting people to work together.	1	2	3	4
15. I neutralize a situation by using humor or by using analogies or stories.	1	2	3	4
16. I substantiate my proposals by pursuing different lines of reasoning.	1	2	3	4
17. I make trade-offs to get what I need.	1	2	3	4
18. I find common ground by emphasizing similarities and deemphasizing differences.	1	2	3	4
19. I generate a team spirit by pointing out the strengths of others.	1	2	3	4
20. I push for reaching a compromise to avoid an impasse.	1	2	3	4

Go to the end of this chapter for an interpretation of your score.

STRATEGIES THAT GET YOU WHAT YOU WANT

To assist you in expanding your interpersonal power and influence, use the Influence Planning Worksheet shown in Figure 6-3 as a planning tool. This worksheet lists items needed to account for when influencing others. It gives a framework for planning your influence strategies and becomes a starting point for improving your influence skills.

GOALS

RELATIONSHIP

RESISTANCE

Points   Counterpoints

STRATEGIES

Preferred

Alternate

FIGURE 6-3. Influence Planning Worksheet.

When planning your influence strategy and selecting the appropriate influence skills, first identify items such as work goals (what you want to accomplish), anticipated resistance (barriers set up by those from whom you need cooperation or approval), power accorded the other person, and your relationship with that person. Work goals usually fall into four main categories: (1) obtaining assistance for your own job, (2) initiating a new organizational program or system, (3) obtaining benefits (promotion, salary increase), and (4) improving your coworker's job performance. These items woven together form the fabric of social interactions that give life to conflicting goals, cross purposes, hidden agendas, and paradoxical behavior. Each one must be carefully analyzed when planning your influence strategy. Now let's review steps to follow for planning your influence strategy. These steps guide you in completing the Influence Planning Worksheet in Figure 6-3.

Steps to Follow

Step 1: Setting Goals

The first step of influence management is identifying work goals, what it is that you want to achieve. Your goal will partially determine influence strategy and skills utilized. For example, presenting yourself as a viable candidate for a higher-level position requires selling yourself by being convincing and assertive. On the other hand, proposing a new program or system requires you to make the benefits of such change personally attractive to your listeners; or you can inspire others with a vision of improved change. When you identify your goal, you expose any cross purposes. You are also less likely to overreact during an emotionally loaded situation if you keep the subject on goals.

Step 2: Defining the Relationship(s)

Your relationship with another person or group determines whether it is cooperative, emotionally loaded, or confrontive. Your involvement with the other person also plays a major role when interacting. You will be less strained if you know each other, feel comfortable together, and are familiar with your idiosyncrasies. The opposite is true, of course, if you have just met. For example, a new manager is more likely to create an uneasiness and apprehension even if the previous manager was viewed as ineffective. At least you knew what to expect from the former manager. Position power held by the other person also carries weight and should not be underestimated even in an entrepreneurial culture; structure and elitism are inevitable parts of any organization.

Relationships can be complex and encompass several layers of involvement. If you deal with your boss on both a social and business level, examine your work relationship and friendship. In some cases, friendship can be beneficial and in others, potentially detrimental. In the case of male friends, the "old boys network" becomes an added advantage. Close friendships, depending on the trust involved, can open Pandora's box if boundaries between business and pleasure are unclear. These cases span the spectrum of relationships and are examples of how they affect influence strategies.

Step 3: Dealing with Resistance

Resistance among people can range from outright refusal to complying with an order, to playing the role of "devil's advocate," to making excuses, and finally to indifference stemming from a lack of understanding and involvement. Beyond recognizing these attitudes, you must also deal with resistance by examining the content of the discussion, the words spoken and points made. To plan your strategy write down the points you want to make and also anticipate counterpoints (objections based on self-interest and occupational point of view). List counterpoints even though they may not come up in the discussion. If you employ a strategy of connecting, (identifying mutual interests or goals as opposed to a strategy of convincing), then verbalizing counterpoints may be inappropriate, self-defeating, or counterproductive.

Step 4: Selecting the Most Effective Strategy

Influence strategies can be roughly divided into two main categories: cognitive (thinking) and affective (feeling). Cognitive or thinking influence strategies provide factual knowledge to convince someone of a logical argument or prescribe a certain direction to follow. These strategies emphasize objectivity (using facts, figures, and data to justify an argument). Affective or feeling influence strategies at the opposite end of the spectrum. Identify with another's feelings, point of view, and personal experiences when using these strategies. You will be empathetic when finding common ground with the other person. When viewed on a continuum from thinking to feeling, various influence strategies are placed as shown in Figure 6-4.

The various types of influence strategies and their supporting skills from Exercise 6-3 are described briefly in the following text:

Convincing

I prepare and use facts, figures, and supporting data to help solve problems or propose changes in programs or systems. I am logical in my presentation of details, arguments, and opinions to support my position. I use persistence and determination in attempting to sell my ideas to others.

Skills from Exercise 6-3.

1. I persist in presenting new ideas and suggestions even if they are not readily accepted the first time around.
6. I support my proposals with facts, figures, and other data.
11. I sell my proposals by stressing the advantages and positive outcomes.
16. I substantiate my proposals by pursuing different lines of reasoning.

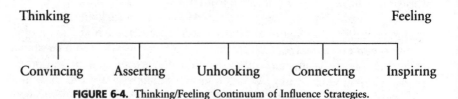

Thinking   Feeling

Convincing   Asserting   Unhooking   Connecting   Inspiring

FIGURE 6-4. Thinking/Feeling Continuum of Influence Strategies.

Asserting

I am direct and open when expressing my position, wishes, and expectations. I let others know what I need from them while being realistic and understanding potential obstacles. I am not afraid to express my opinions and feelings either positive or negative. I use bargaining and negotiating to achieve work goals.

Skills from Exercise 6-3.

2. I clearly state my expectations in a given situation.
7. I give feedback to others in an objective and helpful manner.
12. I openly state my feelings without abusing others.
17. I make trade-offs to get what I need.

Unhooking

I am able to stand back, unhook myself from the emotional aspects of the situation at hand, and view the process objectively. If others don't see my point of view, I do not take it personally but think of an alternate strategy to use. In a group situation I facilitate the discussion and assist in reaching consensus. By recognizing diverse needs and objectives, I emphasize what is realistic and doable while keeping long-range plans in mind. I am able to detect the emotional climate of a situation and defuse the situation with humor, analogies, or call for a break.

Skills from Exercise 6-3.

5. In emotionally tense situations I am able to step back and recognize what is really happening.
10. When interacting with others I am able to look beyond the spoken words and can recognize hidden agendas.
15. I neutralize a situation with humor or by using analogies or stories.
20. I push for reaching a compromise to avoid an impasse.

Connecting

I rely upon listening skills to discover the needs, ideas, interests, and problems of others. I convey my understanding of their point of view by listening empathetically. I also point out mutual interests, tasks, and ways that we can work together in reaching common goals. I make every effort to find common ground for accomplishing a task despite differences in work style, occupational frame of reference, and generational values.

Skills from Exercise 6-3.

3. I make every effort to gather the viewpoints and opinions of others.
8. When others run into problems, I can empathize with them.
13. I accurately describe differences in opinion between self and others.
18. I find common ground by emphasizing similarities and deemphasizing differences.

Inspiring

I use my enthusiasm and excitement surrounding my vision of a workable solution, new program, operational system, or product. I share my perceptions of changes for the better in terms of cost savings, time savings, employee morale, and customer satisfaction. I point out the strengths and expertise of others contributing toward improvements. I facilitate cooperation among others by pointing out exciting possibilities that can occur. I gain commitment from others by enabling them to see a common vision.

Skills from Exercise 6-3.

4. I share my vision of exciting possibilities that are realistically attainable.
9. I show my excitement and enthusiasm for new ideas and suggestions.
14. I point out company goals as a way of getting people to work together.
19. I generate a team spirit by pointing out the strengths of others.

INFLUENCING WITH MAXIMUM IMPACT

Now let's examine how mini-entrepreneurs use these influence strategies. Larry Buxton, an engineer from Chapter 2, relies on the technical knowledge of software engineers for writing new business proposals. He explains how he gets their cooperation using primarily convincing and asserting influence strategies. He uses connecting as a secondary strategy:

> *If I have been working with that person for a long time, it's very easy to get agreement because they know what I am trying to accomplish. When I interface with someone who I have never worked with before, I'll explain the situation with enough detail to convince the person that's it's not so important to me but to the company. I tell him that what he will be doing will affect company goals; how many pieces of equipment we sell.*
>
> *If I run into a person who is a little stubborn and has priority problems then I'll bring his supervisor into the act so we can mutually agree upon some deadlines*

and level of effort. I'll tell the person, Look, if there is a problem with priorities, I'll talk to your boss about it, and then the three of us can work it out.

Penny Sumner is attempting to persuade the executive committee to implement a career development program by using influence strategies of inspiring, connecting, and unhooking:

> *I had written a detailed proposal for a career development program including workshops in career planning for interested employees. I included an action plan, cost schedule, etc. In presenting it to the executive committee I could tell from the looks on their faces and their lack of enthusiasm that they couldn't imagine what it was I wanted to do.*

> *So I thought about how I could get sell my program. I decided to use a film showing how another company had implemented such a program and was successful. I showed it to the committee. After seeing the film they were excited and essentially said, "Let's go for it!" What I really did was literally rally them around a common vision.*

Now let's view Penny's Influence Planning Worksheet in Figure 6-5.

To effectively use influence strategies, you need to devise a plan with flexibility because you may need to change horses in midstream to achieve what you want.

LINKING YOUR PEP TO INFLUENCE PLANNING

You can come closer to influencing others with maximum impact by assuming the roles of communicator, collaborator, and realist. The skills listed in the Mini-Entrepreneurial Skills Inventory overlap and complement influence skills. For example, item 4 in Exercise 6-3, (I share my vision of exciting possibilities that are realistically attainable), is similar to item 34 in the Mini-Entrepreneurial Skills Inventory (Envisioning the end product/result before the project begins and communicating the vision to others). By making these connections, you can easily breakdown and analyze roles and skills for improvement to enhance your influence strategies. This information can be incorporated into your Personal Effectiveness Plan shown in Figure 6-6.

CONCLUSION

Within the entrepreneurial culture of excellence, mini-entrepreneurs gain leverage and achieve results by using influence. The culture supports mini-

GOALS

Implement a career development program.

RELATIONSHIP

Executive committee has decision-making power. Functional relationship with high degree of dependence on their decision.

RESISTANCE

Points	Counterpoints
Program may be acceptable to employees.	It has worked in other companies.
Let's start small by outlining career paths.	Let's present a comprehensive program enabling employees to take more responsibility for their career planning.

STRATEGIES

Preferred

Convincing

Alternate

Inspiring

FIGURE 6-5. Influence Planning Worksheet for Penny Sumner.

entrepreneurs who are influencially agile, flexible, and adaptable to the dynamics of a situation.

To successfully influence others, assume the roles of communicator, collaborator, and realist. You also must utilize multiple skills for effectively planning and adapting various influence skills to a social encounter. These include listening attentively and perceptively and tapping into the networks of interpersonal communities throughout your organization. Remain flexible and "in tune" with the content as well as the process of an interaction. And most of all, you need to be "in touch" with organizational powerwielders, who get what they want when they need it.

Interpersonal relationships lay the groundwork for influencing others so they need to be nurtured and managed with care, planning, and foresight. The

SKILLS

Strengths

1. _____

2. _____

AREAS FOR IMPROVEMENT   ACTION STEPS

SKILLS

1. _____   _____

2. _____   _____

WORK STYLE GAPS

    Ideal   Actual

1. _____   _____

   _____   _____

ROLES

PARTICIPATION

1. Communicator (related to Influence Strategies) — Practice using assertive communication.

COMMITMENT

1. Collaborator (related to Influence Strategies and Skills) — Practice using strategy of connecting and asserting.

CREATIVITY

1. Realist (related to Influence Strategies and Skills) — Use strategy of inspiring.

FIGURE 6-6. Personal Effectiveness Plan.

Influence Planning Worksheet is a tool for gaining leverage by clarifying your goals, anticipating resistance, recognizing the parameter of your relationship, and utilizing the most effective influence strategies. Skill identification and skill improvement for influencing others can be included in your PEP.

ANSWERS TO EXCERCISE 6-1. Examining Your Influence Patterns

A. *If you scored 27–40 points, you have developed a pattern of using power and influence as a way to get information and support from others to accomplish your goals.*

B. *If you scored 26 points or below, you are not accustomed to using your power and influence to achieve results. By using the Influence Planning Worksheet and enhancing your influence strategies and skills, you can improve your influence management competencies.*

ANSWERS TO EXERCISE 6-3. Assessing Influence Strategies

In the blanks next to each number, rate each item of the exercise (1,2,3, or 4).

1. ___	2. ___	3. ___	4. ___	5. ___
6. ___	7. ___	8. ___	9. ___	10. ___
11. ___	12. ___	13. ___	14. ___	15. ___
16. ___	17. ___	18. ___	19. ___	20. ___
___	___	___	___	___
Total	Total	Total	Total	Total
Convincing	Asserting	Connecting	Inspiring	Unhooking

Your highest score indicates what strategy you rely on in your current job to influence others. Your lowest score indicates which strategy you use the least. Think about how you can become more flexible and adaptable by using influence strategies and skills and include ideas in your PEP.

7

TEAMING UP FOR EXCELLENCE

Working Together in a Corporate Environment

SUMMING UP TEAM PLAY

Craig McMillen finds himself on the same project team as Andy Bertoni, a former coworker from a company with a weak entrepreneurial culture that veers toward authoritarian. While Craig is assigned to Engineering Services, Andy's job is in the Finance department. During a meeting, Craig notices that Andy is unusually quiet and seems perplexed by what is taking place. After the meeting ends, Craig approaches Andy:

CRAIG: This must be all new to you. I know when I came here, I went through a real adjustment, culture shock in fact.

ANDY: I am so surprised by how much information is so freely passed back and forth, especially around budgets. Before when we worked at LBT, I was told to keep certain facts and figures under my hat. Here it's out in the open. I'm not so sure that it's such a good idea.

CRAIG: Listen, everything around here is done in teams. I'm on four different project teams, and information is like water—you need it to survive. It's also necessary for company survival. After all, a few good ideas can save the company a lot of money. It's different here. People can go at it, lock horns, but it's OK. Everyone is given a chance to speak their mind, even if someone else might think it is nonsense. It's not like where we worked before where people hoarded information. There they were out to get the other team so they could look good. But here, everyone works together. We're called "team players."

ANDY: I've been given so much responsibility for budgeting and accounting that I feel like I need more control.

CRAIG: Look, it's not your personal budget. It's the team's budget for this project. I'm also responsible for accounting for how the money is spent. And we also have the team's experience and brainpower behind us. You're not in this alone. Don't worry. We'll keep you in line.

ANDY: I guess I need more time to learn the ropes around here. What goes on in a team meeting is certainly a lot different than where we worked before.

What new roles and skills will Andy need to learn in order to perform effectively in this team-oriented culture stressing team play and team accountability?

If you use influence strategies and skills with appropriate timing and emphasis within a group, you are likely to build team cohesiveness and promote team productivity. However, unlike one-on-one interactions, multiple needs of team members make it more complicated to influence the group. Sometimes job needs and perspectives clash as in the classic case between the Engineering and Manufacturing departments. What the engineer designs, the manufacturing people might find difficult to produce. To have a tight team, everyone's needs must be considered, although not necessarily followed. A part of your job, then, is to be alert to both your needs and those of others while keeping in mind group goals. It's like listening to two conversations simultaneously, one from your inner voice and the other from team members. You will need breathing space to step back and observe team dynamics when you see others struggling with an issue. In this situation, you are wearing the hat of facilitator. Similar to using influence strategies, teamwork demands flexibility and adaptability.

Ideally each person should have equal time to express viewpoints and influence the group's agenda. Like cards in a deck, influence should be dealt with everyone playing out their hand. To become an effective team member, you are asked to play a variety of roles and apply multiple skills. You might find yourself changing hats and playing musical chairs when attempting to see another person's point of view, playing devil's advocate, or pushing for group consensus. Even though you can rely on influence strategies such as convincing, connecting, asserting, and so on, you must also be an effective team member by contributing to group consensus. In certain situations you might find yourself representing others by taking their argument and defending them. Primary roles assumed, from the Mini-Entrepreneurial Skills Inventory, fall in the categories of initiator, team member, collaborator, and innovator. These roles enable you to participate within this team-oriented culture, commit yourself to the organization via the team, and sell your creativity to the organization at large.

TEAMS: VEHICLES FOR INNOVATION

My role is to tie everyone together in a team environment.

When your name is listed on the action plan as a 'team player,' you are labeled as such and are committed to the team.

Our company is very team-oriented. We do our product development as a team.

I have to promote a team effort because there's no other way of getting things done. If one person drops the ball, it doesn't matter how good everybody else is.

The synergy of a team is exciting, and you get a better end product.

These are examples of how a team-oriented culture generates an understanding of roles and group ties, a commitment to the team, and an excitement surrounding team accomplishment. You'll find that teams are the vehicles through which improvements and innovations take place in the entrepreneurial culture. Improvements may range from designing a new product, to installing an automated system, to implementing a management development program. Whatever the goal, brainpower meshed within a team produces innovations and better decisions. Team members cut across organizational boundaries and confront multiple viewpoints that they would not find in a one-to-one situation. When you are with a group and actively discuss the issues surrounding a decision, the probability of that decision being accurate increases due to a cancellation-of-individual-error effect. In other words, the group cancels erroneous arguments of its members. In fact, it outperforms even its best individual member. And when it does, it reaches synergy.

Increasing Individual Competence

In addition to improving the accuracy of decisions, teamwork can improve each person's capabilities. In other words, the team helps potentially less successful people shake off the anxiety of failure and pulls them up to a level of maximum performance. Research shows that team spirit plays a powerful force in decreasing a person's fear of failure. In fact, the Achievement Motivation Theory of Atkinson and Feather supports that people with strong motives to succeed tend to choose goals that are challenging, neither too easy nor too difficult. People with strong motives for failure tend to choose goals that are too easy, which assures them success. If the goal is too difficult, they can say, "I tried, but it was silly of me to think anybody could do that." Using this theory as a basis for his experiment, Alvin Zander found that when individuals with high fear of failure are placed in central roles within a cohesive group, they act like high achievers. Group responsibility and team spirit, then, can pull people paralyzed by fear of failure out of their comfort zone and confront them with their competence.

Working in teams, as opposed to working alone, also has humanistic payoffs related to employee morale and job satisfaction. In general, you will see that teamwork reduces deep-seated conflicts, provides job coherence through a clear definition of job role, educates while solving problems, and gives you access to information, resources, and peer support. Lou Ann Bender, a manufacturing cost analyst of a computer division, describes how she presented mini-training sessions to help increase understanding of accounting terminology and concepts. In so doing, she built positive working relationships with managers within the manufacturing area:

> *I presented a group of 8 to 10 training sessions for all the managers and supervisors in the manufacturing area regarding "targeting" on our new system. It included how to stay within budget, how to read the reports and what kind of implications it had for them. I put together packets for educating them and giving them the most help we could.*
>
> *It made our working relationship much better. Instead of my asking them questions four weeks after the reports came out and bugging them, they could now come to me and help me pinpoint discrepancies. The training session to them meant that we cared enough.*

The enthusiasm surrounding a team effort flows over into other work-related teams, generating a team feeling throughout the organization.

The following examples show that teamwork cuts across levels and organizational boundaries and draws together disbursed talent and expertise. These are actual comments of team members.

Learning

When people work together on meaningful issues, they learn through problem solving and generally feel more productive. The group provides a social environment where learning occurs through feedback. A mini-entrepreneur speaks of the glamour attached to team learning:

> *Even though I was hired as a product consultant assigned to a certain region with the sales force, I am spending all of my time training coworkers on our software product as it operates on the Eclipse computer. Because I was a former employee of the company which built the Eclipse computer and know the ins and outs of the machine, I have been asked to train others. So I am traveling to the different regional offices bringing them the word. In some ways I feel like a roving ambassador for the company, building teams through learning.*

Teaming Up

The entrepreneurial culture takes advantage of our natural inclination to act as groups. We live, learn, and work in groups. Within the entrepreneurial culture of excellence, teams range from impromptu communications between two people from different functional areas, to quality improvement teams, task forces, or "start-up teams," to intact formalized work groups composed of peers and a supervisor or team leader.

Working in Pairs

> *Before the salesperson and I go into a sales meeting with a potential customer, we put our heads together to discuss how we are going to approach the meeting. We decide how much in-depth technical information to give them and how to find out their needs. We pool our knowledge and share experiences so that when we are with the customer, we can "key-off" each other's ideas. I'm coming from a training background, while she is coming from a marketing background. Together we can address their questions.*

Two or More Spontaneously

> *Even though all the systems analysts/consultants work separately on various projects, if one of us has a design problem and feels up against a wall, then that*

person would call upon the others for help. That person would call an impromptu meeting. We would brainstorm, coming up with different ways to attack the problem. We all do this for each other. Where someone might get stuck, someone else might fly through it like a breeze. It all was a team effort anyway because our company was so small that when someone succeeded we all did.

Quality Circles

When my supervisor told me that we were going to be a part of a quality improvement process, I wasn't quite sure what to expect. After we had all gone through a training program on techniques in problem solving and communicating as a team, I was really surprised to see how well we worked as a team. What one person found difficult to accomplish in the past, we could now do as a team. We rewrote some manufacturing procedures which eliminated several steps without reducing any control. It amounted to several thousands of dollars in cost savings.

Task Force

I have been temporarily assigned to a Research and Development committee which is developing a new product. I am sitting in as the financial representative giving them information on costs. Other people are from Marketing, Manufacturing and R and D. I am there to help them project costs. It's a joint effort. We'll be meeting for the next three to six months.

Intact Project Teams

There isn't any other way to survive as a company without everyone working together on a team. You are on somebody's team, a team's captain, and you commit yourself to the team goals. For example, our plan may read, 'By next fiscal quarter we will meet these goals' and they are listed. If everyone does their job, we will reach our goals. Team members include an engineer, project coordinator, Manufacturing person, and a Finance person.

Before analyzing the elements of an effective team, you should assess your relationship to your team and overall team effectiveness by completing Exercise 7-1.

EXERCISE 7-1. Examining Your Relationship to the Team

1. Describe your functional relationship to the team (What is your role)?
2. What are the team's goals?
3. Describe your satisfaction with how the team operates. Consider how tasks are accomplished and how people communicate with one another.
4. What are your personal goals in relationship to this team effort?
5. How are decisions made (consensus, unilaterally)?
6. List obstacles related to meeting team goals. Are these external or internal to the group?
7. List obstacles you face as a team member.
8. Describe your working relationships with other team members.

Now that you have accumulated some baseline data on team effectiveness, you can begin to link team building strategies to your own situation.

What Makes an Effective Team

This chapter focuses on intact teams whose lifecycle spans several months with accountability to the organization measured in one form or another. They have certain common characteristics that include: (1) a reason or charter for working together; (2) member interdependence; they need each other's experience, expertise, and commitment to reach mutual goals; (3) member commitment to the belief that joint or group effort is more productive and innovative than working alone; and (4) team accountability to the larger organization.

Craig McMillen breaks down the elements of "good teams and bad teams:

In the good teams, there's so much conversation going on that it's hard not to understand what's going on. They might be discussing new plans from management, new product ideas, or something that's being built right now. You're not left in the dark.

The project leader is able to answer every question. He's done his homework and gives us details of the big picture. Other team members are very dedicated to the company. They are very proud of working here, and they'll tell us in a second that they love the company.

The people on the bad teams are not likely to say that. One basic trait that I've noticed is that the "hyper" individuals are on the bad teams. They are probably that way because their programs are out of control. They get vicious, point fingers, accuse each other, not answer questions. They get into screaming matches, and the people who can help out will refuse to help.

The engineers who have the answers are intimidated by the whole situation. Nobody ever told them when they were in school that they would have to deal with these kinds of confrontations. They thought that they were just going to design great things. So they end up smoothing things over and walk out without the problem being resolved. Then it hits the fan again the following week. It goes on and on, and it costs the company a lot of money.

Team effectiveness consists of what a team gets done and the climate in which decisions are made. Looking at it another way, team effectiveness can be broken down into hard data, (results and measured output), and soft data, (how people feel about the way consensus is or not reached and how they feel about working together). You can be sure then that team effectiveness includes means and ends. To function as an effective team member, be committed to the group and be sure that an interdependence exists. After all, group goals cannot be met unless everyone is pulling together. Equally important, each person must feel that they have an equal chance to influence the team's agenda, whether it be goal setting, coordinating a project, or resolving quality issues. Beyond hard data, teamwork involves a "synergy," a medical term describing a proliferation of energy. When two mild drugs are used together, they have a more powerful effect than when used separately. You'll find that linking the brainwaves of others causes an explosion of brainpower, like dynamite, that results in innovative and creative ideas.

Involvement

As a team member you naturally want to make a personal contribution so that the team can move closer toward organizational goals. Your involvement may include a range of information sharing from simply relating an experience, to giving technical advice, to stating what makes sense from an intuitive rather than logical standpoint.

Cooperation

Within the team, your inclination to cooperate takes root, grows, and replaces competitive win/lose urges. When your team problem is solved collaboratively, members are clear about their roles, job satisfied, and effective performers, both inside and outside of the team. You will see that collaborative problem solving allows members to have equal influence, engage in open communication and conflict resolution, and support innovation and experimentation. Your team thrives in an atmosphere of trust among members including the supervisor or team leader.

Todd Miller, a senior personnel representative, tells how he sold managers on streamlining procedures for screening college recruits by emphasizing the win/win approach he used:

I proposed to the managers that I would take on a certain amount of their responsibility and would provide a better service by doing that. They wouldn't have to take x number of hours each week to make decisions on applicants. I would take on that responsibility, if they would control the process within their department. That was the deal.

We changed it so I was more involved, and the system would run more efficiently. At first they couldn't understand how I, a nontechnical person, could review a resume and made a decision to determine if they would be interested in the person. I convinced them I had picked up a great deal of technical information just by being in Employee Relations for the last three years. Also I stressed that by sitting down and talking to them about their needs and expectations, I could do the initial screening of applicants.

Todd successfully sold his proposal because he pointed out the benefits for both Employee Relations and the technical managers.

Trust

Once you establish a climate of trust, you won't shove disagreements out the door but will view them as chances to clarify and acknowledge differences without bearing personal grudges. Each person, including you, holds the ticket of a potential contributor, regardless of personal values or point of view, and is given time to be heard. Amazingly, people will be sensitive to the reactions and feelings of others and will deal with each other honestly and openly. "Hidden agendas" and self-interests are less likely to distort the task to be accomplished. Feelings of resistance and doubt can be discussed and resolved when they are experienced rather than sitting on them until a "blow out" occurs. Trust, once established, creates a tolerance for conflict. But, you will feel a creative tension. Remember, it is a climate of trust that gives birth to creative conflicts and makes confrontation and assertiveness valuable tools for the effective team communicator. Within this climate, you and team members can both support and confront one another.

Cohesiveness

While collaborative problem solving sets the ground rules for task accomplishment, cohesiveness provides a sense of group affiliation, the yearning to belong. You belong to a cohesive team if members want to remain in the group. In certain types of teams, such as quality circles or professional associations, members may want to be part of the team because the group satisfies certain social needs. Within one company, each quality circle chose a name which was printed on T-shirts. Each month the company displayed photographs of the quality circles that made the most improvements in productivity or cost savings. In this case, the corporate culture provided external support to the team for internal cohesiveness. Cohesiveness, however, can become hazardous when you are pressured to conform to group thinking. To counterbalance conformity to group thinking, you need open communications and equal influence.

Open Communication and Equality

The purpose or aim of the team, which is to increase innovative problem solving and ultimately productivity, demands that members have diverse expertise and experiences. Everyone, including you, usually deals with problems from an occupational frame of reference. But when you put together multiple perspectives, you can snap members out of their tunnel vision. Since the best solution arises from working through differences, you should place a premium on communication and influence.

Chris McMillen recalls a situation where meshing multiple perspectives actually averted a potential crisis:

> *The team was trying to decide which supplier to select for manufacturing a particular part for our product. We narrowed it down to two suppliers. The engineer could see no difference in specifications or reliability. The accounting person pointed out lower shipping costs of one supplier. The team decided to go with this supplier, but the manufacturing person pointed out weaknesses in being so dependent on the one supplier. So we eventually decided to use both of the suppliers. Several months later one of the suppliers went bankrupt. If we had selected only one supplier we would have been in big trouble.*

This situation illustrates how open communication and equal influence was critical to team success.

Decision Making by Consensus

Keeping in mind that team decision making as opposed to individual decisions produces better results, it is valuable to recognize that group consensus also produces better decisions. Research studies compared three decision-making techniques: (1) decisions by an individual and/or a minority segment of the team; (2) decisions supported by a majority of team members; and (3) decisions based on agreement of all team members. These procedures have been called minority control, majority vote, and consensus techniques, respectively.

The minority control technique is the least effective method of decision making because it relies on a few people's competence rather than on the collective brainpower of team members. In other words, the number of people contributing to the decision is minimal. Although more people are included in decision making with the majority vote technique, it reduces conflict and quelches differences of opinion. But if you rely on consensus, all group members can share equally in the final decision. Nothing is approved until all team members have voiced their opinion. To understand how consensus works, you must understand conflict resolution, apply interpersonal skills, and be sensitive to the use of group power.

Tom Atwater, a software product consultant within the telesupport area (telephone support), explains how he uses consensus to reach agreement with his team:

> *Part of my job is to write a newsletter which is sent out every quarter to our customers. What will typically happen is that I'll call a meeting with a person from R & D, marketing, and technical writing. Before the meeting I'll go through two of the three stages of the process.*
>
> *In the first stage I'll write the newsletter. The technical writer reviews it in the second stage, and in the third stage the team will meet to approve it. The meeting really is a give-and-take situation, and we use consensus to reach agreement. It's important that we come up with a compromise.*

Interdependence of Individual and Team Goals

As an effective team member you will balance individual needs against organizational needs. You will feel a sense of responsibility for group success and assist others in meeting their work goals while simultaneously working toward organizational goals.

While testing an accounting software prototype with clients, Tom Atwater acts as a messenger, constantly providing feedback to other members of the Research and Development and Marketing team. In describing how the feedback process works and how individual and team goals dovetail, he emphasizes the sense of ownership felt by the team:

> *I work very closely with the clients. At the end of the three month period of beta testing, we have an evaluation. We sit down and discuss the problems we encountered. It is very important to have the proper flow of information from the client to me to R & D. My goal is to make the client feel that they aren't just another number. I try to be friendly and helpful, to give a little more. It's also an approach we are using in our product line, and it's really a goal which our entire department has. We are excited about product, and we want to give them a little extra.*

Now that you have an idea of the interworkings of team effectiveness, begin determining how you can contribute to building a more effective team. You have already analyzed your relationship to the team in Exercise 7-1. To gain a more indepth assessment of team effectiveness, complete Exercise 7-2.

EXERCISE 7-2. Assessing Team Effectiveness

Listed below are descriptions of either how you might feel about your team involvement or how the team operates. Think about how often you experience or observe them. Circle the number that corresponds to the following frequency.

Often = 4   *Seldom = 2*
Sometimes = 3   *Almost never = 1*

	O	ST	S	AN
1. Team members communicate frankly and openly with one another.	4	3	2	1
2. I feel that I don't have to be very cautious about what I say.	4	3	2	1
3. I am committed to agreements made in our team meetings.	4	3	2	1
4. I am creative when attacking a problem and making suggestions.	4	3	2	1
5. Team members trust and have confidence in each other.	4	3	2	1
6. Team members take an interest in what goes on even if it does not affect them directly.	4	3	2	1
7. I am given enough time to speak my mind.	4	3	2	1
8. Team members talk to the whole team and do not form cliques.	4	3	2	1
9. Team members support each other and build on each others' ideas.	4	3	2	1
10. If I feel strongly about something, I feel that it's OK to voice it.	4	3	2	1
11. When I am with the team I feel valued as a person.	4	3	2	1
12. We make decisions based on team consensus.	4	3	2	1

EXERCISE 7-2. *(Continued)*

13. Team members listen attentively
    and do not prejudge what others say.   4   3   2   1

14. I feel as those I am an important
    member of the team.   4   3   2   1

15. Team members are informal and
    spontaneous when they are with
    each other.   4   3   2   1

16. I rarely feel defensive when I am with
    the team.   4   3   2   1

17. Everyone is willing to help me
    when I need it.   4   3   2   1

18. I feel a sense of belonging
    to the group.   4   3   2   1

Refer to the end of the chapter for an interpretation of your scores.

Now that you have some notion of how teams function effectively and your part regarding role and commitment, begin concentrating on how to contribute to building a well functioning team.

Doing Your Part for Team Effectiveness

As mentioned earlier, the main issues involved in team effectiveness focus on task accomplishment and interpersonal dynamics. Another way of judging team effectiveness is through a sense of team tightness. Like listening to a band playing in unison, you know if there is rapport, camaraderie and if they are "in tune" with each other on a feeling level. They play as if they were one body, not disparate parts trying to harmonize. Craig McMillen describes a tight team: "If an engineer mentions in the meeting that he wants something done, I'll just nod my head and say that I'll take care of it. That's all it takes. It's all a matter of trust."

Achieving Team Tightness

Team building is a method for improving group dynamics so that each member with varying occupational frames of reference and job experiences will feel supported, heard, and influential in contributing toward group goals. Tapping the source of positive group dynamics deals with group morale, feelings, atmosphere, styles of influence, conflict, cooperation, and so on. Some groups actually decrease time discussing task accomplishment to increase time and attention analyzing how the team is functioning interpersonally (Who are the low participators; Who has the most influence; Are there cliques within the team?). Their aim is to improve their ability to overcome obstacles in building a cohesive and productive team. In some companies, an external or internal consultant or facilitator leads the team building session.

However, you do not need to be part of a structured team building session to use team building skills. As a member of one or more teams, you can pave the way for you and others to become influential, insightful, and effective team members by expanding awareness of team building techniques. One technique requires understanding roles people play.

Clarifying Individual Roles

Clarifying roles people play within the team setting can be helpful to understand team communication patterns, decision-making approaches, and leadership styles. By identifying how you and others behave in groups, you can determine if behavior is productive or counterproductive. You can contribute to team effectiveness by undertaking certain roles. Sometimes you may be deeply involved in a debate with others over an issue critical to your job. At other times you may find yourself disengaging and observing others. In either case, you are involved but playing different roles, which fall into two categories: task and team building. Both contribute to goal achievement. A third type of role that is generally counterproductive is called self-serving. The primary concern of the person playing this role is to satisfy a personal need or achieve a self-serving goal while disregarding group goals.

Successful teams, those able to reach goals over an extended period of time, have members who play both task and maintenance or team building roles. Effective members not only help accomplish goals but also build team stability by assuring positive interactions. Groups that limit their scope solely to task functions have been found to be productive for awhile but tend to disintegrate. Groups that focus solely on team building functions tend to be "touchy–feely" with a supportive atmosphere but are devoid of goals that bind them.

Task Roles

Mini-entrepreneurs, when concerned about how to accomplish a task, assume task roles that focus on the content of a discussion and the current problem or task. These roles are shown in the types of behaviors and examples listed in Table 7-1. Begin pinpointing your skill improvement areas by connecting these roles to those listed in the Mini-Entrepreneurial Skills Inventory.

Team Building Roles

Mini-entrepreneurs who assume team building roles are concerned about and sensitive to group dynamics: how members interact and the feelings generated. They want to avoid destructive conflicts and separate cliques that dampen team spirit. Concerned about team morale, they try to create an atmosphere that allows each member to participate, to lay their feelings out on the table. Table 7-2 lists the roles, behaviors, and examples of each type of interpersonal role. Keep in mind that unlike task roles, team building roles require detaching yourself from the content of the discussion so that you can be "in tune" with the feelings beneath the words spoken.

Self-Serving Roles

Table 7-3 lists self-serving roles with a brief description. While they may be easily recognized in others, you may find it more difficult to recognize them in yourself, so be careful.

Using Roles in Team Efforts

Now let's examine how mini-entrepreneurs put these skills to work within the team. Marta Dunlap emphasized the importance of playing the roles of information seeker and clarifer. She describes how pinpointing the needs and objectives of others (skill 19 from the Mini-Entrepreneurial Skills Inventory) is linked to team building:

> *I am working with two other people on a particular document. When we met this morning, I realized that one of them wanted the document to be a certain way because he had already committed himself to getting out a similar document. He felt by doing it the same way, he could kill two birds with one stone. I don't yet know how the other person wants to approach it and what he is going to get out of it. So I'm trying to find out what the three of us are going to do together. I need to figure out their skills and capabilities. They're probably trying to figure me out also. But that's part of the team process. If you don't continually clarify this and that, you can't get anything done.*

Marta is aware of the need to play task roles that clarify personal and group goals and interpersonal roles that play gate opener to find their strengths.

TABLE 7-1

Task Roles

Task Roles	Roles from MESI*	Behavior	Examples
Initiator	Initiator Innovator	Proposes new ideas or alternative ways of viewing the problem. Gets the ball rolling.	Bob, what you really need to do is. . . .Have you considered this?
Information and opinion seeker	Initiator Communicator Collaborator	Asks for clarification of facts, feelings, and attitudes related to a task.	Am I on target? Tell us a little more about what you mean by. . . .
Information and opinion giver	Communicator Innovator	Offers facts and personal experiences to problem solve. States beliefs, feelings, attitudes related to group task.	My reaction to that is . . . . From past experience I think that you ought to. . . .
Clarifier and elaborator	Communicator Team member Collaborator	Integrates ideas or suggestions. Unravels confusion. Elaborates by giving examples, using stories, or analogies.	Tell us how this relates. . . .Let's back up and explain. . . . I can give you an example of. . . . That may be, but have you thought of. . . .
Consensus pusher	Communicator Collaborator Team member	Questions the direction the team is moving. Summarizes agreements made. Restates decisions made. Forces the issue.	We don't seem to be making much much progress right now. Am I correct in believing that we decided. . . .

*Mini-Entrepreneurial Skills Inventory.

TABLE 7-2
Team Building Roles

Team Building Roles	Roles from MESI*	Behavior	Example
Supporter/ gate opener	Collaborator Team member	Encourages others to participate. Uses praise to point out others' expertise.	Liz, we haven't heard from you on this issue. Bill, this seems right up your alley.
Harmonizer	Communicator Collaborator Team member Realist	Mediates disagreements. Resolves differences and relieves tension.	It seems that you two agree on these points but disagree on these points. Bill you see this problem this way, and Liz sees it another way.
Compromiser	Communicator Collaborator Realist	When conflict arises, makes trade-offs for compromising.	I can live with this part but I stand firm on. . . . I'll make a deal with you if. . . .
Team overseer	Collaborator Team member Realist	Observes team progress and gives feedback on how well team is working together.	We seem to be stuck on this issue. It seems as though we are getting ahead of ourselves.

*Mini-Entrepreneurial Skills Inventory.

At one time, Tom Atwater worked in the Research and Development department and is now a consultant in the telesupport unit. He addresses the advantages of team work and also describes how he plays the roles of harmonizer, clarifier, and elaborator when getting involved in collaborative problem solving (skills 11 and 28):

> In our team meeting this morning, we were discussing our quarterly newsletter written for customers. There's a question and answer section. The R & D person, Jack, thought that one of the questions which I had written should be rephrased. So he proposed a new question but the others didn't understand his interpretation of the question. I more or less understood what he was trying to

TABLE 7-3
Self-Serving Roles

Behavior	Example
Being aggressive: Attempting to belittle, attack, or criticize harshly someone's suggestions or ideas.	That doesn't make sense at all. You don't know what you are talking about.
Blocking: Being negative by opposing someone's ideas for the sake of being difficult. Critical of group goals. Being cynical or resistant.	That will never work. We've done it this way and it always works so why change it now.
Dominating: Trying to take over the group by manipulation, coercion, deceit, or flattery, using the group to express personal feelings or judgments that have no bearing on group tasks.	As the senior member of the group, I know what is best for the group. I speak for the group when I say. . . .

say. So I said, "I think this is what you mean. . . ." He agreed. I think that it's important not to tear him down because he has a different viewpoint. I should be able to express his viewpoint. It may be different than mine, but that's OK"

In this situation, Tom was flexible enough to change horses in midstream and in so doing changed roles. He shifted from initiator and consensus pusher to harmonizer. Since he was the only person who understood Jack, he rescued Jack for the benefit of the team.

TEAM BUILDING THROUGH YOUR PEP

For Marta, a team building strategy for reaching group goals will help her work through the many issues involved in writing a final document. Similar to planning your influence strategy, a plan for optimizing effective teamwork is helpful. It is important to remember that at certain times you need to exercise flexibility and adaptability when changing hats. At other times you just want to sit back and "ride it out" until a more opportune time. In either case, a plan of action helps you maintain objectivity and act in the team's best interest. Here your Personal Effectiveness Plan can be an effective tool for reaching team effectiveness. Using Marta as an example, the PEP can be completed as shown in Figure 7-1.

SKILLS

  Strengths

  1. _____

  2. _____

AREAS FOR IMPROVEMENT   ACTION STEPS

  SKILLS

  1. _____

  2. _____

WORK STYLE GAPS

          Ideal   Actual

1. _____   _____

ROLES

PARTICIPATION

  1. Initiator (related to team building)   Practice role of
                                               consensus pusher

COMMITMENT

  1. Collaborator (related to team building)   Practice role of
                                               compromiser.

  2. Team Builder   Practice role of
                                                 consensus pusher

CREATIVITY

  1. Innovator (related to team building)   Practice role of
                                               information and
                                             opinion seeker.

FIGURE 7-1. Personal Effectiveness Plan.

CONCLUSION

Teamwork within the entrepreneurial culture of excellence is necessary for company survival. Opportunities exist for the informal and formal arrangement of teams, from pairs of people preparing for a sales call to intact project teams. Within a team situation, multiple needs of team members should be considered for team effectiveness to occur. Teamwork demands juggling your needs as well as those of team members. To do so, you need to play a variety of roles of initiator, team member, collaborator, and innovator.

Teams have certain common characteristics that include a reason or charter, member interdependence, belief in the benefits of teamwork, and team accountability to the organization. In addition, other aspects contribute to a team functioning cohesively and productively. They include member involvement, a climate of trust, cohesiveness, open communication and equal influence, decision making by consensus, and achievement of individual and group goals.

To do your part for team effectiveness, you must assume multiple roles. These roles include both task and team building roles. Beyond listening to the discussion, you must also be aware of group dynamics. Remaining objective, flexible, and adaptable within the team setting paves the way for you to become a valuable team member.

ANSWERS TO EXERCISE 7-2. Assessing Team Effectiveness

Rate each item in the spaces below. Then total your scores for each column. Each total reflects the degree of openness, trust, and interdependence operating within your team.

1. _____	2. _____	3. _____
4. _____	5. _____	6. _____
7. _____	8. _____	9. _____
10. _____	11. _____	12. _____
13. _____	14. _____	17. _____
15. _____	16. _____	18. _____
TOTAL _____	TOTAL _____	TOTAL _____
OPENNESS	TRUST	INTERDEPENDENCE

ANSWERS TO EXERCISE 7-2. *(Continued)*

INTERPRETATION OF YOUR SCORE

If you scored:

A. 21 points or more, says:

TRUST

I trust the team and also see the team climate as trusting as opposed to threatening and putting people on the defensive.

OPENNESS

I feel free to express my feelings and opinions. I see team members as being open and spontaneous and not hiding behind facades.

INTERDEPENDENCE

I feel connected to the team and feel each team member's presence and contribution is necessary for accomplishing team goals. I see the team functioning well as a unit.

B. 18−20 points, says that some of the characteristics are present in your group to a certain degree. However, overall team effectiveness can be improved along each of the lines listed in the exercise.

C. 17 points or less, says that team effectiveness is relatively poor and in great need of improvement along the lines of trust, openness, and interdependence.

CREATIVE CONFLICT MANAGEMENT

What to Do When People Disagree

AGREEING TO DISAGREE

Joanne Navarro bumps into Lisa Ishimoto as she leaves the cafeteria during lunchtime. As they walk down the hallway, Joanne asks Lisa for some advice:

JOANNE: You know I was in a meeting recently and found myself confused as to whether or not to add my two cents.

LISA: Why? What happened?

JOANNE: I found myself caught in the midst of a very heated argument on pricing. Mark was adamant about raising the price, while Marta was arguing for the opposite. It seems as though she was playing devil's advocate just to give Mark a hard time.

LISA: Listen, we all play devil's advocate for one another at sometime. It's an essential part of keeping everyone on their toes and to really help them think through all the worst cases and alternatives possible. If there are 20 ways of doing something, I want to hear them all so I can take the shortest and most effective route. It saves everyone time and money.

JOANNE: But I thought it was important to be use influence skills to tactfully persuade others of your argument.

LISA: Around here you need to be all things to all people. Sometimes you need to be supportive and at other times you need to play devil's advocate. There's an ethic which conveys the message that it is OK to disagree. It's part of challenging us all to keep the entrepreneurial spirit, to be innovative. After all, how can we be innovative without questioning and disagreeing at times?

JOANNE: I'm not sure how to handle conflicts. I tend to take them too personally.

LISA: Remember we are all tied to company goals, a common vision. If you remind yourself of that then you can work things out and deal with others productively.

JOANNE: I'll have to keep that in mind next time I am in a sticky situation. I tend to want to be the harmonizer because I'm not sure how to take all the yelling. I'd like to find out more about exactly what how to handle conflict. But right now, I need to attend a meeting. See you later.

As Joanne walks down the hall, she wonders about how she can handle differently the conflict that she anticipates will occur in her meeting. She also is puzzled by Lisa's accepting attitude toward conflict, as if it were a part of the rules of a game from which she is disqualified.

This chapter helps you tie together all your prior learning. Your first task is to realize that situations demanding interpersonal roles (communicator, collaborator, etc.) are not mutually exclusive but really overlap. Because they do, you will often face conflicting signals. Managing conflict, then, is tied to managing paradox. In fact, managing paradox is a prerequisite for managing conflict. Juggling several ideas, jumping into the chaos of decision making, overstepping traditional boundaries, and following your instincts are all a part of managing paradox. Ultimately, they are ways of creatively managing conflicts. Take a moment now to complete Exercise 8-1 and examine your style of handling conflict.

EXERCISE 8-1. Examining Your Style of Handling Interpersonal Conflict

Listed below are descriptions of how you might handle interpersonal conflict. Circle the rating that corresponds to the following rating descriptions.

OFTEN = 4   SELDOM = 2
SOMETIMES = 3   ALMOST NEVER = 1

	AN	S	ST	O
1. I try to examine all sides of a problem to find an acceptable solution.	1	2	3	4
2. I argue my case to point out the merits of my position.	1	2	3	4
3. I use my inside contacts who can help me get around an obstacle to reach my goals.	1	2	3	4
4. I try to remain neutral and avoid taking a stance.	1	2	3	4
5. I point out how tasks and goals relate to overall company goals.	1	2	3	4
6. I try to integrate my ideas with others to come up with a joint decision.	1	2	3	4
7. I use my authority to force a decision in my favor.	1	2	3	4
8. When I recognize conflicts that cannot be resolved because of personalities or deadlines, I find other means of reaching the goal.	1	2	3	4
9. I avoid being put on the spot by deemphasizing differences.	1	2	3	4
10. I try to keep a focus on a vision to counter arguments motivated by self-interest.	1	2	3	4
11. I encourage others to state their concerns so they can be addressed.	1	2	3	4

EXERCISE 8-1. (*Continued*)

12. I stand firm when settling an issue.	1	2	3	4
13. I gain the cooperation of others who are influential to help me reach a common goal.	1	2	3	4
14. I avoid unpleasant exchanges and strive for peaceful coexistence.	1	2	3	4
15. I explain how things should be if everything were "in sync."	1	2	3	4

Refer to the end of this chapter for an interpretation of your score.

To manage conflicts creatively, you must draw upon roles and skills presented in previous chapters (communication, influence, and team building). While influence and team building skills require you to change hats and play various roles, managing paradox within the entrepreneurial culture gives you permission to contradict yourself. You can be tough at one time and supportive and caring at another. This is expected of mini-entrepreneurs within the high-tech entrepreneurial culture built upon loose-tight principles that operate between individual autonomy and firm central direction. Shared values and a common vision, unlike standard operating procedures, provide the guiding light for your actions. Your ability to "stay loose," to adapt to changing circumstances beyond control, makes conflict something you need not fear. It is an everyday occurrence, something to be worked through rather than avoided or shoved under the rug.

TYPES OF CONFLICT

My role has changed from doing technical training to more design work, and I'm not so sure I like it as much.

Sometimes you just have to force the issue. They may not see that it is necessary to do what you want, but you do.

Our team leader is so afraid of losing control of the group that he has overlooked some things such as listening. One guy pointed out some oversights to him and then made the mistake of saying, "I told you so." They started arguing and attacking each other. It got out of hand.

A year ago, our group was called a "bunch of wild-eyed incompetents" willing to sell the customer anything. But that has changed.

These examples show how conflict can create job dissatisfaction, damage relationships, and destroy goodwill. To manage your relationships, you need to manage inner, interpersonal, intragroup, and intergroup conflicts. By understanding how to manage conflicts creatively, you will realize that conflict is not always counterproductive. In certain cases it should be tolerated, stimulated, and creatively channeled into collaborative problem solving.

Conflict is any kind of opposition between two parties, perceived by these parties or by a third party. Your inner conflicts stem from role conflicts: the confusion and frustration surrounding your preferred skill, values, and role expectations as opposed to job demands. Once you have identified your strengths and career values, you can deal better with inner conflicts.

Interpersonal conflicts occur between two individuals or more, while intragroup conflicts arise within a group or team. So far you have worked with tools to enhance your communication, influencing, and team building skills. These skills will help you manage your work relationships either on a one-to-one or group basis.

Intergroup conflicts involve disagreements between two or more groups when their representatives quibble over authority, territory, or resources. This type of conflict results from different perceptions of tasks to be accomplished, differences in subcultural norms, need for joint decision making, and dependence on shared resources.

This chapter focuses on intrapersonal, interpersonal, intragroup, and intergroup conflicts. Chapter 7 presented roles and skills for becoming an effective team player. These roles and skills somewhat overlap with those required for managing conflicts. To manage conflict creatively, you need to assume the roles of communicator, initiator, collaborator, team member, realist, and innovator.

Inner or Intrapersonal Conflict

You have already examined your skills and career values in relationship to your current job and corporate culture in Chapters 3 and 4, which also introduced tools for expanding your personal power. These tools enable you to identify your skill strengths, areas for improvement, career values, and work style in relationship to the high-tech entrepreneurial culture. Understanding intrapersonal conflict and how to resolve it will help clarify your job role.

Inner or intrapersonal conflicts occur when you expect to perform a particular role while others demand that you assume another. This mismatch causes a role conflict that can be overcome by a technique called role analysis. Role analysis forces you to examine the purpose of your role, its primary and secondary tasks and activities, and its relationship with other roles.

Role analysis can be made on an individual, group, or intergroup basis. You may want to clarify your role with your boss, team leader, or members of a team. Follow the steps outlined as follows:

STEP 1. Initiate the discussion of your role. Allow others to discuss the purpose of your role and how it fits in with the goals of the team and/or the company.

STEP 2. List the activities that comprise your role and ask others to discuss the activities/tasks that they see as essential to your role. This process aims to add new tasks that result from the discussion or drop the overlapping tasks with the roles of others.

STEP 3. List your expectations of the other person or persons. A discussion of both expectations will clarify role interdependencies and where you and others need to exchange advice and expertise.

STEP 4. Write the main points of the discussion, such as primary and secondary responsibilities, tasks and, activities. This information can be transferred later to a role and mission statement, which will be discussed in Chapter 9.

Role analysis technique can help you focus on tasks expected to be performed and those demanded of you by others. It also helps you differentiate between your strengths and preferred activities, those you "like to do" and activities that are primarily important to your role and those that you have "got to do."

Intragroup Conflict

Disagreements or differences among team members concerning group goals, tasks, and activities lead to intragroup conflict. The causes of conflict stem from task structure, group composition, cohesiveness, and "groupthink."

Whether a task is simple or routine, or complex or nonroutine, depends on its task structure. A routine task has clearly defined goals, includes a few steps, and has concrete solutions. For example, soldering and wiring material to a circuit board is an example of a routine task. A complex or nonroutine task is not spelled out specifically and does not always have a verifiable solution. Designing the circuit board is an example of a complex task with a verifiable solution. In contrast, designing a management development workshop is complex without a verifiable solution because results desired are intangible, subjective, and long term.

When a task is more complex the possibility for conflict to occur increases. Then conflict is unavoidable because large numbers of knowledge workers bump into each other in the high-tech environment. Consequently, you ought to view conflict as a natural occurrence that can lead to creative solutions. To safeguard team creativity, guard against groupthink; it can infiltrate healthy debate and cripple critical thinking.

To counter groupthink, call upon your team building skills. Chapter 7 showed that team effectiveness consists of both task functions and team building or maintenance functions (between content and process). You were presented with roles to play that supported both of these functions. Beyond team building, you need to problem solve collaboratively to manage intergroup conflict creatively and set up win/win situations. At the opposite extreme, when you get dragged into win/lose orientations to conflict, you put on blinders and see interests and goals as mutually exclusive.

Craig McMillen points out the importance of team communication and its impact on a project:

> *Communication is a real big deal around here. Regardless of what level you're on, your input is always appreciated and respected.*
>
> *I've seen schedules saved by people at lower levels. They were experiencing something which seemed to be insignificant to them. But they brought it up in a meeting and found out that the problem was bigger than anyone thought. Someone was smart enough in the room to say, "Hey, let's talk about this."*
>
> *It turned out that a part that was manufactured on the outside was giving us problems. The manufacturer changed their design and didn't tell us, and it started impacting the performance of the computer. Someone at a lower level spoke up and saved the company time and money.*

Remember that collaborative problem solving differs from compromising. In a compromise situation, you may settle for less than your full needs or desires. You are likely to give up something to end the conflict. Robert Bolton calls the compromise method the mini-lose/mini-lose method. Collaborative problem solving, on the other hand, involves a win/win method in which people put their heads together to find a much more innovative solution then they could on their own. It requires redefining the problem, generating alternative novel solutions, and focusing on mutual goals. But you need a positive frame of mind. Lou Ann Bender points out the difference between reaching consensus and collaborative problem solving:

We have developed an attitude in the group which assumes that nobody is going to get everything he or she wants. You can get hung up on the belief that if it doesn't meet everyone's criteria, it isn't an alternative. To try to get an alternative that meets everyone's criteria is immobilizing. You're crossing over too many lines to get consensus. You have the material function, the manufacturing function, the accounting function, an engineering function, and subgroups under them. It's difficult to meet everyone's criteria, so we try to get to the point of saying: "This is our goal, and this is how we want to reach it." It's a matter of trade-offs. To give up this, we are going to get this. It's working pretty well. We are no longer immobilized.

The steps for collaborative problem solving are outlined in the following text. All the skills that you have used previously should now be summoned as you apply these steps.

STEP 1. DEFINE THE PROBLEM. Define the problem in terms of mutual goals to be accomplished rather than quick solutions. When you find yourself in a conflicting situation with another person or persons, you'll undoubtedly be anxious to find solutions to the perceived problem. Restrain yourself by first listening to others needs and desires. It is crucial to the problem solving process to define the problem through contact with other team members; through joint effort, real problems are isolated. Any preconceptions that you have to the problem-solving session should be set aside.

STEP 2. BEGIN WITH FACT FINDING. Each person or persons should explore the "facts." By sharing perceptions, you can begin exploring each person's understanding of the facts. You will find that one person's understanding may differ vastly from another person's for the same set of facts. These questions will enable you to explore the facts, as well as challenge your listening skills: What are the issues? What are the needs? What is known? What is assumed?

STEP 3. LIST ALTERNATIVE SOLUTIONS. List a range of possible solutions for each problem identified. Here, you and others with varying perspectives will have the chance to shuffle through solutions from various vantage points and occupational frames of reference. By examining a range of solutions, you will broaden your perspective and ensure that an indepth solution will be reached. How well you can handle controversy, differences, or objections that arise depends on the level of trust within the group.

STEP 4. SELECT THE SOLUTION. The most effective solution is the one reached through consensus. Tips for achieving consensus include:

1. Present your position clearly and logically but listen to other people's reactions without getting defensive.
2. Push for win/win solutions that are acceptable with every team member.
3. Do not change your stance merely to avoid a conflict. Explore the reasons behind the solutions to make sure everyone agrees for similar reasons.
4. Avoid majority vote and other tactics that circumvent constructive confrontation. Since differences of opinion are inevitable, capitalize on them by seeking everyone's opinion for quality decision making.

Intergroup Conflict

Intergroup conflict results from clashing perspectives on how a task should be accomplished, subcultural norms, occupational values, and a need for joint decision making. Conflicts between line and staff are classic examples. Complex interdependencies can make you uncertain and cause conflict if you don't define and deal with them. For example, ambiguities over authority and responsibility between functional areas, such as purchasing and engineering, cause further confusion. Mini-entrepreneurs deal with these conflicts head on by looking toward teams and cultural values for guidance. They also tolerate ambiguity and jump into team play in spite of it. In one excellent high-tech company, the job applicant interview form actually includes "tolerance for ambiguity." Remember this when conflicts seem intolerable.

Your collaborative problem solving skills will rescue you when managing intergroup conflicts. These skills show the importance of superordinate goals. Robert Blake and Jane Mouton suggest that superordinate goals unify members of conflicting groups because these goals cannot be attained by one group alone. Mini-entrepreneurs look toward superordinate goals, like guiding stars, to reduce intergroup conflict.

Mark Malone, purchasing specialist for an integrated circuit manufacturer, explains how decisions are made as a team and how superordinate goals are respected:

> *Everyone comes into a situation with their blinders on, so it's good to have a team to reach quality decisions. The decisions which we come to, we come to as a team. Engineering doesn't decide this, or Purchasing doesn't decide that. We'll let the vendor know that this is not a decision made exclusively by Engineering or Quality Control or by Purchasing. We all agreed that this is the way we should go. We share the responsibility.*

In this corporate culture, a sense of team play elevates common goals and facilitates group decision making. Brooke Tierney, a sales program developer, explains further:

I have found that when people logically think about how to resolve a conflict that most parties come very close. If you just open up the communication lines between the two conflicting parties, you really come close to solving it without a real hassle.

After all you have common goals. Sometimes you wonder why we are arguing over this when you look at the big picture.

USING CONFLICT TO YOUR ADVANTAGE
Accelerated Problem Solving

Mini-entrepreneurs view conflict as something that should not be avoided or has solely negative consequences. Rather, they view it as a natural and inevitable part of reaching creative solutions. It is tolerated and accepted as an avenue leading to innovative outcomes. Organizations with little or no conflict may stagnate because conflict is vital for productivity and change.

You can see that shared values, a team structure, and a participative management style create an environment for healthy conflict to thrive. They force resourcefulness even though you may lock horns. "Horn-locking" problem solving becomes normal in some organizations, such as Intel. Andrew Grove, president of Intel, uses the phrase "constructive confrontation" to describe Intel's way of dealing with conflicts. He explains that it is a method for putting aggressive energies to work for the organization:

Constructive confrontation accelerates problem solving. It requires that participants be direct, that they deal face to face. It pushes people to deal with a problem as soon as possible, keeping it from festering. It encourages all concerned to concentrate on the problem, not on the people caught up in it.

In our formal course to teach new Intel employees about constructive confrontation, we explain the reasons for using the technique: the need for conflict resolution and the desirability of speeding this process up.

Within this corporate culture, conflict when properly managed can unleash creativity. In other companies, such as Cognos, conflict is viewed as central part of healthy debate.

In another excellent high-tech company, the "road to Abilene" is the metaphor used to encourage people to "speak their mind" and also to emphasize that a price is paid for avoiding conflicts for the sake of harmony.

As you may recall, the story of the "road to Abilene" speaks of individuals who had nothing to do and nowhere to go. Nobody took the responsibility to make any suggestions, until someone suggested that they go to Abilene, which they did. When they arrived, they were upset with where they ended. Within the high-tech entrepreneurial culture, speaking your mind, confronting others, and questioning the usual way of doing things is all in a normal day's work.

Teams, internal networking, informal and open communication give you opportunities to collaboratively problem solve. When you get involved in collaborative problem solving, you are less likely to engage in power struggles that damage another person's self-esteem. Remember, you want to raise self-esteem not lower it. Destructive power plays are out of style in the entrepreneurial culture. Instead, you can engage in a healthy competition that will push your talent and expertise to the limit. Like other mini-entrepreneurs, you can compete and strive toward personal excellence. Once you accept conflict as a part of daily worklife, it will function as a safety valve, releasing pent-up energy, letting off steam. Your tolerance for conflict will make relationships, after conflict, salvageable and solutions viable.

Tony Scarsdale, a sales program manager for a high-tech company, reveals how she resolves conflicts:

> *Here all of us want to get ahead and be the best in what we produce as well as who we are. I don't let personal conflicts get in the way of business. If I disagree with someone on an issue, well, it's on the issue. If I want to resolve a personal conflict, I will go in and talk to the person. I would say, "It's not personal. I really believe that it's this way." We would resolve it. I don't sit around and wait and let things boil and bubble. It's not worth your time to carry around that burden.*

In chapter 4, one high-tech company emphasized "leveling," communicating honestly. It is written in the corporate philosophy and stressed at every management development workshop. This company realizes that teams create a greater need for problem solving because conflict multiplies in teams. Points of contact among functional areas increase and create potentially more interface problems. However, the collaborative ethic can clarify rather than muddle issues, as long as a willingness to work things out exists. Penny Sumner explains that defining her management role was a collaborative process:

> *I came to the company knowing that the Human Resources function was decentralized. The Corporate Management Team helped define my role. I found out from each one of them what their "gripes" were, what they loved and what they wanted to change. We decided that I would play a supporting role to*

the managers. They pushed that concept. They helped set mandates for my job. Now I know that my role is to tie everyone together in a team environment.

Conflicts have benefits as long as the collaborative ethic, a tolerance for ambiguity, and a bias toward constructive confrontation are in place. Keep in mind that conflict needs to be managed, not eliminated.

Stimulation

The other side of the conflict management coin is conflict stimulation. Traditionalists view conflict as destructive and something to be eliminated. This view prevailed during the nineteenth century through the mid 1940s. During the late 1940s and early 1950s, behavioralists recognized that all organizations encountered conflicts. While arguing for its acceptance, they concluded that the way to manage conflict was to resolve it. Most organizations operate under this philosophy, upholding anticonflict values that stress obedience to authority.

Stephen Robbins points out the need for a third philosophy, which he calls interactionist. Advocating the necessity for conflict, he defines conflict management to include stimulation as well as resolution techniques, and considers the conflict management a major responsibility of all managers. The interactionist viewpoint stresses that an organization cannot survive without some level of constructive conflict. Survival results when an organization can adapt to environmental changes. Adaptation is prompted by change which, in turn, is stimulated by conflict. This chain reaction is illustrated in Figure 8-1. Conflict then is the catalyst for change. High technology companies live out this dynamic interplay, as they adapt and respond to customer, employee, and marketplace needs and technological developments.

HANDLING INTERPERSONAL CONFLICT

The value you place on conflict and how you handle conflict situations will determine its outcome. Conflict can be interpreted as a collision between personal and mutual goals. These two sides separate different styles of

Conflict --➤ Change ---➤ Adaptation ---➤ Survival

FIGURE 8-1. Conflict Survival Model. *Source*: Stephen P. Robbins. *Managing Organizational Conflict: A Nontraditional Approach.* Englewood Cliffs, NJ: Prentice-Hall, 1974, p. 20. Reprinted with permissions.

handling conflict. The relationship between a concern for reaching personal and mutual goals and styles for handling conflict is illustrated by the conceptual model in Figure 8-2. This model places a premium on superordinate goals, a common vision, collaborative problem solving, and circumventing an obstacle (a strategy used by mini-entrepreneurs in the high-tech entrepreneurial culture).

Going Around the Problem

Previously, mini-entrepreneurs have explained how they have used various strategies to skirt obstacles. The principle thinking behind this strategy is similar to the rationale behind aikido, a Japanese art of self-defense. Instead of using your own force to overtake your opponent, aikido uses your opponent's moves and energy to your advantage. You never use any more force than is necessary and try to blend your movement with those of your opponent. In Chapter 6 when Lisa Ishimoto used her peers to speak on her behalf to her boss, she was circumventing an obstacle, her boss, to accomplish a mutual goal of getting a department computer. She was successful because her ego or personal feelings did not interfere with reaching a common goal. She did so because she sensed that using the Rapport Matrix techniques would not be effective with her boss. She used her internal network to get around an obstacle. Yet as a manager, she uses the "road to Abilene" metaphor as a lever to get her people to speak up. While managing conflict, she manages paradox. How she manages her boss and her people are not necessarily the same, nor should they be. In the entrepreneurial culture, consistency and control are not achieved through conformity, but through shared values that let people know what really counts.

Other mini-entrepreneurs have also circumvented obstacles as an effective

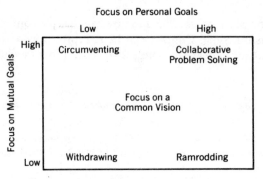

FIGURE 8-2. Styles for Handling Interpersonal Conflict.

means for reaching a goal. Craig McMillen explains why he finds it necessary to bypass the Purchasing department in his fast-paced environment demanding quick and decisive action:

> *Sometimes the manufacturing work is going faster than purchase requisitions are being processed. You've got your fingers crossed that materials will arrive on time. Once you detect that problem, you have to recover from it to stay on schedule. So when this happens, I won't allow purchasing to step in. I'll call the vendor myself and order the materials. Then the vendor will end up telling the purchasing guy, if I don't get to him first. The purchasing guy, if he is a professional, will understand why engineering had to go around him. He knows that you did the company a favor.*

In this case, the superordinate goal of getting the product out the door on time overrides documentation, the paperwork for purchasing. Although a potentially combative situation exists, it is pushed aside in pursuit of a common vision.

Styles and Supporting Skills

The various styles for handling conflict and the value judgments associated with each one are outlined in the following text. The supporting skills from Exercise 8-1 also are listed. Figure 8-3 illustrates how individuals interact when using different styles of handling conflict.

Ramrodding

I try to dominate the conversation with my arguments. By presenting my arguments logically and forcefully, I can convince others of their merits. I try to make others understand and agree that my goals should take precedence over others. I view conflicts as power struggles where someone wins and someone loses.

Skills from Exercise 8-1

2. I argue my case to point out the merits of my position.
7. I use my authority to force a decision in my favor.
12. I stand firm when settling an issue.

Collaborative Problem Solving

I make every effort to discover creative solutions with others. Conflict is inevitable, and agreement can be reached by working through the issues in question. I see interdependencies as a fact of organizational life. By involving everyone in problem solving, we can achieve more innovative solutions. I try to attack the problem not the person.

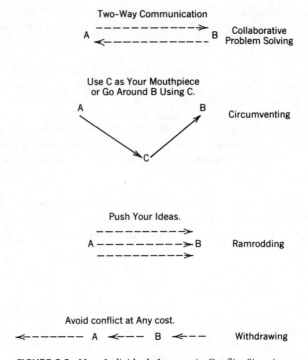

FIGURE 8-3. How Individuals Interact in Conflict Situations.

Skills from Exercise 8-1

1. I try to examine all sides of a problem to find an acceptable solution.
6. I try to integrate my ideas with others to come up with a joint decision.
11. I encourage others to state their concerns so they can be addressed.

Lou Ann Bender describes how her task force works at solving common problems. Within the cost accounting area of Manufacturing, she joins others from Product Engineering, Manufacturing, and Materials working out inventory control problems. She explains how her function is perceived by Manufacturing and ways to get around this negative perception to work for common goals:

Accounting is the bad guy. You kind of wear the gun and the black hat because you're saying that you can't do this or that. You're going to lose control of material or tracking or whatever. But we're really not saying that. What we are saying is that it is important to you also.

So we try to get accounting into a support role by saying: "We are working with you. You tell us what you want to do, and we'll help you develop your plan. We can ensure that the controls are there within that plan but you are getting your end result." When we started to do that, it became a real turning point.

Withdrawing

I believe in peaceful coexistance between conflicting parties. Collaborative problem solving is not needed because our department can solve our problems better by ourselves. Collaborative problem solving only confuses matters. It is better to isolate ourselves from conflict and work on those problems that don't concern other people.

Skills from Exercise 8-1

4. I try to remain neutral and avoid taking a stance.
9. I avoid being put on the spot by deemphasizing differences.
14. I avoid unpleasant exchanges and strive for peaceful coexistence.

Circumventing

It is better to skirt an obstacle in situations in which conflict may be destructive or too difficult to resolve objectively or time does not permit working things out. I tap my internal network for support depending on the situation. I also break rules when it means honoring commitments and reaching overarching mutual goals. I try to remove my ego from a situation and keep my objective in sight. It is not essential that I get credit for accomplishing a task, as much as it is to reach a common goal.

Skills from Exercise 8-1

3. I use my inside contacts who can help me get around an obstacle to reach my goals.
8. When I recognize conflicts that cannot be resolved because of personalities or deadlines, I find other means of reaching the goal.

Focusing on a Common Vision

I try to stress interdependencies and overarching company goals and values such as service to the customer. By focusing on realistic achievements together, others are able to give up self-interests. An emphasis on team play helps rally everyone around a common vision. For example, Research and Development people need to see that, unless the Marketing people also help define the product, they will not be successful in getting the product to the marketplace. I engage in constructive confrontation because it clarifies superordinate goals and fulfills commitments.

Skills from Exercise 8-1

5. I point out how tasks and goals relate to overall company goals.
10. I focus on a vision to counter arguments motivated by self-interest.
15. I explain how everything should be if everything were "in sync."

Let's examine how Lou Ann Bender gets team members to rally around a common vision, a common goal:

> *Initially people tend to feel threatened because you're talking about changing their little empire. Not that it is really like that, but it is really important for everyone to see that we have a common goal. We try to define a common goal and specifically define action items which they could take so that they felt some ownership.*

MANAGING PARADOX

The changing views of and value placed on conflict make it more complex to manage your relationships. When outlining steps to follow, your judgment and discretion, when changing roles and applying skills, are critical to managing conflict creatively; for all is not what it appears to be on the surface. To manage conflict creatively, you need to be versatile, adaptable, and engage in contradictory behavior. To manage paradox means "to stay loose." You may need to influence others through inspiration around one issue, such as a new marketing strategy, while being assertive and confrontive when implementing this strategy within the sales force. In reality, you need to be both tough and supportive at different times.

Team Play

As a team member you may play a supporter/harmonizer role one minute, then change to information giver. In this situation, depending upon the agenda, you can avoid conflict at one point by initially "tippy-toeing" around issues and later on confronting one another. A newly formed team is likely to avoid conflict until team members are more familiar with each other. To make this transition, first stimulate conflict to get the issues out on the table and then resolve them. For example, the supporter role may be needed to get others to open up and state their opinions if members seem distant and reticent to speak at the beginning and seem to be nodding their heads in agreement. You should switch to the harmonizer role when the ice has been broken and team members are at a point where conflicts arise and polarize the team.

Penny Sumner recounts how she created conflict to make a group more cohesive:

> I recruited a number of trainers from various parts of the company to assist me in presenting a series of career development workshops. These people were from different buildings and had not even met each other until the train-the-trainer session. While leading this session I sensed that there was distance and even a competition between them. None of them really came prepared as they were supposed to. So I became very forceful in stating my expectation that they come prepared to the session. By so doing, I created conflict between myself and them. It set up the old "we/they" split, but it rallied them together. They all saw each other in the same boat. I was the "heavy." During lunch they all seemed more congenial toward one another. The barriers had been initially broken because I created a conflict between me and them.

In this situation, an external threat (the workshop leader) created a conflict that strengthened group cohesiveness. It required Penny Sumner's ability to switch roles.

Influencing Others

You will mostly rely upon influence skills when you want to gain the cooperation of others for information and resources. Chances are you do not want to alienate the other person. On the other hand, if you face passive resistance and indifference, you can force a conflict and pry loose a debate to get the issues out. It's best to follow your instincts when performing a task that conflicts with your better judgment. Steve Thomas, a manufacturing productivity improvement specialist, explains how he confronted others, created a conflict with coworkers, and was, in the end, appreciated:

> I am kind of a maverick. If my boss or anyone else tells me to do something which I find disturbing, I don't necessarily do it. I was asked to drop a quality "gate." In other words I was asked to lower standards of inspection on a product so we could meet our shipping schedule. I said that I wouldn't do it because it would hurt us in the long run. It wasn't a real popular decision. They resisted at first, but after I talked to them about it later, they understood and said it was a good decision.

In this situation the quality of the product was at stake. Steve confronted the issue head on, knowing that in the end a higher objective would be reached. So in this case this mini-entrepreneur influenced others by dealing with a conflict without being coercive.

In addition to being influentially agile, conflict management requires versatility enough to engage in contradictory behavior. What works in one situation may not hold water in another. Consistency, when disciplining children is admirable and effective for compliance, but is second to innovation when everything is in a state of flux. You need to count on people for fast thinking and sound judgment. Mini-entrepreneurs display their commitment to excellence by working smarter not harder. They separate efficiency (doing things right) from effectiveness (doing the right things). Don't forget that the right thing is a matter of judgment.

Guarding Against Groupthink

A cohesive team is a productive group of people working toward mutual goals and bonded together by an espirt de corps. However, a team loses its creativity when "groupthink" sets in like rigor mortis. "Groupthink," a term coined by Irving Janis, is introduced when a cohesive group finds it more important to get along than to find an innovative solution to a problem. Then the question is: If cohesiveness is needed for teamwork, when should conflict be present for the healthy and productive functioning of a group? You can find the answer in the research findings of Jay Hall. He conducted a study of both well-established and ad-hoc groups. He found differences in how the two groups handled conflict. A variety of opinions is beneficial to an established group but disruptive to an ad-hoc group. Members are not likely to see clashing opinions as threatening in an already well-established group because they view disagreements as a natural result of their efforts. They do not read them as hostile acts but of attempts to uncover the issues.

In addition, established groups produce unique solutions that are better, on the whole, than average individual findings. Their solutions tend to be creative, while ad-hoc groups arrive at compromise solutions. Conflict, then, is a healthy process for intact teams whose members are familiar with each other.

These findings hold up several red flags. An awareness of team development stages is essential for managing intragroup conflicts. If you are in the habit of playing one role, you need to step out of the comfortable role and assume others that may give better results. Craig McMillen warns about the dangers of getting caught up in their wave of groupthink:

> *There's a fine line between being on the team and handling the team concept and knowing where to end it. For example, I was on one team and was asked to purchase a bunch of material. The customer came to us and handed us a design instead of having us design it. Because of the schedule, the program manager*

wanted to go out and buy the material based on their design. I objected because I knew the design was going to change. I told them that it was not a smart way of doing business. In the long run, after a fiasco, I was proved to be right.

In this case, a mini-entrepreneur trusted his better judgment and went against the team's decision.

An examination of your values about conflict situations may well be in order. Table 8-1 lists cultural stimulants, ways the entrepreneurial culture encourages healthy conflict.

FINE-TUNING YOUR CONFLICT MANAGEMENT SKILLS THROUGH PEP

Creative conflict management requires playing many roles but in particular those of analyst, collaborator, and realist. The skills that support these roles overlap and complement skills needed to handle conflict. The skills from Exercise 8-1, which outlines different styles of handling conflict, can be incorporated into your PEP as shown in Figure 8-4.

TABLE 8-1
Cultural Stimulants of Conflict

Message	Source/Channel of Communication
Question the usual way of doing things.	Metaphors, stories such as the "road to Abilene."
Let yourself experiment. Tolerate mistakes.	Participative management style granting the freedom to take risks and make mistakes.
Communicate openly and honestly.	"Level" with people. Replace "finger pointing" with problem solving.
Don't get caught up in "groupthink."	Engage in constructive confrontation.
Change is necessary for survival and growth.	Fix problems as the company grows. Don't stop growing to fix problems.

SKILLS

Strengths

1. _____

2. _____

| AREAS FOR IMPROVEMENT | ACTION STEPS |

SKILLS

| 1. _____ | _____ |
| 2. _____ | _____ |

WORK STYLE GAPS

Ideal	Actual
1. _____	_____
_____	_____

ROLES	ACTION STEPS
PARTICIPATION	
1. Analyst (related to managing conflict)	1. Practice using skills for withdrawing.
COMMITMENT	
1. Collaborator (related to managing conflict)	1. Practice using collaborative problem solving skills.
CREATIVITY	
1. Realist (related to managing conflict)	1. Practice using skills for circumventing.

FIGURE 8-4. Personal Effectiveness Plan.

CONCLUSION

An unspoken social contract within the entrepreneurial culture, agreeing to disagree, shapes the way people manage conflicts creatively. In reality, conflict is an inevitable aspect of organizational life. Confront it through healthy debate or constructive confrontation. Certain instances exist, however, when you should circumvent conflict because the price to pay may be too costly, such as damaging fragile relationships or slipping schedule. Because managing conflicts creatively requires self-contradiction, you need to be versatile enough to be assertive and individualistic at one time and a team player pushing for consensus at another.

Within the entrepreneurial culture, conflict actually stimulates creativity. Shared values such as respect for the individual, a structure of teams, and a participative management style create an environment for a healthy level of conflict. Serving as a safety valve, conflict releases pent-up energies.

Manage conflict creatively, by also managing paradox. Be tough in one situation and caring and supportive in another. When changing roles and applying various skills, judgment and discretion are critical to personal effectiveness.

You have already acquired skills for dealing with various conflicts in the introduction to communications, influence, and team building skills. These skills overlap and complement one another. Various types of conflict (interpersonal, intrapersonal, intragroup, intergroup) demand different strategies for resolving conflict. Role analysis and collaborative problem solving are solutions to intrapersonal and intragroup conflicts.

By analyzing your style of handling conflict as well as examining other styles, you can better manage conflicts creatively and effectively. Within the entrepreneurial culture of excellence, focus on a common vision, collaborative problem solving, and circumventing are supported and made legitimate.

ANSWERS TO EXERCISE 8-1. Examining Your Style of Handling Interpersonal Conflict

First rate each item of the exercise in the following spaces. Then total your scores for each column.

Focusing on a Common Vision	Collaborative Problem Solving	Circumventing	Withdrawing	Ramrodding
5. _____	1. _____	3. _____	4. _____	2. _____
10. _____	6. _____	8. _____	9. _____	7. _____
15. _____	11. _____	13. _____	14. _____	12. _____
_____	_____	_____	_____	_____
TOTAL	TOTAL	TOTAL	TOTAL	TOTAL

There are no correct answers for this exercise. All five styles of handling conflict are useful depending on the situation. Within the entrepreneurial culture, focusing on a common vision, collaborative problem solving, and circumventing are more prevalent styles of handling conflict. To determine your prevalent styles, refer to the break down of scores.

Interpreting Your Score

Look at your scores for each column that represents the frequency with which you use this style (circumventing, withdrawing, ramrodding, etc.) If your score fell between:

A. 11–16 points, you tend to rely upon this style for handling conflicts. You are more adept at using this style and, therefore, find it more comfortable to use. You need to think about how it serves you. What are you gaining or losing by using this style?

B. 10 points or below, you may find that you occasionally use this style. Certain circumstances and personalities that you confront may force you into using this style. Again, think about what you are gaining or losing by using this style.

Refer to explanations in "Handling Interpersonal Conflict" for descriptions of these styles.

9

SETTING INNOVATIVE GOALS

Individual Objectives in a Corporate Culture

TAKING OWNERSHIP OF YOUR JOB

In Chapter 1, we left Carol Callahan wondering whether she would fit into the high-tech entrepreneurial culture and asking what additional information was needed to better picture her career choices. Now ready to make a change, bored and unchallenged by her job, she contacts friends, such as Marta Dunlap and Lou Ann Bender, who work in high-tech companies.

CAROL: Can you tell me what you find most satisfying about your last job?

MARTA: Moving the division toward a product and a process. Here you get a chance to make an impact, to really take ownership of your job.

CAROL: What exactly do you mean by that?

MARTA: My boss and I organized a project for long-range planning for the division. It was a difficult, multifunctional process, and we got everyone to work together as a team. As a result, people know where we are going. The common vision is set. We have everyone going down the same path. What I enjoyed most was making that team process work. It was fun! I was also given a long leash to do it.

CAROL: So you feel that you have opportunities to challenge yourself, take the bull by the horns, and be innovative?

MARTA: Most definitely. What we did was really a concept leap. What I mean by that is that we used new methods. We got the sales people, who work together on a tactical basis, to look at long-range plans. We got multifunctional teams to do more strategic planning, from the marketing side and from the engineering side. That was a new concept for the organization. This position was a first and only position. So I got a chance to formulate what to do. There was no precedent.

A week later Carol meets with Lou Ann Bender to ask her some of the same questions.

LOU ANN: I've just recently moved from an analyst position to a supervisory position in cost accounting, and I'm finding it very challenging to be a supervisor.

CAROL: How so?

LOU ANN: I now have my old job under me. I am constantly rethinking my role. In the beginning I felt as if I wasn't producing a lot of work. I'm dealing with personnel issues and making sure that the same level of detail is getting accomplished without doing it myself.

CAROL: What advise would you give to me, if I were to come to work here.

LOU ANN: I think that you and I are a lot alike in that we need challenging goals. We both have higher expectation of ourselves than most people do. Here, if you are willing to be challenged and step out, you can really grow. You can take ownership of your job. It's really fun and very interesting.

CAROL: Can you give me an example of your taking ownership?

LOU ANN: In my previous job, I set a personal goal of being the expert on a new system called Orbit. It was meant to be a sales order system not an accounting system. There were a lot of bugs to work out. Nobody really had the time to analyze the data, so I did most of the problem solving with the programmers, making changes to the system, and interfacing with manufacturing people. I also taught classes on the system, classes which I developed and presented myself.

What I was doing was not really expected, but if I didn't do it, I couldn't broaden my knowledge and be much of a contributor. It's taking that extra step that's important to your career and to the company.

CAROL: Do most people take ownership of their job?

LOU ANN: The people who are considered to be successful certainly do.

For these mini-entrepreneurs, an impassioned personal search for excellence propels them toward outstanding performance. They take ownership of their job through targeting and a sense of excitement.

Michael Potter, Chairman and Chief Executive Officer of Cognos, points out how grass roots job ownership led to innovative changes in product development. He explains how new product development actually arose from people who stumbled onto a new idea and ran with it:

> *Our early product development was not a result of extensive corporate strategy sessions. It happened because individuals lower in the organization said, "Here's a great idea, let's work on it ourselves." The company only provided a supportive environment.*

Real job ownership comes from taking advantage of a chance to make things better and doing it. This knack of mini-entrepreneurs is achieved by being nimble, seeing a need, and jumping to satisfy it. Sometimes this means shifting gears, trying something that hasn't been done before. It means setting some off-the-record goals.

Do you clearly understand what mutual goals are expected of you on the job? Are they in writing? Have you set for ourself some innovative or stretch goals that will improve and make a difference to your department and to you personally? Stretch goals are those that help you chip away at your personal and professional growth (by forcing you to learn something new) and also add to organizational improvement. If you answer these questions affirmatively, you are taking ownership of your job and becoming a mini-entrepreneur. For mini-entrepreneurs are self-directed goal setters who take the initiative to improve themselves and the company.

Now it is probably clear to you that mini-entrepreneurs are architects of their careers. They set innovative or stretch goals. They go beyond merely meeting routine goals for maintaining the status quo. If you set innovative or stretch goals, you will be taking great strides toward personal excellence.

Innovative goals produce something new (new product, service, or process) that results from looking at products from a different angle. Innovative goals take you beyond what has been done in the past. Stretch goals improve your knowledge and skills of an existing service or process. You then become an expert as a result of reaching stretch goals. Marta's process for long-range planning is an innovative goal that represents a concept leap, a change in methods of strategic planning. Lou Ann's personal goal is really a stretch goal.

Now let's review steps for building your career, steps that were outlined in Figure 2-3 in Chapter 2. Previous chapters outlined some of the roles (communicator, team builder, etc.) for accomplishing each step in detail. You also assessed your strengths and areas for improvement, pinpointed your career values, compared them to corporate cultural values, and recognized job dissatisfaction resulting from this mismatch. By now you are aware of the necessity of interpersonal skills—communicating, influencing, team building—for job accomplishment and how they are linked to building a support system.

At this point you need to step back and look at the big picture. These steps will begin to make sense to you as you begin setting some personal and professional goals. You have already harvested a bundle of self-knowledge. This yield has also, undoubtedly, planted additional seeds of areas to explore, items to clarify and follow up. Let's now take this self-knowledge and put it to work, because goal setting is really a self-investment.

HOW TO BUILD YOUR CAREER

The following steps outline the way for you to take ownership of your job, to become a full-fledged mini-entrepreneur. They are all a part of the mini-entrepreneur's cycle of learning and career success. They give you specific actions to take while "taking that extra step," which is so necessary for pursuing personal excellence.

Step 1: Assessing the Needs of the Environment

You are successful to the extent that you can make a contribution by improving methods or techniques, or implementing new concepts. Mini-entrepreneurs not only fulfill routine organizational goals but push themselves further by satisfying other unmet needs. Like an entrepreneur who meets a need in the marketplace, mini-entrepreneurs strive to fill gaps internally and perfect methods that are thought by others to be impractical or impossible to achieve.

Tim Allen has been recently promoted from product marketing engineer to manager of quality and reliability engineering for an entire division. As a mini-entrepreneur, he starts out by listening with an open mind, zeroing in on a need, and reaching out to satisfy it:

I did a lot of listening when I first moved into this job. I came in with no preconceived notions of how things should be done, although with my previous experience, I know how I would like things to be done. When meeting with the other managers, I listen and try to identify unmet needs, needs which my group can satisfy.

For example, in doing our reliability projects, we use a box to put the part in. We were being charged $800 for the box. I found out that we could build it internally for $100 and could save the company $700. Within a few months we saved $42,000. Because we needed a greater number and it was taking too much time, this year we decided to set up a contract with a company to build them for $150. So it's a matter of being open and looking at a better way of doing things.

This mini-entrepreneur proposed a new way to meet an organizational goal, saving the company money by building a better mousetrap.

Lou Ann Bender already spoke of personal goals when she described improving a new accounting system. She and the company benefited from her efforts to "debug" the system and share this information with coworkers. Craig McMillen gives us another example of a personal goal, one that has less of a direct impact on the company but more of an effect on his career. His goal of distinguishing between "bad teams and good teams" has assisted him in getting ahead. His desire to become a member of a "good team" stems from a desire to learn and grow professionally. By improving his skills, he inevitably upgrades the overall competency level of the company:

As a new guy I was put on a team which was the worst in the league. I had to deal with that mess. But I've learned a lot. It was like a real good boot camp. When I get into a real war I know what's going on.

I've learned how I can really contribute when I get on the good teams and why I want to stay on the good teams. I've also learned how to become a good team player.

Craig's goal of learning to distinguish between good teams and bad teams is a stretch goal that has a long-range impact on team professionalism and effectiveness.

So the first step involves scanning your work environment to focus on unmet needs, needs that you jump to fulfill. This step requires wearing the hats of communicator, analyst, collaborator, organizer, realist, and self-developer. Let's examine how mini-entrepreneurs have assumed these roles and what action steps they have taken. Tim Allen's action steps are outlined in Figure 9-1.

GOAL: REDUCE PURCHASE PRICE OF BOX FOR RELIABILITY
TESTING.

ROLE	ACTION STEP
Communicator	Listen to others. Sit back in meetings and learn from others rather than give advice. Pinpoint areas for improvement.
Analyst	Do research to determine whether to make or buy box. Compare prices. Do feasibility study.
Organizer	Develop plan to build box internally. Identify who can do it, at what cost, and time frame.
Collaborator	Ask other managers for information on outside contacts for company that can build box at reasonable cost.
Realist	Envision the end product and results and communicate the vision to others.
Self-Developer	Research new methods and apply them on the job.

FIGURE 9-1. Goal, Roles, and Action Steps.

Seeing How You Can Contribute

This step forces you to put your curiosity to work. Innovative goal setting can
be categorized by two processes: outside–in and inside–out.

Outside–In

Scan the environment outside the company to research new methods or
resources available that can be introduced into the company. Tim Allen's
efforts in developing a contract with an outside company, which manufactures reliability boxes at a reasonable cost, is an example of an outside–in
process.

Penny Sumner is another mini-entrepreneur who creatively solved the
problem of replacing trainers for her career development workshop program.
She convinced her boss that the most ideal trainer could be found outside the
company, in career planning offices at the local universities. Connected to
this network of professionals, she recruited a few to assist her. This was a new
method of recruiting trainers that was cost effective and upgraded the quality

of the program. This is another example of importing certain expertise to satisfy an internal need through the special efforts of a mini-entrepreneur.

Every job can be improved by the application of new developments in science, technology, management, and organizational effectiveness. You need not invent or create the method, device, or principle. It does, however, require a healthy curiosity about new developments or expertise existing outside of the organization. You also need an openness and receptivity to new ideas to set innovative goals. Like a satellite dish receiving signals from afar, you need to raise your antennae and continually ask yourself, "How can I use this information, technique, or method?"

To increase your chance for successfully implementing a new method or technique that takes root within your organization, follow these steps:

1. Research the new idea and acquire a layman's understanding of it, particularly if it relates to new technology. You may discover it through reading, attending a seminar, consulting with experts, or visiting a location where it has been applied.

2. Conduct a feasibility study to determine whether or not the technique, method, or ideas will meet the needs of your organization. This study includes cost estimates and also determined whether the idea will solve problems or create additional problems.

In this step you should also anticipate the impact on your corporate culture. What adverse effect could the new idea have?

3. Set a plan to gain the support of others and management approval. Peers with similar needs can be helpful.

4. Install the new method, technique, or idea. Start out on a small scale, perhaps using a pilot project in an area where you have an active supporter. By implementing the idea on a small scale, you will have better control and can circumvent disastrous errors.

Inside—Out

Take a closer look at how you can contribute by improving or expanding upon existing methods or ideas and sharing them with others within the company. Each improvement triggers a chain reaction and ultimately impacts company growth and customer needs. First scan your work environment to see how you can make an impact.

Lou Ann Bender has already given an example of a personal goal that she set as a cost analyst: to become the expert of the Orbit system and improve it for production cost accounting purposes. She has made an improvement within her area which in turn improved other areas of manufacturing and information systems. Although manufacturing gets the product to the customer, they continue to do so because the accounting folks stay on top of dollars spent. Lou Ann's efforts, begun inside her area, affect those outside her area and beyond to the customer. The steps that she followed are outlined in Figure 9-2.

This is an example of setting a stretch goal, improving an existing system inside the organization, becoming an expert on that system, and spreading this knowledge throughout the organization to manufacturing, information systems, and accounting. Lou Ann looks back a year later from a supervisory position and acknowledges the progress she made as a cost analyst in improving the Orbit system: "It's doing great. We made unbelievable progress in the last year. It's really rewarding."

GOAL: IMPROVE ORBIT SYSTEM FOR PRODUCTION COST ACCOUNTING BY REDUCING THE NUMBER OF ERRORS.

ROLE	ACTION STEP
Analyst	Identify discrepancies and errors in the system. List examples.
Communicator	Speak to manufacturing and pricing people to get more information on discrepancies and variances.
	Discuss examples of discrepancies with programmer to determine changes to be made to the system.
Organizer	Compile information on problems. Document it. Complete maintenance requests to give to programmer.
	Plan and design training sessions with people in manufacturing and accounting.
Collaborator	Exchange information on improvements made with others in accounting and manufacturing through informal training sessions.
Realist	Envision result and communicate them to others.
Initiator	Take corrective measures on own authority.
Self-Developer	Assume new tasks beyond normal job duties.

FIGURE 9-2. Goals, Roles, and Action Steps.

She has high expectations now as a supervisor of cost analysts. She possesses the spirit, the drive, and dedication that allow her, as well as other mini-entrepreneurs, to stand head and shoulders above others.

When you are an analyst, you have ownership of a certain system. Ownership means that you know that system better than anyone else in this division. If there are any changes or questions about the system, you can determine what is best.

One of the analysts was asked by a user to delete a portion of the system which he did. My feeling on that is he should have questioned the person, pointing out the impact of the change and asking about the result that was really wanted. That takes a real dedication and ownership of your job. There are different degrees of that feeling of ownership.

I think that you can make an important contribution by going beyond what's been done in the past. For example, defining new reports, or automating something which is manual or going one step further in analysis. It's taking it one step further and being a real consultant to people. It's very important in our company because they're looking for initiative to make changes.

Mark Malone gives a more obvious example of the inside–out goal setting. Excited about the Quality Improvement Program, Mark has written articles from the viewpoint of a purchasing specialist, articles that have been published in journals and for which he received company awards and recognition:

The Quality Improvement Program has been so successful in the materials end of it that I put together a few articles. I thought that it was time that the world heard about it. The articles describe what we are doing and how serious we are about quality.

With his enthusiasm, vision, and caring, he can't help but feel pride in a job well done. This is the backbone of ownership.

Steps 3–7: Exercising Your Personal Power

When you combine roles and skills in an effective way, you are exercising your personal power. Like anything else, it all comes together as if it were second nature, like riding a bike or driving a car. Remember, exercising your personal power, becoming personally effective, forces you to stretch your interpersonal muscles within the corporate culture. Interpersonal skills such as communicating, influencing, and team building all lay the groundwork in building productive working relationships and, ultimately, building a support system for striving toward excellence.

Marta explains how she taps into the cultural norms of informal and open communication, management by wandering around, and team play (step 3). She called upon these skills as she approached the chief engineer and she can't help but expose her enthusiasm in being a part of the corporate culture. A natural by-product of her actions is a support network (step 4).

I have been exposed to people who are good to get to know and fun to get to know. It's the building of internal relationships. When I'm out in the field getting a better understanding of what customers really want and really think of our products, I can then feed back that information to product managers. I'll have a professional base not only with product managers but with engineers. That's important.

As she moves into the position of customer marketing manager, she again sets goals and creates an action plan (step 5). Her new action plan is listed in her PEP in Figure 9-3.

Marta's personal search for excellence, her need to play to succeed (step 6) becomes apparent as she describes what motivates her: the need to achieve, to learn, to succeed:

In the long run you grow, you learn. During the last six months prior to my becoming a customer marketing manager, I wrote a document. I achieved something within the company that other people haven't been able to do. It has value to the company.

Writing the document was really tedious at times. But that doesn't mean I wasn't committed. I know that if I didn't care down to the nth degree, if I didn't

WORK GOALS

JOB GOALS	ACTION STEPS
Alleviate problems in installation of equipment.	Speak to customers, engineers, sales, and marketing people.

INNOVATIVE OR STRETCH GOALS	
Get a "feel" for customer needs.	Go out into field to talk to customers.
	Listen to complaints and needs.

FIGURE 9-3. Personal Effectiveness Plan.

do the very best possible job I could, I would disappoint myself and not meet my
own standards. I had to do the very best, and I was dedicated to that. I had
ownership of this document. It feels like mine.

Mini-entrepreneurs like Marta close the loop by measuring how far they
have come (step 7) based upon their personal criteria and formal performance
evaluations. Extrinsic rewards come in the form of raises, promotions, and,
occasionally, company stock. Intrinsic rewards come from knowing that
you have done your personal best by taking ownership of your job, setting
stretch or innovative goals, and persisting until you reach your target.

TARGETING: SETTING JOB GOALS

Each company has a system, especially for managers, for goal setting. Some
companies use MBO (Management by Objectives), while other companies
use other types of systems such as RMO (Responsibilities, Measures, and
Objectives). Whatever the system, set job goals regardless of your rank
(management or nonmanagement) to operate in an entrepreneurial culture.

Within the entrepreneurial culture, this is not a mechanical process, one
that fulfills a requirement, but a process that gives direction and meaning to
mini-entrepreneurial action. The process helps everyone stay in touch and in
tune with company goals. The time period involved for goal accomplishment
varies. Managers are usually expected to accomplish their goals within a year.
For others, such as Craig McMillen, goals are set weekly. He explains how his
system works within his entrepreneurial culture:

Here you do a lot more reporting than was done at LBT, my former company.
The first part of the weekly report consists of a summary. We are mainly
concerned about shipment of a product. The second part consists of goal
accomplishment from the previous week. So each week you set goals as a
guideline and write down how much you have accomplished.

The third part of the report includes general accomplishments. For example,
maybe you met with another group, such as accounting and came up with a
better way of tracking the dollars. I would sit down with my boss and review
this. He may question whether this was an accomplishment. He may think that
it was part of the job and not think that it is an accomplishment.

The next part of the report consists of accomplishment by project which is
something extra which you did beyond the parameters of the job.

Within the entrepreneurial culture, organizational goals are circulated like
flyers on the street corner, making these goals common knowledge among the
crew. Information on goals becomes the commodity of exchange when

responsibility is pushed down to a grass-roots level and job ownership is handed out to the takers. In Craig McMillen's company divisional goals are like beacons of light providing guidance to individual action:

> *Every month we all get a milestone calendar which tells us where we should be and where to put our efforts. This is given to everyone, even the secretaries, so that we all understand what the divisional goals are.*

> *If I need something from document control on the Eagle product, I know they will respond quickly because it is a priority, it's first on the list. This calendar is set from market requirements, and it moves the division.*

Dovetailing Individual and Organizational Goals

Setting personal goals is unavoidable and expected within the entrepreneurial culture. Organizational goals are announced loud and clear through many channels: written material, quarterly meetings (state-of-the-company addresses by the president), training sessions, celebrations, and informal get-togethers. Ignorance of organizational goals is ignorance of your job. Although some companies are better at articulating superordinate or overarching goals, mini-entrepreneurs become successful when they align their goals with those goals of the organization.

What are overarching goals? According to David Bradford and Allan Cohen, overarching goals are similar to superordinate goals and give coherence, excitement, and meaning to a department's work. Like superordinate goals, they cannot be accomplished by one person alone. It becomes a collective effort to fulfill them with every individual action shaping the values of an organization.

These organizational goals need to be reinterpreted and broken down for each department or unit. In reality, it is the entrepreneurial manager, the visionary, who can articulate goals in ways that excite and mobilize the troops toward a common vision. This is the up side. The down side of this issue is that not all are blessed with entrepreneurial managers. You do, however, have the ability to question and dig until an overarching goal surfaces. That is your charter, your responsibility to yourself and the organization, as you strive to become more entrepreneurial.

Lou Ann Bender articulates her understanding of her department's goals and how her personal goals dovetail with them:

> *Ultimately we have to please the controllership. So our ultimate goal is to advise, be flexible, and be a service organization to manufacturing. This is in everybody's best interest.*

My personal goal is to gain more control by educating people in manufacturing. I want them to want the same controls that we have and encourage them to see that it is in everybody's best interest to have those controls. It's not easy because they have different goals.

Suggestions for meshing department goals with individual goals are listed as follows:

1. Find out from others (boss, peers who are "in the know") what makes your department stand out, achieve its mission in ways that are different from similar departments.
2. Assess your departmental environment to identify an unmet need.
3. Look at this need as an opportunity to create a job goal for yourself.

Penny Sumner tells us how she followed these steps while serving as training and development manager:

When I came to the company, there was a whole new change in top management, a new general manager and director of Human Resources. Prior to my arrival, the employees all decided by voting to keep out the union. The name of our department had been changed from Industrial Relations to Human Resources to give a new image to the department, a more people-oriented, employee sensitive image.

Although my primary goal was to implement a management development program, after I had successfully gotten that program off the ground, I began focusing in on employees needs. We organized a secretarial training workshop, career counseling, and retirement planning. All of these programs helped to turn around employee attitudes toward our department. Yet they were secondary goals which made a big difference.

Setting Job Goals with a "Feel" for the Organization

Fortune magazine states that *In Search of Excellence* is the business book of the century, selling more than 5 million copies. It gives us a character reading of American business since the turn of the century. Most of all, it tells us that the people in excellent companies are not cut off from their feelings, from a passion for excellence.

Setting job goals with a "feel" for the organization means being in touch with superordinate or overarching goals, your role and mission, and results desired. It is with this overall feel plus specific action steps that target excellence. Marta Dunlap puts it all together, as she further describes her project for division long-range planning:

> *What I found most satisfying was making that team process work. We took 130 people off site for three days to explain the process, work, and answer question. What we did was get everybody to "sign up." Everybody had a hand in implementing the results.*
>
> *What also was satisfying was not only setting up a difficult process and getting it to work, but coming up with a document which is really good. It was a team process.*
>
> *We've got the division moving with everybody knowing where we are going. I think that it's really neat; it's fun; it's unusual.*

Marta's example points out that personal alignment with company goals leads to synergy with spirit.

Seeing the connection between individual and overarching goals excites the mini-entrepreneur and pushes that person to greater heights of performance. Brooke Tierney, a sales program developer for a personal computer manufacturer, describes her company's efforts to enable its people to get a feel for where it is headed:

> *I have attended four communications meetings in the last two weeks. They tell us what the company's goals and strategies are for the next fiscal year. We know exactly what the company's goals are. It makes it easier to incorporate them into our personal goals and to make sure our personal goals are in sync. Anytime you start a project you can relate it to what's important to the company. It's knowledge that has to flow from the top down which allows you to do that.*

Determining Role and Mission

A statement of the department's role and mission really tells the scope and nature of the work to be performed. In the position of project coordinator, Craig McMillen sees his role as acting as the "right-hand man" to the project manager or team leader. It is not difficult to see him in a quasi-manager role, using influence management skills.

He expresses his department's mission, "We are here to support a schedule, to make sure everything runs smoothly between engineering and manufacturing."

Articulating and clarifying your role and mission become the starting points for determining results, objectives, and action steps. The following questions will help crystallize your thoughts on roles and missions:

1. Why does our department exist?
2. Who do we primarily serve? Internal customers/users or external customers. Are we a production or support operation?
3. How can you improve this relationship?
4. What is our common vision? What are we striving for?

Working Smarter—Identifying Results

Without a clear picture of results to be achieved, you'll spin your wheels needlessly. Key result areas help you determine where you should be investing time, energy, expertise, and where to make your mark.

Pareto's Law of 20/80 has important implications for setting priorities, for working smarter not harder. For every problem or result achieved, the 20/80 rule can be assumed to be in effect. This is the rule of the vital few and the trivial many that explains how results follow a certain pattern. The following examples illustrate this rule:

- 80 percent of the sales come from 20 percent of the customers.
- 80 percent of the quality errors are made by 20 percent of the operators.
- 80 percent of the grievances are filled by 20 percent of the employees.

By concentrating your efforts on the vital 20 percent, your payoff will be greater. Identify those areas where results are important enough to devote your time, attention, and expertise.

Categorizing Goals

If job ownership means taking over responsibility for meeting organizational and personal goals, then create a plan to learn, stretch, and develop professionally and personally. Within the entrepreneurial culture of excellence, pacing yourself to succeed and outperform your personal best takes planning through goal setting. Mini-entrepreneurs set various types of personal goals, as Marta Dunlap explains:

Every six months we write our objectives through a MBO process. At the end of six months my boss and I sit down and evaluate them. We also had private goals or objectives, those things which were important to getting your job done but you didn't want to write down.

I had three sets of goals: the public ones which were written down, the private ones which were written down and the private–personal ones, which I didn't share with my boss. One private–personal goal, which I didn't let my boss know about, was to work with him closely so we would develop as a better working team. At the end of a long period, we were talking about my evaluation, a conversational evaluation, not a written evaluation. I said to him, "You know, six months ago I set out to work on making our working relationship click." To my surprise he said that he also had made that same goal for himself. We both had the same private agenda which neither of us confessed to upfront. We both understood the need. That's probably why it worked.

An example of a private goal would be to build credibility and earn respect from a particular engineer.

Set innovative goals by following these steps: establish job goals through a formal process such as MBO; identify personal goals that force you to stretch, learn, and grow beyond your present capacity; set personal–private goals that allow you to expand, to bite the bullet and make a difference on some level.

Completing the goal setting section of your PEP forces you to differentiate between expected job goals and innovative or stretch goals. Innovative goals enable you to fine-tune your expertise or knowledge in a given area. Stretch goals build productive working relationships. Innovative goals can be either private (unwritten or written and shared only with your boss or peers) or personal–private goals (goals only you know about and pursue).

After transferring from one division to another, Marta Dunlap, now in Customer Marketing, lists her goals that are shown in her PEP (Figure 9-4).

WORK GOALS

JOB GOAL	ACTION STEPS
To produce a technical document on a product line for customers and sales people.	Gather information through interview. Write draft. Have draft reviewed. Arrange printing and reproduction.

INNOVATIVE OR STRETCH GOALS

To become knowledgeable about product lines.	Gather information from others. Push for valid information.

FIGURE 9-4. Personal Effectiveness Plan.

In the process of digging for information and striving toward her stretch goal (becoming knowledgeable on a product line), Marta becomes more of an expert on this product line then she originally anticipated. In other words, she surpasses her own personal standard:

My personal goal was to learn about the product line very well. I've done that. What I also have learned is that I understand it more clearly than people around me.

I have been working with one of the chief engineers. It's always a delight to run down the hall to ask him a question because I always learn something. Last time he wasn't sure about an answer to my question. I said to him, "If you don't know who does?" He got up from his chair, and we both walked down the hall to the switch room. We probed around, traced some things, and found the answer to the question. He was willing to take 10 minutes and figure it out.

When he started reading the first 60 pages of my document, he was then aware that I knew some of the things that the product managers didn't. That surprised him, and I gained credibility with him.

Now as customer marketing manager, I can carry that which I know one step further. I am looking forward to being out in the field dealing with customers whom I haven't worked with before.

Marta has accomplished her job and stretch goals and is now ready, through her new position as customer marketing manager, to pursue new goals. The cycle continues.

Setting Innovative or Stretch Goals

Setting innovative or stretch goals requires more than merely jumping through organizational hoops. You should continually strive to improve the company and you. The following steps list procedure for setting innovative or stretch goals. The case of Sam Edgars shows you how to apply these steps.

STEP 1. BE AWARE OF SUPERORDINATE OR OVERARCHING GOALS. As the manager of the companywide Quality Improvement Program, Sam was acutely aware of the company's superordinate goal of improving the quality of integrated circuits so that fewer errors occurred.

STEP 2. BE AWARE OF YOUR UNIT'S ROLE AND MISSION. Sam explains his unique and innovative role and how it differs from other departments:

My task is to change the way everybody in the company thought about quality, to change the way they do their jobs so that there would be fewer errors, fewer rejects created. There are several things which are key to this task. Instead of trying to control quality by inspectors, we are trying to make quality a part of everyone's job.

What we mean by that is that we are going to change the way people come to work and change the way they react and relate to one another. We want to change things in terms of the kinds of demands they make on each other, the requirements they make of each other and the kinds of services they perform for each other.

Step 3. Set Innovative Goals or Stretch Goals

By doing this we realized that it was going to be a massive change. We were going to change the way 11,000 people think. My goal then was to make this happen. I made it my goal to understand how people work together, how they interface with each other.

Step 4. Don't Overload Yourself With Impossible Goals

I knew that it would be a slow process. In five years I would say that I got it started. I wouldn't say that it was finished by any means.

Step 5. Introduce New Ideas From Outside the Organization

There were systems around, some ideas generated by consultants which were useful. We borrowed heavily from people who had gone before. We studied those changes and created a step-by-step process for making it happen and a strategy for putting it into the company.

Step 6. Clarify Areas of Responsibility

We did have a quality and reliability function in the company. That was a separate function from my own. All the inspectors, and quality and reliability engineers were in that area.

Step 7. Determine the Impact of the Corporate Culture. Consider what the adverse effect on certain groups will be and determine what can be done to minimize these effects:

The company wanted to build quality into the culture. As the people became better at building quality into their jobs, the quality and reliability department wasn't needed anymore. So the people in that department had to change their role. They had to stop being policemen and start being helpers.

That was a tremendous change. The people in that department had the perception that they would be losing their authority. What we did was to help them eliminate those tasks which had minimal payoff for them such as some of the paperwork they did.

Step 8. Set Criteria by Which to Measure Progress

Some terrific things did happen. The quality did improve a whole lot. We had some conventional ways of measuring defective parts. The number of defective parts dropped 50-fold. The number of errors in the sales ordering department also dropped by 10 percent.

When you implement innovative goals, you'll find that the impact of the change can create stressful situations. After you have set innovative goals, strategies for managing change will get you through difficult transitions. Managing these transitions will be addressed in Chapter 11.

Now that you have some examples and guidelines for setting innovative and stretch goals, you can plan for yourself by using the goal setting section of your PEP. Use the form in Figure 9-5 to complete your own goals.

WORK GOALS
_____

JOB GOALS   ACTION STEPS

_____   _____

_____   _____

                                    _____

_____   _____

_____   _____

                                    _____

INNOVATIVE OR STRETCH GOALS

_____   _____

_____   _____

                                    _____

_____   _____

_____   _____
_____

FIGURE 9-5. Personal Effectiveness Plan.

CONCLUSION

Setting innovative and stretch goals helps focus in on what is important to you and the organization when striving for excellence. Merely meeting routine goals, maintaining the status quo, is not enough to become an mini-entrepreneur.

Innovative goals produce something new such as a product, service, or process. Innovative goals take you beyond what has been done in the past. Stretch goals, on the other hand, improve your knowledge and skill of an existing service or process. They assist you in becoming more of an expert in a given area.

The steps for building your career give you a framework for job ownership. By following these steps, you can make a real contribution by improving methods, techniques, or implementing new concepts and, ultimately, exercise your personal power. These steps require you to assume a number of roles such as communicator, analyst, organizer, initiator, collaborator, realist, and self-developer.

Personal goal setting involves dovetailing individual goals with organizational goals. Your first step is to become aware of superordinate or overarching goals, goals that give coherence, excitement, and meaning to a department's work. You also need a "feel" for the organization, knowing what shared values carry weight and meaning.

When setting job goals, you must have a clear picture of departmental roles, mission and results expected. Keep in mind types of goals and their relationship to each other and take ownership of your job and targeting excellence. Setting individual objectives that are in line with the corporate culture has a payoff both for you and the organization.

Part III

MANAGING FOR SUCCESS

10

HOW TO MANAGE YOUR BOSS

Defining What You Need from the Relationship

WORKING WITH, NOT FOR YOUR BOSS

Carol Callahan digs for more information from Lou Ann Bender about working within the high-tech entrepreneurial culture. She is particularly curious about how much leeway bosses given their employees:

CAROL: It sounds like you are given a long leash to do what you think is important.

LOU ANN: I don't feel like I am working for my boss, but with my boss. I think that we all feel that we are working together, but we recognize that certain levels have veto power. We all feel very comfortable about having the right to speak up and to present our views.

CAROL: I can't say that about where I work now. If you speak up too loudly, you'll find yourself out the door.

LOU ANN: The nice thing about my job as an analyst is that I am expected to be the one that knows the most. They rely on that. I have reconciled reports that were thought to be irreconcilable and redefined them. So I have been the expert. It goes back to taking ownership of your job. So then my boss defers to me in understanding the problem.

You feel like you want to make a contribution, because they instill you with this responsibility.

CAROL: How does that change how you work with your boss?

LOU ANN: It puts you in the driver's seat. It puts you in a position of really wanting to work things out with your boss. In my last job my supervisor was very analytical, while I am very expressive. What I had to do was to stretch, to understand her.

I would give her the bottom line, and she wanted to know how I got it. I had to be patient. I had to back up and go through all my steps of analysis. It was important to her. So in order to manage her, I had to stretch and understand her needs.

CAROL: It sounds like it was difficult.

LOU ANN: Initially it was like hitting a brick wall because it was very frustrating. I felt that she should trust me. Then you work at it and realize that there are trade-offs. If you want her to understand, then you have to go through this process. It also gives you the ability to be quite honest and frank.

CAROL: So what suggestions do you have for me in this regard?

LOU ANN: Remember, instead of your boss managing you, you need to manage your boss. It helps you to meet job goals and feel like you have some control over your career.

Undoubtedly you have had bosses who were difficult to work with in some way. Yet there is no getting around that your boss plays a very vital role in your career. Let's face it; depending on how your boss sees you doing your job, this person can limit the career options available to you in the company. In a favorable working relationship, your boss can open doors to higher management, if that is your preference, run interference for you, serve as a mouthpiece for you, and also as a mentor. On the other hand, an unfavorable relationship with your boss can become a roadblock, an impediment to advancing vertically or laterally within the organization that frustrates your efforts. Your current performance greatly determines opportunities for moving in the organization.

You must determine how you want to be treated by your boss. If you want to be treated with respect and recognition of your expertise and ability to accomplish things, then you need to draw upon two very important roles that have already been discussed: committing yourself to goals and managing conflicts creatively. Goals enable you to find common purpose and direction and to lay common ground between the two of you. If you deal with conflicts creatively, you will be dealing with differences in a productive way. You will better manage your boss if you call upon skills such as communicating, team building, influencing, initiating, and self-developing.

The phrase, "managing your boss," may sound contradictory. However, you can shape your professional destiny by building a productive working relationship with your boss. The choices you face, the decisions you make based on your skills, personal preferences, and career values all determine your career success. Your boss controls you to the degree that you give up your inalienable right to job satisfaction, job freedom, and pursuit of excellence. You can transform your relationship with your boss to make it mutually beneficial. First examine your own needs and expectations so that you can be objective. Before developing strategies for managing your boss, first you need to take an honest look at your needs, expectations, and attitudes toward this important figure in your career.

DECIDING WHAT YOU WANT FROM YOUR BOSS

Anna Lew, a training specialist who recently made a career move from a financial services company to a high-tech company of excellence, reveals what she needs and expects from her boss:

> I can always make progress on my own. But with a little bit of guidance I can take bigger leaps. I want a boss who can give me a little bit of guidance. The kind of guidance I want includes knowledge about the organization: what direction we are headed, what is happening at other levels and at other divisions. My boss has access to people in other divisions while I don't.

> That kind of information is valuable to me because then I can look at trends and patterns. She is very open to giving me that kind of information. It is up to me as to how I make use of that information. I may not act on it right away. But it will sit in the back of my mind, and I know that it will influence my projects.

> Right now I am working on a project. I want to find out what other divisions are working on this project and what they are doing with it. I've done as much as I can with what I have. I'm ready now to extend. What I found out from my boss is that we are leading the group. So it is up to me. But what I want to do will depend on my boss's sense of where the division is headed. That will give me guidance.

> *I am very fortunate to have her as my boss because we operate in the same way. We are both fairly independent. Given that, we touch base when we feel there is a need.*

Anna is aware that she wants a boss who provides the guidance she needs to be a valuable contributor.

In contrast, Todd Miller, a senior personnel representative, is in quite a different situation:

> *If my style, and my desires because of that style, are different than my managers, then my manager and I have to reach some sort of agreement on how that potential conflict is going to be handled.*
>
> *If my style is to approach something aggressively and my manager's is to approach the same situation casually, then that difference can create a lot of conflicts. For example, I like to sit down, work out a problem and be done with it. While my manager's style is more casual, let's wait and think about it.*
>
> *If you are more proactive than your manager, and if you go off to get something started, you run the risk of being seen as going around your manager and not communicating with your manager.*
>
> *I think the ultimate solution is to go on to other things. If your career is being slowed down by somebody, then you need to decide whether to stick it out or go off and do something in another job.*
>
> *In the last two years I've had two managers who were new managers. And the styles of these two managers were amazingly different. Under my former supervisor we got a lot done. The style was such that she would say, "You tell me what needs to be done, and if it sounds like it makes sense to me, great, we'll go ahead and do it." It was a time that we got new systems developed and new equipment and changed a lot of processes.*
>
> *My manager now is saying that she has to wait and she has to learn. For somebody who is aggressive and has gone through an aggressive period, to stop and wait can be very frustrating.*

Obviously, Todd has reached a point when he should consider whether to stick it out or to leave. As he shows later, he will make every effort to deal constructively with this work relationship. Unlike Anna, Todd should decide if he has benefited and developed sufficiently to move ahead.

Marta Dunlap, when she was a new business planner, sums up what characterizes a good working relationship with her boss:

> *This is a loose–tight organization. People can go off and do the best they can. My boss is there for guidance, but he doesn't hang over me. It's part of the ethic, management style here. Some people are better at it than others.*

If you work with people who do a really good job of being a part of the culture and the company, you can learn from them. But you see, someone can give you a long leash, and they're not there when you need them. But if you've got someone there to talk to, it's a safe leash. That's what I have with my boss.

As in all relationships, you are one-half the equation and your boss makes up the other half. To make it work, first acknowledge your strengths, weaknesses, and personal style. This does not mean changing your personality to please your boss. It means that you must be aware of personal preferences that are likely to interfere with this relationship.

What is it that you expect from your boss? What are your needs and expectations at this point in your career? How are you going to get what you want from our boss? To what extent are you willing to examine your own attitudes and change your strategies for dealing with your boss? Remember that nothing remains static. What you valued and was important three years ago may not be true today. To help you answer these questions, complete Exercise 10-1.

EXERCISE 10-1. Assessing Your Working Relationship with Your Boss

1. Are you willing to work out differences in style existing between you and your boss?
2. Is there mutual trust between you and your boss?
3. When new conditions arise (change in assignments, change in schedule such as traveling), do you seek clarification of expectations?
4. Is it OK with you if your work style differs from your boss's? If not, how much are you willing to bend or confront your boss to achieve agreed upon goals?
5. Are you receptive to suggestions for improvement and discussion of professional development?
6. Do you see your boss as a role model for you? If not, why?
7. If differences exist, are you certain how to handle them in a productive way?
8. Do you keep your boss's best interest in mind as well as your own?
9. Do you use your boss as a resource for getting your job done?
10. Do you accept the relationship with its limitations?

If you answered the questions in Exercise 10-1 honestly and still feel hopeful, then your working relationship with your boss is manageable. If answering these questions leaves a bad taste in your mouth or creates a gnawing sensation in your stomach, look realistically at your needs and expectations. Keep in mind that you have the power to improve a shaky relationship. You need not wait for the other person to move first. Of course, some bosses are ill-suited for their jobs. Dealing with them is beyond the scope of this chapter.

TAKING A GOOD LOOK AT YOUR RELATIONSHIP WITH YOUR BOSS

Bosses have the upper hand, even in the entrepreneurial culture where they are expected to take off their authoritarian hats and replace them with that of coach and mentor. The boss not only makes judgments and contributes to decisions about pay and promotions but also can help you develop professionally and give you credit where credit is due.

By virtue of your boss's position, he or she represents the organizational needs and goals. Yes, your boss like you, has individual needs and goals. Yet it is easier for your boss to see overarching goals because of background and training. From a different vantage point, your boss is, more often than not, in a better position to see the big picture, while you may be just learning. You both have a hand in moving and shaking the organization. It's just that your boss is more influential because of prior experience and expectations. For these reasons, you are dependent on this person to help you carve out your role and plan your steps so that they are in line with organizational goals. If your needs conflict with those of your boss, clarify your role and working relationship with your boss.

Larry Buxton, recently promoted to a program manager, is aware of how his boss's perspective and pressures differ from his own:

> *When we come to a conflict I'm comfortable enough to tell her that I don't agree with her. I can tell her that I'm doing something a certain way. I can tell her that I see her doing it differently, and I'm not so sure that it is right. Basically we handle our differences by talking about them.*

> *She is more detail oriented than I am, a little more picky than I am. I think that the more important issues are left aside. For instance, I think that major issues should be addressed such as problems with customers or with manufacturing. I think that she is willing to address them, but she has pressure on her to get the administrative details done.*

This mini-entrepreneur confidently confronts his boss when something does not seem right.

The truth is this relationship is one of mutual dependence between two fallible human beings. Failing to recognize this fact can cause unnecessary grief and frustration. Remember, your boss also has a boss, to which he/she is accountable. Your boss needs your knowledge and expertise to accomplish goals. To do an effective job, this person needs your cooperation and commitment.

Even though you may be assigned to a number of teams, the team work that develops between you and your boss is crucial to your career. This person can play a vital role in linking you to other departments, making sure your priorities are in line with organizational needs, and obtaining resources to get your job done more effectively. Part of working smarter is making an extra effort to make your relationship with your boss work. You need to "debug" any underlying resistance or resentment.

Mini-entrepreneurs do not assume that their boss can read their minds. Instead they seek the information and guidance they need, like Anna Lew. The rule of thumb to remember when managing your boss is to have a sense of him or her as a person, work style, needs, strengths, and weaknesses. With these insights, you can better work together as a team.

THREE GOOD STRATEGIES

Strategies for managing your boss fall under three distinct categories: making a contribution to your boss's goals: keeping your boss informed; and understanding your boss' work style. All three are essential for managing your career.

Let's begin where the last chapter ended: goal setting. You can find common ground by negotiating goals during a goal setting session with your boss. Do not wait for your boss to initiate it. This session sets the stage for ensuing discussions.

Making a Joint Contribution

Part of managing your boss is being aware of the goals and pressures facing him or her. To identify these pressures, clarify your own goals and establish priorities. Using the goal setting process is a convenient and useful tool for discovering your boss's goals and pressures. Your boss will most certainly throw out those unnecessary items. In this way, you will get a sense of where the organization is headed and what you must do. Mark Malone briefly sums up the process of setting objectives with his boss: "We go through a negotiation process on RMOs (responsiveness, measures, and objectives), and I eventually agree to them."

Tim Allen, recently promoted to manager of Quality and Reliability, points out the pivotal role that goal setting plays in managing your boss:

> *It is really important to know what your boss's goals are. If you don't know that, you have no opportunity to please your boss. In the past I was probably insistent to a point of irritating my boss. I wanted to know what her responsibilities were.*
>
> *If I understand those, it would certainly make my job a lot easier. Then I don't have to ask her whether I am doing a good job or not. I know that I am doing a good job. I know what the bottom line is.*

This mini-entrepreneur has taken the initiative by meshing his responsibilities with those of his boss.

Another mini-entrepreneur, Todd Miller, explains how the goal setting process can avoid misunderstanding later on:

> *I want the goal setting process to be a bit more formal than my boss does. Over the last year or so I've been assigned some responsibilities that are very invisible. We have a small division of about 150 people who are housed in this building. I have become the quasi-personnel manager for them. I still am retaining my responsibilities in my own division, however.*
>
> *I spend a great deal of my time in the smaller division. But I really don't report those activities to my immediate boss. I report those activities to the personnel manager. I essentially have the authority to do anything I want.*
>
> *Because those activities are invisible, they could become a problem. We need to figure out how much time I should be devoting to them and how much time I should be devoting to my division. If in fact there are some conflicts, we need to figure out how to balance those scales. The only way to do that is through a formal MBO process.*
>
> *Part of the process should include naming what should be accomplished over the short term, how much time will be required and how I am going to be evaluated. If XYZ things don't get done, am I going to be considered a bad individual? Or is it OK because of all the other responsibilities I have?*
>
> *Without going through a MBO process very formally, you cannot arrive at that state. So you are really going through two stages. One is deciding on how you are going to arrive on goals. The other is actually sitting down and going through the process of establishing objectives.*

This mini-entrepreneur steered his boss toward clearly defined objectives. Without Todd taking such a proactive stance, he might find himself being improperly evaluated during performance review time. Through this discussion, Todd and his boss agree on primary and secondary objectives. They both then put their efforts into mutually agreed upon goals and jointly make a contribution to their organization. Getting to this point takes a certain amount of commitment and tenacity on your part.

Steps to follow to get to this point and to ensure that you and your boss are on target are listed in the following test. These steps (presented to you in Chapter 9) on goal setting should become focal points for your discussion with your boss. Topics for the goal setting session should include: department role and mission, result areas, priority groupings, and innovative and/or stretch goals.

After your discussion with your boss, you should answer the following questions. In so doing, you will better understand your supervisor's pressures and goals:

1. What does your boss want to achieve over the next year? What does your boss foresee as being most important?
2. What innovative goals does your boss have that you can support?
3. What are your boss's priorities?
4. How does your boss's relationships with other department managers affect what you want to achieve?
5. What ideas or positions does your boss understand or not understand?

Knowing the answers to these questions will increase your chances of accomplishing the agreed-upon goals. By assuring that you are looking through the same window, it becomes less of a strained effort to gain commitment and support.

Selling Your Ideas to Your Boss

You have been placed in a position because of your expertise. Bosses don't have all the right answers and may not attempt to give them, nor can they do what you can. You are separate and distinct individuals. Your boss, then, relies on you for carrying out certain tasks and depends on your professional judgment to zig where he or she may zag. For these reasons, your brainpower is needed to point out better or more innovative ways to get things done. Although open to improvements, bosses need sound justification for making changes. They need to be sold on an idea. Let's consider the steps Todd Miller followed in selling his idea to a former supervisor:

First you do a lot of homework, figuring out why you want to do something and what the benefits are. I consistently look at the down side. If you are going to buy a new piece of equipment or whatever, you need to ask yourself: "What is the down side?"

About a year ago I sold my manager on the idea that we could do a better job of tracking job applicants, of maintaining an applicant pool by a personal computer. What I did to get to that point was to talk to people who were familiar with software which I wanted to use. I found out the positives and the negatives. And I found out the requirements for the hardware.

Also I had to find out what the corporate office was doing in terms of giving us a system. I essentially convinced my boss that we could do a better job with the system which I was proposing. I also convinced her that I could develop a better system using the software package. We discussed it over lunch. We tend to do things informally around here. She said, "Great, go ahead and do it."

We are using it right now. Actually, one of the conversations I had yesterday with one of the managers was on how we can create a system which is even better than the one we currently have.

Todd successfully sold his ideas to his boss because he did his homework. You should follow these steps when preparing to sell your ideas.

STEP 1. KNOW YOUR IDEA OR PRODUCT. Take your idea apart and analyze it. Arrange the pieces so that they can be easily understood and accepted.

STEP 2. CONSIDER THE IMPACT OF YOUR IDEA. You should address these questions:

    A. Who may benefit besides you and your boss?
    B. Who else needs to be involved?
    C. How do you plan to enlist their help?
    D. What difficulties will you encounter? For example, is the timing right?
    E. How can these difficulties be minimized?

STEP 3. KNOW YOUR BOSS. Determine how your boss receives information. Does he or she prefer a written proposal so it can be studied, or to discuss it face to face?

STEP 4. CAPTURE YOUR BOSS'S INTEREST. Present the idea from the point of view and the language of your boss. Point out how your idea will contribute to the goals of the department and the company.

STEP. 5. GAIN YOUR BOSS'S SUPPORT. Don't insist on a spot decision. Give your boss time to think it over. In the meantime, supply additional material such as back-up information, magazine articles, or results from a similar program or product.

STEP 6. ANTICIPATE BOTH A "GO" OR "NO GO." Be prepared for either a negative or positive answer. If you get the approval, be prepared to implement it. If the answer is no, postpone your idea but keep it on the back burner. Also keep in mind that you will be making a joint effort if you get the signal to go ahead with your idea.

Todd called upon several roles and skills from the Mini-Entrepreneurial Skills Inventory to sell his ideas. They are listed in Table 10-1.

TABLE 10-1
Goal, Roles, and Skills Used for Selling an Idea

GOAL. To sell the idea of using a personal computer to track job applicant.

Role	Action Step	Skill No. and Description
Initiator	Talk to people familiar with software.	2. Asking the right question to get needed information.
Analyst	Find out positives and negatives of software.	24. Diagnosing a situation and maintaining an objective viewpoint by seeing all sides of the problem.
Innovator	Check with the corporate office.	31. Introducing new ideas and products that are precedent setting.
Communicator	Persuade boss to accept the idea.	19. Pinpointing the needs and objectives of others.
Realist	Persuade boss to accept the idea.	34. Envisioning the end product/result before the project begins and communicating the vision to others.

Getting Support for Your Ideas

When you feel resistance or reach an impasse with your boss, get others to help sell your idea. Take advantage of working in a team-oriented environment by calling upon team members to support. Sam Edgars provides clues on how and why to do this:

> *If you and your boss disagree, go get support. By that I don't mean be insubordinate. I'm not talking about unions. You may have a perfectly good idea, and your boss doesn't see it. Maybe he doesn't see it because you can't present it logically enough; or because it is coming from you; and he doesn't appreciate your expertise in that area. But you can go get support from team members. The team then becomes a proving ground for ideas and gives validitiy to them. The ideas then come not only from your boss. So part of managing your boss involves getting support for your ideas.*

In the Chapter 6 section on Influencing Others Successfully, Lisa Ishimoto relied upon her peers to sell an idea to her boss. Influence skills are valuable for managing your boss. Marta Dunlap speaks about style clashes between herself and a former boss and how she used influence skills to get her job done:

> *I honestly felt like I was beating my head against the wall. I would propose things to try, and I would get stymied. What I would do sometimes, during the review cycle for this document, was to go to his boss for advice on whether something should be included in this document which I was writing.*

> *When my boss brought up certain ideas and I didn't think that they were important, the next time that I met with his boss, I would bounce them off him. If he felt that they were important I would do it. I was using my boss's boss to manage my boss. This is a classic example of using other people to manage my boss.*

> *Because I had recently transferred to this division, I hadn't established a peer group, and I couldn't rely on them. When I was in the other division, I would manage someone who was a boss of a peer. But there I knew the organization, the people, the situation, the personalities. I felt effective then, because I had that down.*

In these two cases, managing your boss primarily requires using team building and influence skills. But selling your ideas and getting support are only parts of the broader spectrum of boss management. For instance, you must keep your boss informed.

Keeping Your Boss Informed

The cardinal rule for managing you boss is: no surprises. It is up to you to keep your supervisor informed of potential pitfalls that you may encounter.

Never leave your boss out in the cold. With changing conditions in the fast-paced high-tech environment written information, such as progress reports, are not enough. Craig McMillen tells why:

> *There are some things which you can't get out of a memo. I always make it a point to let my boss know what I'm doing whether he likes it or not. It's important to let him know where I stand. If he is going to do a proper job of managing, he needs to know what I am doing. If I never talk to him, I'm not too sure he can do his job correctly.*

Mini-entrepreneurs who work effectively with their bosses are alert to changing conditions and priorities and check them against their boss' view of events. By testing their assumptions against their boss's and maintaining an ongoing dialogue, they react appropriately and timely and avoid presenting unnecessary surprises. For the good of the organization, your boss, and you, your boss needs to hear both the good news and the bad news.

How much information bosses need about what you are doing depends upon their style of managing, the situation they are in and the trust between employees. To play it safe, you should provide more information then he or she actually requests. The more responsibility you acquire, the higher you go in the organization, the more the responsibility falls on you to keep your boss informed. In his new position as manager of Quality and Reliability, Tim Allen explains how his reporting relationship works:

> *I wrote these objectives and asked him what he thought. He said, "Fine." We don't talk about the specifics. For example, one of my objectives read: "Forecast accurately reliability plans for releasing new products plus or minus one week." He wouldn't tell me to change it to five days or two weeks. He leaves it up to me. My peers understand this objective better than he does and depend on me to do it well.*

This mini-entrepreneur, Tim Allen, receives minimal direction from his boss. Tim is, however, wise enough to know that at his level, part of managing is keeping his boss informed.

Understanding Your Boss's Work Style

Work styles and styles of interacting with others differ in varying degrees. Your job in managing your boss is to put aside your personal judgments and try to find productive ways to work alongside what may seem like idiosyncrasies. This means experimenting with your style by adjusting your behavior to get what you need from the relationship.

Disagreeing with Your Boss

A part of managing conflict creatively is being able to disagree with your boss and still advance in your career. In fact in the entrepreneurial culture, working out differences in point of view is considered part of the creative process. By disagreeing you are testing assumptions and fine-tuning the decision-making process. Mini-entrepreneurs like Todd Miller are not afraid to speak up:

> *I tend to feel OK about disagreeing. And I'll do it very adamantly, not from an emotional standpoint, if something is not being approached correctly. If we are going to implement an idea, we need to look at the down side. I try to keep it constructive. But I am a firm believer in looking at the up side and the down side.*

> *In disagreeing I very much try to keep it positive. I usually say, "I agree with what you are saying, I want to implement it. But here's the down side. How do we deal with it?"*

> *I think it's important not to be afraid to speak up. If you see something that bothers you and if you don't give feedback upfront, it might be too late somewhere down the road. And someone might be wasting a great deal of effort, because there is a roadblock. They eventually may find it. But, at least you can get them thinking about it.*

> *They can either overcome the obstacle when they get to it. Or they may never get to it, because they've adjusted for it on the front end.*

> *That's part of the creative process. I would hope that I'm never associated with a place where you can't talk about negative issues.*

When you have good reasons for facts and feelings and can back them up, then disagreement is expected and desired. A careful examination of your motives for disagreeing will help you determine if you are disagreeing for the right reasons. Your goal should be to improve a situation and contribute to the company's operation.

Encouraged to speak their minds in the entrepreneurial culture, mini-entrepreneurs like Todd Miller manage conflict creatively by risking disagreement with their bosses.

Managing Differences in Work Style

Working out differences in style between you and your boss is really a measure of your ability to adapt to your situation and manage your career. According to Peter Drucker, it is one of the few indicators that tells which younger people in the organization are going places and which are going nowhere.

You can spot the comers because they do something about managing the boss.

Lou Ann Bender points out how she uses constructive confrontation to work through differences with her boss:

My new boss is a real driver. She'll say, "Here's what I want done. I don't care how it's done." It is different with her than with my former boss. She doesn't want the personal openness. To have a working relationship with her, I had to understand that she didn't want the personal side of things. She is extremely bright. I respect her, and she respects my capabilities. We have that basic understanding.

I've had to curb my emotional side. Actually, one time I told her that I wasn't going to roll over and play dead because she wanted something. What we had to do the first couple of months was to set the ground rules. I thought we had to confront each other right upfront. She needs to listen a bit more than she does. I told her that she doesn't listen, and she told me that I don't listen. We agreed that we need to make a bigger effort.

She is able to dissociate her feelings when she deals with manufacturing people. She has a goal and she wants to meet it. She can say, "I don't care what they want, this is the way it's going to be." I am the opposite. I have worked very hard to develop a relationship with manufacturing. So I explained to her that I am more emphathetic. I asked her if we could be more flexible. She tends to think that if I don't give her a straightforward answer I'm taking it personally. I am trying to get her to see that some people don't disassociate, not personal feelings but job feelings, empathy toward another group's point of view. You may have to look at the way you are isolating or alienating them.

With my boss now, the biggest challenge is to be able to work with her, knowing her frame of reference, and get the response from her that I really need. Yet I want her to feel that she hasn't compromised her objectives.

Because Lou Ann recognizes her boss's strengths, weaknesses, and blind spots, as well as her own, she can manage the differences in an open and objective way.

Another important aspect of managing differences is to adjust your work style to meet your boss's preferred work style. Peter Drucker separates bosses into "listeners" and "readers," just as there are right-handed and left-handed people. If your boss is a reader, don't stalk into his or her office to talk about an idea. Write your ideas down to give to your boss, then you can talk about it. If your boss is a listener, don't send a memo or written report beforehand. Go in and talk about it first; then you can leave the written document.

Resolving differences in work style can be as simple as switching from writing a memo to using the telephone. Consider the case of Peter Rodin:

As a product consultant, I am out in the field providing technical support to the sales people. I found it difficult to catch up with our regional manager, since we are both in and out of the office so much. Whenever I had a question or needed to give him some information I wrote him a memo. Then one of the sales people suggested that I leave a message on our computerized phone answering service. I did and he started responding to my calls. I should have figured that one out, since he is a former salesman who used the phone as a life line.

By checking with others you gain insight into how to change your behavior to get what you need.

Understanding Your Boss

Beyond assessing your boss's work style, you must truly understand what lies beneath the style, what values are important, what is taboo, and what buttons you should not push. By knowing what your boss really cares about, you understand how to handle certain situations. What gives him or her the greatest pleasure: developing people, developing new ideas, wanting to be liked by employees?

Sam Edgars tells how he handled differences in values between the boss and himself:

I had a boss who had a value of playing together. He thought that everyone should play together outside of work. He wanted to extend the workplace into our social lives by having beer busts and parties at each other's homes. It was his value but not mine.

It was a difference in values which was small. But it could become real irritating if I always had to go to these social events. I managed it by going to just enough social events to meet his needs in that area. I found plausible excuses to not attend as many as I could. Now his needs were met because I was available for enough social stuff so that he thought I was playing the game. My needs were met because I wasn't spending so much of my time with him socially.

Sam managed differences in values by balancing his needs against those of his boss.

Timing

Another important factor when dealing with your boss is timing. Some bosses are morning people while others are afternoon people. You need to determine when your boss is at his or her best to address your concerns. Your boss's assistant is the person who is likely to provide this information. Listen to Penny Sumner's story:

Before I discovered that my boss was at his best in the late afternoon, I would walk into his office in the morning and found him to be foggy in his thinking and unanimated. Then I found out from his secretary that he is at his best around 4:00 in the afternoon. From then on, I made sure that if I wanted something from him, I would see him late in the day. If he was busy I would stay late to see him. It worked. He seemed like a different person.

Taking the time to discover bits of information to increase your chances of communicating clearly is a strategy for boss management.

MAINTAINING YOUR INTEGRITY

In entrepreneurial cultures, in which decentralization is a way of life, mini-entrepreneurs are expected and encouraged to talk back to the boss. In fact the Dana Corporation, as explained by Tom Peters and Nancy Austin in *Passion for Excellence*, used exactly this phrase, "talk back to your boss," in an advertisement placed in *Fortune, Forbes* and *Business Week* magazines. It was their unique way of announcing to the world their commitment to humanistic management practices of trusting and treating people as adults. They contend that bosses don't have all the answers, so they must listen to their people. It surfaces in improved productivity.

When you stand your ground because of integrity, you are taking the acid test of mini-entrepreneurialism. If you pass, you can stand among the ranks of mini-entrepreneurs who hold firm to deeply embedded values, such as quality work and service to the customer. Listen to the wisdom of Sam Edgars:

A boss can ask you to do all kinds of things. Probably 95 percent of what has been asked has been OK with me. About 5 percent of what I have been asked to do was uncomfortable with me. I disagreed with it philosophically or I felt I was not competent to do what I was asked to do. I felt that it was legally or morally wrong. On one occasion I was asked by a supervisor to stretch the truth to the customer. I wasn't willing to do that. I found that it was better to make it clear right upfront that I had a problem in doing these things. I worked very hard to set it up so that he found some other way to get his needs met, but not from me. It's important to maintain that self-integrity.

The mini-entrepreneur's raison d'etre is to make a qualitative difference in his or her organization. Ultimately it is to protect the integrity of the organization, what the company stands for, above all else. If asked to compromise your integrity, you not only have the right to refuse but are expected to talk back to your boss. Doing so demonstrates not only your self-confidence but your commitment to a higher purpose, to some shared values that your boss has temporarily lost sight of during a frenzied reach for a quick fix. Your actions serve as reminders of what really counts. Like everyone in today's business world, you are at the crossroads of business as usual and business with excellence in mind. Now is the time to stand up and be counted.

One fact of corporate life is that some bosses are in transition, trying to learn the new norms and values of the entrepreneurial culture. Not all have been lucky enough to have been nurtured in this culture that espouses humanistic management practices. You can help your boss get through this transition by sticking to the new rules. This is, however, no small task.

You can be paralyzed by deciding what actions to take when following your sense of integrity. Even though you may be trying to trust your gut-level feelings, your rational side pulls at your coat tails. To satisfy both your rational analytical mind and your intuition or gut-level feelings, you can use the decision matrix in Figure 10-1 to help isolate the real issues, your feelings, your fears and the possible outcomes.

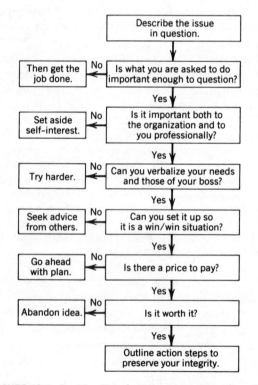

FIGURE 10-1. Decision Tree for Maintaining Your Integrity.

For some mini-entrepreneurs, maintaining integrity is like a knee-jerk reaction. They automatically stand behind what seems right. It is as simple as refusing to ship a product because the ceramic packages leak. This simple yet courageous action on the shipping dock makes a qualitative difference and shapes the values of the organization.

CONCLUSION

Within the entrepreneurial culture of excellence, mini-entrepreneurs feel comfortable about speaking up and talking back to the boss. Dana Corporation uses this phase, "talk back to the boss," to illustrate how increased productivity results from individual initiative.

Like all people, bosses are fallible human beings with strengths, weaknesses, and blind spots. Yet even in this loose–tight structure, your boss plays a very important role in your career. Your boss can open or close doors for you. After all, your performance determines opportunities for moving around in the organization. Given these facts of corporate life, you must rely upon two important roles: committing yourself to goals and managing conflict creatively. Goals lay common ground between the two of you, while dealing with conflicts enables you to deal with differences productively.

Although the phrase, "managing your boss" may sound contradictory, you are in charge of your career. Your boss controls you to the degree that you give up your inalienable right to job satisfaction, job freedom, and pursuit of excellence. You can transform your relationship with your boss by first examining your own needs and expectations.

Strategies for managing your boss include: making a contribution to your boss's goals: keeping your boss informed; and understanding your boss's work style. Using the goal-setting process is a convenience and useful tool for discovering your boss's goals and pressures. Through this process, you are in a better position to know where to put your efforts. When you want to sell an idea to your boss, getting the signal to go ahead with your idea makes a joint contribution to the organization.

Working out differences in style is really a measure of your ability to adapt to a situation and manage your career. How you manage your boss foretells your status as a comer, if you are going to advance in the organization. Tactics for resolving differences can range from constructive confrontation to shifting from written to verbal communication.

Beyond assessing your boss's work style, you need to understand what lies beneath the style, what values are important, what your boss really cares about. On the other hand, you also need to maintain your personal integrity if you are to join the ranks of mini-entrepreneurs. This is no small task and requires talking back to your boss. Your actions speak loud and clear of your commitment to superordinate goals.

=11

CHANGE

Managing the One Constant in Corporate Culture

MAKING CHANGE WORK FOR YOU

Carol Callahan meets with Sam Edgars for lunch to discuss her thoughts about changing companies. She is particularly interested in listening to Sam's comments on the "ins" and "outs" of the fast-paced high-tech work environment and what it takes to survive. She knows people who thrive on it, while others have been burned out. Anticipating a job change, she feels anxious about moving and would like to discuss it with Sam:

CAROL: Sam, you made several job changes within the company when you were working for BCM, and now have just made another. Tell me your secret. I'm having trouble just thinking about changing companies.

SAM: Well you know that with the high-tech business there are always changes. So it's really important to be able to know how to deal with change, to manage change, particularly resistance to change.

CAROL: What exactly do you mean by resistance to change?

SAM: Resistance to change is really nothing more than anxiety and fear.

Because you know what you have now, but you don't know what you'll have in the future.

CAROL: That's what I am experiencing now.

SAM: For me personally, in any of the changes I have experienced, the biggest things are dealing with anxiety and fear. And they can become paralyzing. I had a thousand worries, but I concluded that there wasn't a whole lot I could do about certain fears. Naturally I did my homework.

But five years ago, if I had envisioned the process of getting where I am today, it would have been a much different process. Things didn't happen the way that I thought they would. I thought that I would start consulting very slowly and under the apprenticeship of someone else. It didn't happen that way. I left the company and became a highly paid consultant and am considered an expert in my field.

So the lesson in this is that you can't plan the outcome. All you can do is plan the process in between.

CAROL: How did you do that?

SAM: I asked myself what I could do to move from being employed within the company to being self-employed. There were some things which I did. I served as the spokesperson for our company on quality improvement. So I started a focused campaign to be available for public speaking.

People began to ask me more and more to help me develop a program. So the demand for my services developed. Then I eased out of my job, first continuing to work half time.

CAROL: How did you feel about getting into a situation that demanded you do some different things that were new to you, or that you particularly didn't like doing?

SAM: I had to force myself to do some things that I didn't think I was good at, like selling. But I made a decision that I was just going to do them and I did. I got through them and after a while I found out I was pretty good.

CAROL: So Sam, are you saying that, if you want to make a change, part of making the change process work is to stick to your plan, knowing that you will feel uncomfortable and incompetent for awhile?

SAM: Yes, don't let the fears get the best of you.

Mini-entrepreneurs in the fast-paced, high-tech entrepreneurial culture have been successful because they have dealt effectively with change and handled the stress attached to it. As one mini-entrepreneur expresses it, "You need to go with the flow of things." Whether you initiate the change or it is forced on you, the same symptoms occur: fear and anxiety surrounding an uncertain future. If you survive and thrive within the high-tech environment, you need skills in managing change. You can use these skills to carry out new directions, initiate new projects, or simply accept change. If you rely on these coping skills, you not only get through dire straits but lend a hand to others who may be frustrated and immobilized by fear.

First you need to step back and look at the big picture, how your organization responds to technological, economic, societal, and environmental changes. Since change is the one constant, management requires you to take a positive and proactive stance, not just passively carry out orders or overreact to new situations.

SORTING OUT CHANGE

Marta Dunlap has moved from four different positions with the same company over a period of a year and a half. She has moved from new business planner to product marketing manager in one division and from customer marketing associate to customer marketing representative in another.

Larry Buxton has moved from applications engineer, writing new business proposals, to a program manager within a two-year period.

Phillip Holmes moved from one semiconductor company to another and became a manager. After about one year with the new company, the company filed for bankruptcy.

In all of these cases, each individual initiated the change in his or her career life. In each case it was a step up, a promotion. Change can be divided into two categories: change you initiate (job change/promotion, change resulting from implementing an innovative goal) and change imposed upon you (change in job assignment/priorities, in boss, in organizational structure). A common thread running throughout all these transitions is stress. Even if you have chosen to change, the accompanying stress is real and needs to be confronted. By doing so, you can better channel your energies in a positive direction and let yourself off the hook for feeling temporarily in limbo and vulnerable to criticism.

Harnessing Stress for Positive Change

The stress that accompanies change is a two-edged sword that can help or hurt you. Lack of stress can lead to apathy, lethargy, and poor job performance. It creates a situation in which you are unmotivated and stagnating. On the other hand, too much stress produces anxiety and fear.

When properly managed, stress caused by change becomes a tool for helping you and others as well. Dr. Hans Selye, a leading stress expert, calls good stress "eustress" and bad stress "distress." He states, "Stress is the spice of life. We could avoid it only by never doing anything. But who would enjoy a life of no runs, no hits, and no errors?"

Your goal should be to change potential distress into eustress or negative stress into positive stress. To do so, manage the rate at which you change your life. Rates of change and stress levels can be described as follows:

- No Stress: Stagnation (no runs, no hits, and no errors)
- Optimum Stress: Eustress (personal growth and success)
- Too Much Stress: Distress (anxiety, ultimate failure)

Controlling Your Rate of Change

Everyone reacts differently to varying circumstances and types of changes in their life. Dr. Thomas Connellan has developed a scale for gauging stress and how to control your rate of change, which is presented in Figure 11-1.

As you move from zero to one on this scale, you are stretching yourself without too much danger. However as you move to stress levels three and

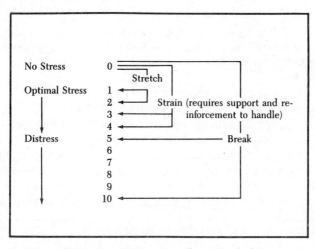

FIGURE 11-1. Stress Scale. *Source*: Thomas Connellan. "Personal Success is only 10 Steps Away." *Data Management*, March 1983. Reprinted with permission.

four, you are likely to feel a bit more strained. Dr. Connellan suggests handling this strain by developing a supportive climate from others that will help you be more personally successful.

If you move too rapidly between stress levels five to ten and reach the breaking point, no matter what type of supportive climate you've built, you can only handle that amount of stress for a short time. As Dr. Connellan puts it, "You can build 'success muscle' the way you build body muscle—a little bit at a time." You start out by achieving something within your reach and then stretch a bit farther.

You can use these insights to deal with challenges now facing you. Before managing change on a personal basis, let's focus on how you can manage the stress of change with others.

UNDERSTANDING HIGH-TECH WHIRLWINDS

ROLM, a manufacturer of communication systems, was recently acquired by big blue, IBM. The mil-spec division of ROLM was bought by Loral Corporation. How will these mergers affect the corporate culture and the way we do things around here?

One day the chairman of the board of Apple Computer, Steve Jobs, has 1500 people reporting to him, the next day he is told by the Board that he no longer has a hand in operations. Several weeks later he resigns to start another company. The change means streamlining and reorganizing divisions. How will I be affected? How will this change the entrepreneurial style of the place, if the maverick entrepreneur doesn't have his hand in operations?

The president of a Signetics Corporation resigns from the company. U.S. Phillips, the parent company located in Holland, sends a replacement. The wheels of reorganization begin to turn. Layoffs are imminent. What's going to happen to me?

These scenarios allow you to put your finger on the pulse of the high-tech industry. Technology, positioning in the marketplace, and foreign competition, like plates deep in the earth, are forever shifting. These shifts force high-tech companies to be agile, to react to rapidly changing cicumstances. They create opportunities for improvement as well as a turbulent environment. Michael Potter, Chairman and Chief Executive Officer of Cognos Corporation, explains how change benefits the organization: "We are always tinkering with the organization and doing something to improve it. Change is something that needs to be managed and sold." For the organization, managing change requires a clear focus on goals and matching individuals to the demands of the situation.

For you, managing the stress of organization change involves two steps: recognizing that corporate agility is necessary for survival and understanding organizational life cycles. Like human beings, organizations grow and develop, entering phases that allow maturation. You are less likely to get caught in whirlwind power plays and free-floating anxiety if you look at organizational change from an aerial view and keep the changing landscape in focus. Power plays surface as people anticipate benefits from real or imagined future events. The level of anxiety increases and feeds upon itself as individuals ask a myriad of questions such as: What is happening? Where is the organization going? How will these changes affect me personally and professionally? What pressures will I face in my job as a result of these changes? By becoming aware of organizational growth cycles, you manage the stress of change and bring order to your predicament.

Using the Corporate Life Cycle Model

Researchers provide several models for corporate life cycle development which are illustrated in Figure 11-2. Every organization goes through an entrepreneurial stage (early innovation, niche formation, creativity), a collec-

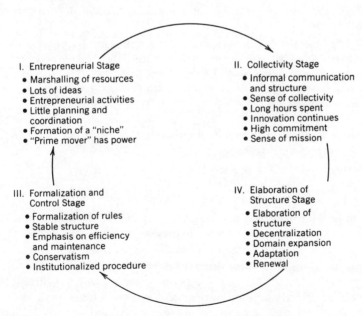

FIGURE 11-2. Corporate Life Cycle Model.

tivity stage (high cohesion, commitment), a formalization and control stage (stability and institutionalization), and a structure elaboration and adaptation stage (domain expansion and decentralization). Like a metamorphosis, organizations transform their structure and style to adapt to the changing environment.

Although the corporate life cycle model is a handy tool for comprehending organizational transitions, not all organizations fit nicely into one of these categories, nor are these categories mutually exclusive. Excellent companies can be both entrepreneurial and still hold on to other stages, for example, IBM, 3M, and Hewlett-Packard. By preserving parts of the entrepreneurial stage such as product development teams and shared values, innovations are produced. It is a way of having the advantages of both bigness and smallness.

In the face of rapidly changing technology and fierce competition, mini-entrepreneurs learn new skills, work near robots, and redefine work relationships. If you accept organizational change as a natural process of life, then you lighten the stress and feel less fearful of new situations.

You must realize that products and ideas also have a life. Some live longer than others. The statement, "nothing lasts forever," is likely to smack you in the face when clinging to the safe and familiar. The notion that ideas have a life cycle makes change inevitable and less shocking when it occurs. In fact, a vice president of a high-tech company gives the following advice when orienting new employees to the company. Lisa Ishimotos describes it:

> *When I first joined the company, I was encouraged to do things differently. He said that the most common human characteristic is resistance to change. But if you have a better or new way of doing things, which you think is better, then you should persevere and sell that idea. We were encouraged to constantly seek ways to improve.*

Being receptive to change and initiating change for the better is a fact of life in excellent high-tech companies.

Dealing with Organizational Transitions

Richard Beckhard and Reuben Harris in their book, *Organizational Transitions: Managing Complex Change*, present a model for thinking about organizational change. A change basically involves moving from a current state of functioning to some desired future state. Complex organizational change also includes a transition; a period during which the current state is being disassembled and the future state is not fully functional.

Excellent companies attempt to ease the pain of change by communicating openly about it. Lou Ann Bender explains how her company handles a change:

There's a lot of dealing with change around here. It can be a real frustration for people. I think that most people interpret change as: "Now what do I have to do?"

What is important to do upfront is to define the change. We have a lot of organizational structure changes. We try to let people know how the change will affect them, what to expect. We try to waylay any fear because it's the unknown that's frightening.

People ask themselves: Will my job be harder? Will I not succeed? Will I have a job next month? Our company is really good at communicating change from the highest level and communicating how that change will affect each individual.

Within excellent high-tech companies certain shared values, such as respect for the individual, remain intact and serve as the guiding light in times of uncertainty, giving definition to specific humanistic management practices. Michael Potter, Chairman and CEO of Cognos, gives an example:

People want to know what's happening in the organization. By letting them know, it makes them feel a part of the place. When the president of U.S. operations decided to leave the company, we spent more time in crafting the announcement. It was a significant change in operations, so we spent a longer period of time preparing for it.

How Mini-Entrepreneurs Manage Change

An awareness of corporate life cycles enables you to anticipate change, read the stress level, and assess what needs to be done in the transition phase. During this phase, the mini-entrepreneur manages the change process with dedication, caring, support, and a personal vision, enabling the company to pull through dire straits. Let's examine how mini-entrepreneurs help manage change.

If you identify the source of change, you can better cope with the situation, understand the reasons behind the change, and envision your job role in the transition phase. Mini-entrepreneurs by definition are change leaders or instigators of innovative change. A number of ways exists in which you, as a change leader, can help individuals and the organization get through any transition by assuming certain roles. These roles include coach, facilitator, and orchestrator. Mini-entrepreneurs who assumed these roles have helped ease the pain of change for others. With empathy, insight, and vision they help others to adapt to changing circumstances.

Orchestrating Small Wins

Take the case of Anna Lew. As a training specialist, she is responsible for coordinating an internal retraining program for production workers whose jobs will be taken over by robotics. She tells how to deal with resistance to change and orchestrate program implementation:

> We have a lot of people moving to other parts of the company through a retraining program. One man told me that, after 17 years in his job, his boss told him to look for another job within the company.
>
> Part of dealing with the negative aspects of change is letting people look at the big picture. We let people know that this is part of the changing work environment, and the company needs to respond to industry needs, market needs, and changing customer needs. These are going to dictate how we run our organization. We tell them that we are going to try our best to match organizational needs with their skills and interests.
>
> Of course there is a lot of resentment initially, but then there is also a lot of assistance provided for these folks. People have time off with pay for one semester to attend classes at the local community college to pick up administrative support skills and a certificate.
>
> There were several administrative support positions which I recruited for. I did an extension PR job. We sent out a newsletter, flyers and gave coffeebreak talks. I had to make sure that we had a good applicant pool for those positions. We had a good number, about 55, and I was happy about that. Now we have more people interested."

Anna's orchestration of the program with an upbeat tone enabled her to turn around initial resistance to change and create small victories for individuals and the program. The roles, skills, and action steps she followed are listed in Table 11-1.

Coaching/Facilitating a Turnaround

A former manager of the Corporate Quality Improvement Program, Sam Edgars assumed the roles of coach and change facilitator. He listened to and empathized with those who were asked to rethink job roles and tasks performed. He recounts how he handled the change in moving several hundred people from the quality and reliability department to other internal jobs. Some of the steps for implementing Sam's program are listed in Chapter 9, section Setting Innovation or Stretch Goals. He further explains how the change was managed:

> We started to create the future state through massive training. People started to make fewer mistakes and defects and, therefore, we could eliminate inspection. We also changed the way in which people operated so that they could be trusted without inspection.

TABLE 11-1
Roles, Skills, and Action Steps of Anna Lew

Role	Skill No. and Description from MESI*	Action Steps
Initiator	30. Taking action on my own authority without asking permission.	Initiated Public Relations campaign.
Innovator	14. Implementing new concepts and ideas despite adversity.	Gave presentations on retrainig progam and dealing with resistance to change.
Communicator	5. Actively listening to others.	Listened with empathy to employees.
Realist	12. Reality checking suggestions and new ideas of others.	Matched employee skills and interests with job slots and program offerings.

*Mini-Entrepreneurial Skills Inventory.

The way which we handled the transition phase went this way. We said, "Today there are some of you who are policemen (inspectors). Tomorrow some of you will have to be consultants." We told them to decide how they wanted to change their roles, what tasks they wanted to eliminate. We gave them the control of managing their own transition. I was responsible for making the transition occur. But they were responsible for designing their own process.

Because they were able to design their own changes, they felt that they had control over the situation. They felt that they were masters of their own destiny. This reduced a lot of personal stress. It made them want to help move through the transition rather than resist it.

Wearing the hats of coach and facilitator, Sam Edgars, sensitive to the stress of change, helped ease corporate growing pains. A breakdown of the roles, skills, and action steps that Sam used is provided in Table 11-2.

Building a Model to Follow

As a member of a task force, Lou Ann Bender is working with manufacturing to convert to a Just-In-Time system of inventory control. As a mover and

TABLE 11-2

Roles, Skills, and Action Steps of Sam Edgars

Roles	Skill No. and Description from MESI*	Action Steps
Initiator	23. Anticipating problems before they occur.	Gave people control to manage change.
Analyst	24. Diagnosing a situation and maintaining an objective viewpoint by seeing all sides of the problem.	Reduced stress by making them masters of own destiny.
Innovator	31. Introducing new ideas and projects that are precedent setting and represent concept leaps.	Put quality into job and eliminate inspection.
Collaborator	20. Working jointly with others inside and outside my work unit to accomplish a task.	Told them to decide how to change their roles.
Realist	34. Envisioning the end product/result before the project begins and communicating the vision to others.	Prepared people for future by training them.

*Mini-Entrepreneurial Skills Inventory.

shaker of the task force, she explains the initial problems encountered and how common goals came about, leading to a clearer direction:

> *One of the problems is getting people to feel ownership for the project. The task force crosses over many functional lines such as engineering, manufacturing and accounting. But no one was really taking ownership.*

> *So what a few of us did was to visit the other divisions to see what they were doing. Then we came back and put together a model for other task force members to follow. So now when there is an action item, they know what to do. The can follow the format. And what is being implied is that you're really not doing a good job unless you do something as in depth as this.*

We tried to move people toward a common goal. We tried to define that common goal within a certain category and define the specific action items so we could address them.

Table 11-3 lists the roles, skills, and action steps that Lou Ann followed while leading others through this change.

These mini-entrepreneurs have jumped into the chaos of innovative change and given a structure and coherence to the transition phase. They have been sensitive to and respectful of certain basic needs of people in transition. They have followed these steps:

Surviving an Organizational Transition

1. Set a common vision. What does that future state look like? If possible, establish a model.

TABLE 11-3
Roles, Skills, and Action Steps of Lou Ann Bender

Roles	Skill No. and Description from MESI*	Action Steps
Organizer	1. Setting reachable job goals.	Set common goals for the team.
Analyst	26. Observing the work behavior of others to collect data and draw conclusions.	Recognized that nobody took ownership.
Collaborator	20. Working jointly with others inside and outside of my work unit to accomplish a task.	Took a trip to other divisions to see what they were doing.
Innovator	18. Enabling others to see my vision using terms that are attractive to them.	Built a model to follow.
Team Member	6. Helping others to see mutual interests and goals.	Identified goals, action steps with others.

*Mini-Entrepreneurial Skills Inventory.

2. Pay attention to individual feelings, reactions. Take time to listen to unexpressed fears. Empathize by seeing through the other person's eyes. Be supportive and tough at the same time by holding people accountable.

3. Provide support and follow through by identifying short-term common goals to which people can commit. Break them down into specific action steps.

4. Give up control but not ownership. Let others participate in defining goals and action steps. Stay loose and open to opinions, suggestions from others.

In addition to easing the pain and frustration and clarifying the transition phase, mini-entrepreneurs stay in tune with organizational needs. Once committed to the future state, they follow certain steps to manage the stress of change. These steps are included in Exercise 11-1.

EXERCISE 11-1. Checklist for Managing the Stress of Change

The following steps are helpful when coping with the stress of change. Lack of information intensifies the fear of an uncertain future. By stepping outside of your fears, you are in a better position and frame of mind to manage the stress of change with others and yourself. Check those steps that you need to improve.

———— 1. Listen to what top management has to say about why the change is needed. An effective facilitator of change must understand where the organization is before explaining the reasons to others.

———— 2. Promote a feeling of common identity and purpose with those involved in the change as well as the targets of change.

———— 3. Have a sense of timing. As a facilitator/coach/orchestrator of change, assess the support for change and judge the most opportune time to make it happen.

———— 4. Adapt innovations so that they are beneficial to all organizational members. Try not to leave others in the dark. Ask yourself, "Who needs to know this information?"

———— 5. Build an open and authentic relationship with others by sharing knowledge and being available for help.

Now that you have some idea of how mini-entrepreneurs manage organization change, let's see how they manage change for themselves.

Managing Personal and Job Changes

As you change jobs internally, you carry a certain amount of excess baggage. This baggage contains the old way of doing things and seeing yourself, old values, and former, perhaps obsolete, work styles. Changes in the work style and peer group are par for the course. For some, these changes increase the stress level. Let's listen to a couple of mini-entrepreneurs describe their job transitions.

Lou Ann Bender recently was promoted from a cost analyst to a supervisor of cost analysts. She speaks of how she reacted to her job transition:

> *Change is hard for me because I go back to the thought that I'm not going to excel or meet my expectation. I went through a three-month period of being very sensitive.*

> *So I think that the most important thing is to be communicative about it. Be open and honest about it. Don't be afraid to admit that you're insecure. Bring it right upfront. I talked to my manager, a prior supervisor who is now a peer, and I even was very open with my employees about it. We talked about my expectations of them and their expectations of me.*

> *I don't want to fall short of their expectations. Yet what they are trying teach me is that my expectations are higher than theirs.*

Robert Devore, a contributor to Chapter 4, replaced Sam Edgars as the manager of Corporate Quality Improvement. For him the job change, moving from manufacturing to a service organization, means adjusting to a whole new ball game:

> *I report directly to the president. My assignment is really a short-term two-year job. They have pulled me up from operations. They need that. They don't need an executive in this job. They really need someone who understands what goes on down there in the bowels of the company.*

> *After two or three years in this job, I'll go back to my regular place in the organization, where ever that is. But in the meantime it is a very interesting opportunity. It's better than getting an MBA, to get to observe what happens on a corporate staff level.*

> *I'm not in competition with the guys I'm dealing with. So I'm not afraid of them. They are not afraid of me. And we don't play the same games that we would play if I were vying for a permanent job at that level. The fear and anxiety thing is not there. If I think they are going off in the wrong direction, I'm not*

afraid to say, "Hey guys, I think you are doing a dumb thing here." They are receptive to that.

There are some parts of my previous job that I miss. I miss the people. And I miss coming into work and knowing exactly that today I have to make a widget. I could draw a picture of it and, at the end of the day, I would know if I made it right. This job is much less concrete.

When Marta Dunlap moved from one division to another, differences in corporate culture surprised her. For her, handling this job transition meant adjusting to a new culture:

The mil-spec division is a much smaller division and I think size makes a difference. We had a really tight family atmosphere. It always seemed to embody the principles on which the company was founded.

I was invited back to attend a management meeting. One of the executives from the new parent company commented on the warmth in the room. It was the camaraderie, the bantering back and forth between the audience and the speaker. Someone would say something and then someone else would counter it. You had a sense of a really good warmth. That organization just hangs together. You can feel it!

The division I am now in is larger, more diffused. It doesn't have the guts of the culture which mil-spec has.

I knew how to get things done in mil-spec. I knew more people. I had my finger on the pulse of the organization, and I know what the top management was thinking. While now, in this division, I am lower in the organization and feel like I don't know what's going on. I feel like I am in the back room, isolated. But over the next six months, my job will be more outwardly focused. So I can do something about my concerns.

In these cases an external change, job change, has provoked internal changes in self-perception, confidence level, and a reevaluation of corporate cultural preferences. As a matter of fact, job transitions can open up Pandora's box, forcing you to question your job competency and throwing your self-esteem and self-confidence into a tailspin. It also forces you to take a stand on work style preferences and corporate cultural values. The way that you previously got things done may be shockingly different and foreign in your new job. All of these changes produce an uneasiness, missing the past and feeling uncomfortable and awkward in the present.

William Bridges, in his book *Transitions*, gives a useful way of viewing personal transitions. He identifies three distinct phases of a transition: endings, neutral zone, and beginnings. Essentially the transition process involves letting go of an old situation, suffering the confusion of inbetweenness, and forging ahead in the new situation.

The stage of feeling betwixt–between or neither here nor there is experienced as being the most confusing and stressful. Job transitions contain private, personal rites of passages for individuals who dare to grow personally and professionally. Let's take a look at the nuts and bolts of mini-entrepreneurial rites of passage.

The Problem with Endings

The problem with endings, leaving one situation for another, is that you are giving up, really losing, something. So facing endings means losing something previously valued. For Marta, changing divisions meant giving up personal power and influence, familiarity with cultural norms, and a peer group. Lou Ann's job transition meant leaving behind her feeling of being competent and an expert as a cost analyst and stepping into the darkness to acquire new supervisory skills. For Robert, his job change meant leaving behind a whole different world that dealt with tools, equipment, and a tangible product.

All these changes threaten feelings of comfort attached to your work environment. Your first step, then, is to admit that you will be pushing yourself outside of your comfort zone. Like an astronaut walking in space, you will feel disoriented yet will know that you are still connected to a home base, the spaceship, the organization.

The second step in coping is to realize what you are giving up. You are, in fact, starting over, starting a new job even though you haven't left the company. You have competed for the position and earned the right to the job. Don't take this achievement too lightly.

Coping with the Betwixt–Between Stage

In the past, primitive people followed a ritual when passing from youth to adulthood. People making this transition left the village and went into an unfamiliar place, the wilderness. There the person would be separated from old connections and stripped of old identity. One of the problems of working in a fast-paced environment is giving yourself a time-out, breathing space, a time to stay in the neutral zone.

This second hoop of the transition can seem like an unproductive period of time. Yet, it is a time of reorganization and self-renewal, time spent inside the cocoon just before emerging as someone different. Marta Dunlap recounts this period.

> There were times when I was doing a lot of proofreading, and it was very boring. I would walk around the office with a set of headphones on. There's just not a lot of professional women who have the guts to walk around the office with their headphones on.

The former head of the division saw me and got my attention. He was laughing. He didn't mind and even if he did, well that's too bad. There's a tolerance here for a broader range of behaviors.

I don't know what I will be doing in six months; or what I will have learned; or where I will expect to be after a year. I've just crossed one hurdle, and now I am in a sitting period. I'm regrouping.

Marta has created a twentieth century, high-tech version of the neutral zone, a time to "regroup."

Take this period to disengage from the frenzy and the familiar and be patient with yourself. Unlike a machine, nothing needs to be fixed or repaired in order to move on.

Robert Devore, in his new job only a short time explains how he is hit from all sides during the transition. For him, changes take place on several levels, a personal transition in the midst of organizational turmoil:

It's a difficult time with the transition. The president of the company left. We're kind of in an interim zone. A lot of reorganization is going on.

For Robert, the "interim zone" is happening on personal and organizational levels. In the midst of this "organized chaos" mini-entrepreneurs live out their own private agenda of personal transitions as a way of dealing with uncertainty.

Tolerating Uncertainty and Ambiguity

Within the dynamic high-tech environment, mini-entrepreneurs are expected to work around experimental structures, a variety of people, new technology, and respond to a changing marketplace. In doing so, they acquire the skill of tolerating uncertainty and ambiguity. Taking a tolerance pill aids in decreasing stress levels and helps you get through difficult transitions. If you can just live in the neutral zone for awhile, you will be increasing your tolerance for uncertainty and ambiguity.

A psychological study of more than 250 managers from AT&T shows that a tolerance for uncertainty, among other traits, goes hand-in-hand with long-term professional success. Some high-tech companies screen applicants for this "tolerance for ambiguity." Some even include this trait on their applicant interview checklist. Let's move on to the next phase of transition.

Starting Over

Having moved through the neutral zone, you can now lift up your head and open your eyes as you undertake your new job. You know what you need and want to accomplish. Let's listen to Marta:

I am looking forward to going out into the field and dealing with customers and people in the field. I haven't had a change to do that before. Those experiences will mean as much to me as any kind of hard product knowledge that I would get over the next six months.

I'll actually be getting up in front of customers and dealing with them. If they say that they really don't like the company, I'll need to know how to handle that.

While I am mulling over my next job in the back of my mind, I'm not devoting full energy to figuring out exactly what I want to accomplish yet. I have too much ahead of me over the next two weeks.

I'll write out my MBOs. It's a good way of getting clarity on where I am going and what's important to my job vis-a-vis what my boss thinks is important.

For Marta, starting over is exciting. She is also aware of where she doesn't want to place her time and energy. For her, leaving a job means leaving behind job tasks she has already mastered:

The strategic planning process which I was involved in at mil-spec is now getting off the ground in this division. They are following our prototype from mil-spec. I can sit back and watch the process and know what's going to happen.

I could be participating in the strategic planning process a lot more than I am. But I am really tired of it. I am spending all of my time getting this document out. It needs to be done. There's a deadline. I have more to gain from it, learn from it. Part of the reason that I'm not dying to get heavily involved in the strategic planning process is because I want a different set of experiences. But I will get involved enough to satisfy my team leader and do some new things which interest me.

For mini-entrepreneurs like Marta, the thrill of learning something new, testing the limits of their capabilities, pushes them to reach for the brass ring of job excellence. You can ease the pain and frustration of a corporate rite of passage by fully experiencing and appreciating each phase.

Awareness of the various phases of a job transition helps you cope with the stress attached to them. Listed in Exercise 11-2 are steps for mapping your job transition.

EXERCISE 11-2. Mapping Your Transition

1. What are you losing as a result of this job change (personal power and influence, peer group)?

    _____

    _____

2. What are you gaining?

    _____

    _____

3. What is getting in the way of making the change (Fear of failure, loyalty to a peer group)?

    _____

    _____

4. List three ways of coping with the neutral zone, the betwixt—between state.

    _____

    _____

5. Who around you can be supportive?

    _____

    _____

6. What new learning needs to take place as you strive to become effective in your new job? How will you go about acquiring it?

    _____

    _____

7. List previous transitions and describe what you did to get through them.

    _____

    _____

CONCLUSION

Mini-entrepreneurs within the high-tech entrepreuneurial culture have been successful because they have effectively coped with organizational change, dealt with the stress of both personal and job transitions, and managed the change process with others. Regardless of whether you initiate a change or change is imposed upon you, fear and anxiety accompany an uncertain future. This fear and anxiety creates stress.

The stress that accompanies change is a two-sided sword; it can either help or hurt you. When properly managed, stress caused by change becomes a tool for not only helping you but others as well.

You will successfully manage change for yourself and others to the degree that you understand and accept organizational transitions. An understanding of corporate life cycles enables you to bend with the winds of organizational change.

Mini-entrepreneurs by definition instigate innovative change. They assume the roles of coach, facilitator, and orchestrator to help ease the pain of change for others. In doing so, they are sensitive to and respectful of the needs of others in transition.

Another part of managing change is coping with personal and job transitins. Job changes provoke inner changes in self-perception, confidence levels, and a reevaluation of corporate cultural preferences. Job transitions contain private personal rites of passage. Phases of personal transitions include endings, a neutral zone, and new beginnings. Your awareness of these phases helps ease the pain of change for yourself and others.

12

PLANNING YOUR CAREER

Getting Where You Want to Be with PEP

THE ILLUSION OF THE FAST TRACK

Carol Callahan makes one final round of informational interviews with her friends Lou Ann Bender and Marta Dunlap. She has pinpointed a major concern, competing with fast-track individuals with MBAs.

CAROL: You know Lou Ann, I'll be giving up a lot of security by leaving the company. Security not only in terms of financial security but also knowing how to get things done. That's half the battle. Also I'm afraid that I'll be competing with those fast track MBAs.

LOU ANN: Listen, they aren't as fast track as you think. I am having talks with one right after lunch on his career.

He is concerned that he isn't moving ahead fast enough. He expects to be promoted into management right away. It just doesn't work that way. You have to prove yourself first and pay your dues.

The best way to get ahead is to do the absolute best that you can do in your present job. Opportunities will be given to you, if you do a good job. If you are always looking ahead, you'll be setting yourself up for failure.

CAROL: What do you mean, to "prove yourself?"

LOU ANN: He needs to learn to take the initiative, to take ownership of his job. He doesn't know how to go about getting the proper information from people. If he can't be an effective cost analyst, how can he become a supervisor?

CAROL: Does that mean that if I became a cost analyst I would have to start all over again?

LOU ANN: Not exactly, you have a track record to fall back on. You've been in the working world for several years. You know how to deal with people and you've acquired a number of skills that you may not even know that you use. You would have to adjust to our culture, though.

But for this guy to think that he can quickly move ahead on the merits of his MBA is just unrealistic, plain and simple.

The following week Carol meets with Marta to discuss her same concern.

MARTA: My boss and I just interviewed a person with an MBA for a job opening. She really left a bad taste in my mouth. My boss said that she really left an unsettled feeling in his stomach.

CAROL: What was it about her that turned you both off?

MARTA: There was one opening in the company working for a friend of mine, Heather, who is one year out of business school. I was talking to the person about working for Heather.

This person responded by saying, "Well Heather doesn't have anything to teach me. She is only one year out of business school." I thought that was terribly arrogant. First of all, no matter who you are or where you are, you have something to learn from everybody around you, above you and below you—secretaries, fellow professionals, and senior managers.

Learning doesn't necessarily happen from those who are ahead of you five years or more. I was really surprised by this comment coming from a person with an MBA. Furthermore, before Heather went to business school she was a top salesperson for her company. She has a set of skills which this person wasn't currently looking for. But they could be very valuable skills. In other words, she felt that Heather wasn't going to offer her the skills which she wanted.

Well I think that's a very narrow perspective on the kinds of things one can learn and one needs to move ahead in life.

CAROL: So you don't think that she would have worked out?

MARTA: No. My boss and I discussed it. She needed to be brought down a couple of notches. What we are looking for was how she dealt with people. That's how you decide if there's a good fit with the company.

I don't think that you have anything to worry about, Carol, in competing with people with MBAs. Your experience speaks for itself. Plus you have good judgment and know to work with people.

Besides, you never really get the perfect candidate, but you want people who can grow with the company.

Leaving Marta, Carol is a bit relieved by Marta's encouragement. She realizes that her background and experience count a great deal. At least she doesn't have unrealistic expectations.

This preoccupation with future-oriented career pathing and moving ahead at all costs sidetracks commitment to the organization and your job.

Building your career begins with focusing on your current job performance, corporate culture and personal skills, capabilities, and values. It means taking stock of where you are right now. Naturally one way of measuring how far you have come is through a performance evaluation. Most companies have a formalized performance evaluation system used to determine compensation and to give feedback. Take this opportunity to look at objectively your strengths and developmental needs. Also use it as a time to look ahead and determine a short-term action plan for self-improvement and set long-term career goals.

Let's now back track and refer to Figure 2-3. By following steps 5-8 of this learning/working cycle, you will finalize your Personal Effectiveness Plan for building your career.

Throughout this book, you have identified action steps to follow in a number of areas: communicating, influencing others, team building, managing conflict, and goal setting. The Mini-Entrepreneurial Skills Inventory breaks down these skills. You should compile the data you have gathered on yourself and develop a final Personal Effectiveness Plan. But first, let's dispel some myths surrounding this career planning process.

SHATTERING CAREER MYTHS
Myth 1: Career Development Is Following a Career Path

Career pathing, outlining job progression lines and requirements needed to move into each progressively more complex job, is only one slice of a comprehensive career development plan. It is helpful only if you are sure that you want to stay in a particular job function. In reality, you can determine your career interests only after being in the working world for a number of years. Mini-entrepreneurs in high tech develop their careers by broadening their skill base and jumping from one career path to another. Paradoxically, it means finding a career direction by first getting lost in a career maze. Immerse yourself into a job so deeply and intensely that you learn what aspects of a job you find most satisfying and at which you are competent.

Listen to Tom Atwater describe the process. In Chapter 4 you have already met Tom, originally with the Research and Development function of a software company and a certified public accountant, Tom transferred to the product support function, providing telephone support to customers. He explains why:

> They needed someone in the product support area who knew both the accounting side and the data processing side of the product. I was the only person in R&D who could handle the accounting side.

> It's quite challenging. In R&D I didn't really get the personal contact with customers. Now I'm more in a consulting role. I also find it quite enlightening because in R&D, I got only one point of view of the product. Here in telesupport I get other viewpoints from the customers and what they actually think of the product. I can give that feedback to R&D.

> It's provided good interaction between myself and R&D and other departments. I'm dealing with people in other departments and other regions. It takes more patience and compromising. When I go to R&D and tell them that this is what we should have on our system, I have a good basis for doing so.

> It takes being able to get along with people over the phone. If I can't do that then I can't sell our product. If you have a happy client, then he is satisfied with our product. Being in telesupport is a lot more regimented. I have to be there hour after hour. But I am better suited to be in product consulting than in R&D. I would like to move towards becoming a regional product consultant. It's more or less a progression for me. I started in R&D and I've moved into more of a marketing role.

Without this job change, Tom would not have applied his interpersonal skills extensively. Taking a detour, getting lost in a career maze, has been beneficial to Tom and the company. Tom's collection of multiple perspectives, like a kaleidoscope, enriches product improvement and innovation.

Myth 2: Going "Up" or "Out" Equals Career Success

Until the mid to late 1960s, career success was thought to be reaching a higher rung on the corporate ladder. Attached to an image of success was more responsibility, authority, and money. Movement upward was thought of as the only way to go. If you faced a roadblock in the road to success, you simply changed companies to get ahead.

Many researchers have found that individuals now follow other career patterns that take on a spiral movement, reflecting changes in job functions. Edgar Schein has given a model of how individuals make career moves within the organization.

He uses a cone to represent career change and career progress. These changes take place along three dimensions:

1. Vertically: Increasing or decreasing rank or level in the organization.
2. Radically: Increasing or decreasing your centrality or degree of being more or less "on the inside."
3. Circumferentially: Changing from one function to another or from one division to another within the organization.

Mini-entrepreneurs follow career patterns as a way of acquiring additional skills and gaining exposure to a new functional area. Now a customer marketing manager, Marta describes her career moves:

I've had to work very hard and long to get where I am, to get the credibility and background to do what I'm doing. I feel fantastic! And yet the company did not have an XYZ career path for me to get where I am now. Sometimes it depends on how an individual does and how fast the company grows for certain things to open up. I don't think that you can plan for a particular job.

I was counting how many different jobs I've had since joining the company. Over a four-year period I've had five different jobs. They haven't necessarily built on each other. They have been different. I've changed job functions. I moved from Finance to Product Marketing in one division to Customer Marketing in another division.

Marta's example, as well as many others, suggests that the notion of linear career progression is no longer common. Lateral transfers are a fact of career life and are legitimate avenues for reaching a long-term career goal and just as "successful" as traditional notions of moving up the career ladder or moving out of the company to move up.

While other companies have formalized job rotation programs, mini-entrepreneurs in high-tech companies create their own. For Marta, like Tom, job changes have definitely followed a career maze pattern as shown in Figure 12-1. As she explains, the idea behind her moves was to rotate through jobs to get into a marketing position:

> *I was really hired in as senior financial analyst by a person who saw me as a long-term employee and knew that I wanted to get into marketing. He knew that I could do a short-term project for six months in Finance and maybe Marketing would hire me. That's exactly what happened. After I did a European business plan and presented the report, I was hired by Marketing. I was hired as a new business planner to do strategic planning for two years.*

Staying within a technical area as opposed to moving into a management position is another acceptable avenue. Success for some does not necessarily mean moving into the ranks of management. Lisa Ishimoto gives an example:

> *There is one person who became a manager and didn't like it. He didn't like having a lot of people directly reporting to him. He has a lot to contribute as an individual contributor. That's what he chose. He is very successful, and it's the right thing to do for him. Nobody is fighting him about it, and he is still being a success. He didn't want the headache of line management. He would rather work on technical problems. For him it's a lot more satisfying. Our company lets technical gurus develop.*

For some people moving into management is not the only way to go.

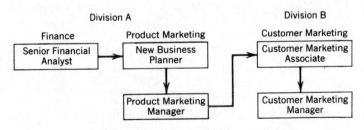

FIGURE 12-1. Example of a Career Maze.

Myth 3: The Company Will Develop My Career

Responsibility for developing your career rests with you. While many companies offer career development opportunities, such as job postings and formal and informal career planning sessions, it is up to you to take action. One study, conducted at Hewlett-Packard in Colorado Springs by Warren Wilhelm, identifies "key career success variables," and indicates that individual willingness to nominate themselves for promotion rather than wait for advanced positions was as important as an outstanding performance or an engineering degree in getting ahead.

Lisa Ishimoto can't emphasize this enough:

Nobody does the career pathing for you. You have to do it yourself. When I give advice to people, I tell them that they should always know what their next step is going to be. If you are effective, you can take any path you want. There is a woman whom I hired as a clerk who is now a programmer. There is another woman with a college degree who started out as a secretary. Now she is a sales manager.

Now that you have reexamined some misconceptions about myths surrounding career development, you can begin to determine what stage you are at in your career by assessing your career needs, values, and career orientation. Remember, career planning is really an ongoing process. You will face many alternatives, career crossroads, and career decisions in your lifetime.

ASSESSING WHAT YOU WANT

As you collect more information about what you need and value and what your talents are, an occupational self-concept emerges. It is only through being in the workplace that you can begin gathering information to determine what you want and how much you want to invest in YOU, Inc. It is healthy to change jobs or careers to search for the best match between an organization or an internal department and your needs, values, and talents.

Career needs change as your job experiences and responsibilities change. Robert Devore and Lou Ann Bender gave some good examples. Their goals and interests have changed from wanting to increase their technical competence to achieving managerial competence. For others, creating a spot for themselves that offers a maximum amount of freedom and autonomy is important. Conversely, some individuals may want to sacrifice some autonomy in exchange for stability in their total life situation.

Career Stages

Age and career stages shape your needs and goals. Career stages include: entering basic training, going through initiation, becoming a legitimate member of the organization (after you have paid your dues), and becoming a mentor for others. The needs and values for each career stage differ. For example, Phillip Holmes, who has been in the high-tech industry for close to 15 years and has been laid off and rehired four times, values security at this stage in his life; it is important and becomes his career anchor:

> *I don't tend to be a person that's really career aggressive. I like getting a promotion occasionally, and if I deserve it that's fine. I've got my family and my hobbies and other things outside the workplace that makeup the rest of my life. I like working hard and doing the best. But as far as getting into that mold of constantly moving up the ladder and achieving, I'm not into that. I wouldn't mind being a training manager for the next 10 years.*

The first three-to five years are valuable years of experience in determining your strengths, values, and attitudes toward work. Within the high-tech industry, after about five years people tend to burn out. For this reason some high-tech companies, such as ROLM, Tandem, and Intel, offer employee paid sabbaticals. After working at Tandem for four years, you can take a six-week sabbatical. At ROLM you can take a three-month leave after six years, and at Intel after seven-years you can take eight weeks.

Sabbatical or not, taking stock after you have gained enough experience to determine your skills, needs and values is essential for further career development.

CREATING YOUR PEP

By now you have accumulated a great deal of information on your strengths and development needs, career values, preferred work style, preferred corporate culture, and your career anchor. You also have, undoubtedly, received feedback on job performance. Let's begin to compile this information in your PEP (Personal Effectiveness Plan) which is included in Figure 12-2.

Two sources of information are available to measure how far you have come. One is from your performance evaluation by your boss. The other is the Mini-Entrepreneurial Skills Inventory. List your most outstanding strength in your PEP. Do the same for your development needs. If possible, ask for feedback from your boss on how you can improve. Determining specific action steps will be discussed later in the chapter.

SKILLS
Strengths

1. _____

2. _____

AREAS FOR IMPROVEMENT   ACTION STEPS
SKILLS

1. _____   _____

2. _____   _____

WORK STYLE GAPS
Ideal   Actual

1. _____   _____

   _____   _____

ROLES   ACTION STEPS
PARTICIPATION

1. _____   _____

COMMITMENT

1. _____   _____

CREATIVITY

1. _____   _____

WORK GOALS
Job Goals

1. _____   1. _____

   _____   _____

Innovative Goals

1. _____   1. _____

   _____   _____

CAREER GOAL

_____

_____   _____

                                               _____

FIGURE 12-2. Personal Effectiveness Plan.

Marta Dunlap gives us her perspective on the whole process:

I just had an evaluation a week ago. We discussed what I need to do over the next six months. By dragging it out into the open and being honest about it, when I make progress he can recognize it. Or if I'm not doing some things that will help me grow, he will know that I'm not doing the right things.

There's a whole set of skills I need to know along the way. If I don't get past those hurdles, I'm not going to rise. And people in different points in their career have different skills they need to learn along the way. Thank God, I have a boss who cares, who is experienced and who can talk to me about my career.

Realigning Your Work Style

You now know what it takes to fit into the high-tech entrepreneurial culture. To realign your current work style with the preferred work style of the entrepreneurial culture is to pinpoint a work style characteristic that needs adjustment. Review Chapter 4 and then complete the section of your PEP under "Work Style Gaps."

Roles to Expand

First review Chapter 2 to determine which roles are critical for accomplishing your current job. Then select those roles that you feel need development. Review Chapters 5–8 to refresh your memory of how various roles support job effectiveness and which action steps need to be followed.

To recall which roles fall under the categories of participation, commitment and creativity, refer to Figure 3-2.

Setting Work Goals

Work goals are broken down into job goals and innovative goals. They are considered short-term goals to be accomplished over the next year. To distinguish between job goals and innovative or stretch goals, review Chapter 9.

Setting Career Goals

As opposed to work goals, career goals are long-term and usually take three-to-five years to reach depending on any number of factors, such as your eagerness to learn, your background, and experience and career opportunities within the company. At this point in your career, you may not have a definite career goal. There are a number of steps that you can take to determine whether or not you want to pursue a particular career goal; one is to take a survey of the field.

People in your own company are a gold mine of information about careers. You already have a number of contacts through coworkers in other company areas. Interview them informally to determine what roles they play in their job, specific tasks and activities undertaken, and basic job requirements. This informal information gathering discussion can take place over lunch or any other time which seems fitting to you and the other person.

Todd Miller, who has an MBA, has been a senior personnel representative for six years. He has previously chosen not to enter the ranks of management; he is now reconsidering that decision. Interested in working in the operations side of the business, he begins speaking to marketing people about what they do. He sees himself eventually getting into the marketing function.

Lou Ann Bender is at the same fork in the road, as she needs to decide her next career goal. Having met her goal of becoming a supervisor, she sees herself in another functional area other than Finance:

> *A personal goal which I have is to decide where I want to go next. I've made a commitment to this job. But I think that I would have a lot to contribute in a marketing role. I don't want to do direct sales, but I would like to do customer training. I still haven't decided whether my goal is to become a controller or to move into customer marketing. In the next two years I will work on that, to determine my career goal, to see if I am going to be committed to finance or branch out.*

> *I will talk to people in the organization, to understand what is available and to find out their job requirements to determine if I can fit.*

> *I've had a chance to do presentations and train people. I know that I would be comfortable doing that. But I don't know if I want to follow a career path in customer marketing. Because I don't have an engineering background, there may be limitations that I wouldn't like. Those are the things which I need to determine.*

Know Yourself

Throughout this book you have had numerous opportunities to assess your strengths and current career values. When identifying a career goal, this information should be considered as well as other information such as satisfying job experiences and reasons for job changes. Lisa Ishimoto explains her reasons for moving from systems engineering manager in one division to sustaining engineering manager in another.

> *There's an opportunity to make a lot more money, and I was looking for more personal growth, personal challenge. I've been with the company now for six years, and I've gone up the ladder so quickly. I didn't see anything changing*

over the next year. I would be taking on new projects but not necessarily learning anything new.

For Lisa the challenge of learning becomes a goal itself as opposed to targeting a position. Again the career maze pattern overshadows the traditional career path model. Lisa's career pattern is outlined in Figure 12-3.

By reviewing the past, your previous jobs, you can plan for your future. An analysis of your strengths, preferred roles, and job experiences that were most satisfying will point you in the right direction. As you begin to pinpoint preferred tasks and job activities, you'll find some common threads.

Let's examine the case of Lou Ann Bender and nail down her strengths, preferred roles, and experiences that were the satisfying to her. Drawing from data from her Mini-Entrepreneurial Skills Inventory, Lou Ann discovers that as a cost analyst her strongest roles were organizer, innovator, and team member. The skills that supported these roles are listed on the Preferred Roles Worksheet in Figure 12-4.

Lou Ann exceeds what is expected of her by presenting training classes on the new accounting system called Orbit. As you may recall from Chapter 9, Lou Ann wanted to become the Orbit expert and made sure that everyone understood the system through the classes that she designed and presented. The skill she applied was "implementing new concepts and ideas despite adversity" (skill 14). By conducting this training she became aware of how much she enjoys training. We also have seen Lou Ann apply the skill of "helping others see mutual interests and goals" (skill 6), as she bridges the gap between manufacturing and accounting and between various members of a

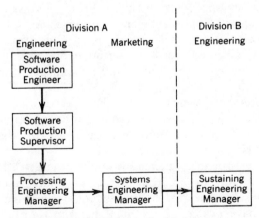

FIGURE 12-3. Career Maze of a Mini-Entrepreneur.

JOB TITLE	PRIMARY ROLES PLAYED	SKILL STRENGTHS
Cost Analyst	Organizer	16. Establishing priorities after reaching agreement with others.
	Innovator	14. Implementing new concepts and ideas despite adversity.
	Team Member	6. Helping others to see mutual interests and goals.
Cost Accounting Supervisor	Innovator	14. Implementing new concepts and ideas despite adversity.
	Team Member	6. Helping others to see mutual interests and goals.

PREFERRED ROLES

1. _____

2. _____

FIGURE 12-4. Preferred Roles Worksheet.

task force. As a new supervisor and as a member of a task force, she again calls upon an old skill (implementing new concepts and ideas despite adversity), as she formulates a model for a Just-In-Time system of inventory control. Refer to Chapter 9 for her description. She also "helps others see mutual interests and goals" by pointing out common goals among task force members.

Both of these skills, which support the roles of innovator and team member, push her toward a customer training position within the marketing function. These skills complement the marketing skills of assessing customer needs and surfacing mutual interests.

By examining prior job experiences, Lou Ann targeted her next career goal: customer training within the marketing function. If you are standing at career crossroads, Exercise 12-1 is a helpful tool for clarifying your thoughts. If you already have a career goal in mind, list it in your PEP.

EXERCISE 12-1. Targeting Career Goals

1. Using the format of the Preferred Roles Worksheet first list your previous job, primary roles, and skill strengths.
2. For each skill strength describe in writing what it is that you did to apply this skill.
3. What did you find most satisfying about these experiences?
4. Now list your preferred roles based on your answers to the preceding question.
5. In light of this information, what career goal would you like to explore?
6. List this career goal in your PEP.
7. What new skills do you need to develop to reach this goal?

Setting Action Steps

To complete your PEP, identify action steps for reaching your career goal. At this stage, if you are uncertain about a career goal, explore possibilities to acquire more information on what it will take to reach your goal. How you go about exploring depends on your learning style.

Examine your skills as a self-developer. A common theme among mini-entrepreneurs is the need to be challenged and the urge to learn, in short, to develop themselves. What has earned them the title of mini-entrepreneur is their ability to passionately seek ways to improve themselves and the company. What separates them from the crowd is their willingness to take responsibility for their learning.

Larry Buxton has recently been promoted from applications engineer to program manager. For him stretching beyond his normal job duties is important:

> *For my own personal growth, assuming new tasks beyond my normal job duties is really important. I can't stand people doing only exactly what they are told and maintaining only that level of performance. That's my own pet peeve. If someone asks me to do something, I do a little more than is expected. I would look for that in someone I was hiring.*

Lou Ann Bender, who has moved from cost analyst to a supervisory position, also emphasizes the need for personal development and making a contribution:

> *I find with this company that, if you are willing to be challenged and step out and do a new job, you really grow. The opportunities are really great.*

I have higher expectations than most people. It's important for me to set challenging goals because I get bored if I don't. I also have personal goals. They're not goals which I have to do on the job, but if I don't do them, I can't really broaden my knowledge. I can't be much of a contributor to the department as a whole.

We have already heard from Marta Dunlap and have watched her career progress. Let's hear about what she finds exciting about her previous jobs. She made these comments when she moved from new business planner to a product marketing manager:

All three jobs which I've had so far were the first and only jobs of that type. They weren't held by anyone before me. That's fun because I got to formulate what I was going to do. There was no precedent.

While developing her jobs, Marta also developed herself, acquired new skill, and broadened her knowledge of the company.

The bottom line in self-development is to take action, to take risks. Lou Ann describes just how risky developing your career can be:

Change is hard for me because I go back to thinking that I'm not going to excel. I want to be an expert right away. When I became a cost analyst I went through the same thing. It was very frustrating for me to not know everything in the first month. But people were great. They told me that I wasn't going to know everything up front and not to worry about it. They were very supportive.

Lisa Ishimoto also points out how the entrepreneurial culture supports risk-taking and self-development:

Our company believes that people are their most important resource. Our culture is very entrepreneurial. The key people, who have left, left to start their own companies for the most part. We develop people who are willing to take risks, people who are creative in their approach, see things differently and see opportunities. But for some people this is totally inappropriate. They want to be the constant people. You need those in every organization. But you let them decide what is right for them. The company is oriented toward that— individualistic determination.

Let's determine what action steps can be taken to develop your career. What steps you take really depends on your learning style; whether you prefer reading or listening to others or jumping into a task or first observing others perform it.

Pinpointing Action Steps

As you pinpoint action steps that will provide the biggest payoff, you also need to consider how you like to learn, through classes, on the job, from mentors. You have already identified your career goal, what you want to do. Now you need to determine how you plan to reach it.

A number of ways exist for gathering more information on how to reach your career goal. Some resources are available within the company, while others are available outside your work environment. Resources include workshops, seminars, mentors, college or university courses, computer-based training, and trade or professional associations. Other ways of learning include simply observing others and keeping a journal of your impressions and feelings. Which option you pursue depends on how much information you already have, your readiness to make a career move, and how you learn best.

Consider Lou Ann Bender's case. At a crossroad, she now faces the decision whether to stay in Finance or to switch to Marketing. If she pursues a higher-level management position in Finance, she may need an MBA degree. Pursuing a marketing position may involve acquiring additional technical knowledge. To tap resources available within the company, she speaks to people in marketing, customer training, and the marketing manager responsible for customer training. She may observe training classes to determine if she can see herself in a training role. Lou Ann learns best by speaking to people who may give her some new insights and observing the behavior of others. Her action steps are listed in Table 12-1.

With this example to follow, you can now complete your own PEP.

TABLE 12-1
Example of Career Goal and Action Steps for Lou Ann

Career Goal	Action Steps
Customer training in Marketing	1. Speak to others (customer trainers, marketing manager) in marketing about job responsibilities and requirements.
	2. Observe customer training classes.

Building a Support System

You already have begun to build a support system through internal networking. You probably built this network as a means of accomplishing your job. In other words, the unstated contract among networkers can be interpreted as, "You scratch my back and I'll scratch yours." You can use this same network to make other career contacts or to get information or support for career planning. Included in your network should be a mentor.

A mentor is a leader or expert in the field in which you are interested who can offer guidance and support. Mentors can be found both in as well as outside your company. Listen to Lisa Ishimoto's comments about her mentor:

> *Our former vice president who is now on the Board of Directors is a mentor for me. I used to go to him with a lot of questions. He is a very people-oriented manager. On Halloween he came in as super manager. He has an engineering degree from MIT but went into marketing. He said that he went into sales because it was a lot more fun.*

> *I listened to what he had to say and it helped me. Sometimes it gave me a different perspective on things. I asked him to speak to a women's organization about marketing opportunities. He did an unbelievable analysis of careers in marketing. He took all the positions in marketing within our company and went through the requirements, the personal skills needed, and listed those which were required or desirable. He also spoke about marketing positions as a function of the type of product. I listened to what he said and realized that it made a lot of sense. I realized that I had gone through the analysis myself in deciding to join the company. I didn't do it in such a formal way. It all fell into place. One thing which he wanted us to understand was the company culture.*

Lisa also acts as a mentor for others as she explains:

> *People also use me as a mentor. They come over from Engineering, Manufacturing, and Marketing and ask me for help. It is not a part of my normal responsibilities, but is is assumed that it is part of my responsibilities as a manager here.*

> *They ask how they can evaluate what their next move will be. It's no magic. All I'm doing is giving them ideas of how they should do their analysis. I don't tell them what they should do in terms of a specific position. I tell them about techniques, how to decide what their next move is, I ask them "where do you want to be in five years?; what are some short-term goals to get to long-term goals?; and what are your requirements for a satisfying job?"*

Muchmore, John and Galvin, Kathleen. "A Report of the Task Force on Career Competencies on Oral Communication Skills for Community College Students Seeking Immediate Entry into the Work Force." *Communication Education,* April 1983.

Mumford, Enid. *Values, Technology and Work.* London: Martinus Nijhoff Publishers, 1981.

Perreault, William Jr., and Miles, Robert H. "Influence Strategy Mixes in Complex Organizations." *Behavioral Science,* Volume 23, 1978.

Peters, Michael L. "How Important Is Interpersonal Communication?" *Personnel Journal,* July 1983.

Rubin, Irwin, M., and Berlew, David E. "The Power Failure in Organizations." *Training and Development Journal,* January 1984.

Schall, Maryan S. "A Communication-Rules Approach to Organizational Culture." *Administrative Science Quarterly,* Volume 28, 1983.

Schilit, Warren K. and Locke, Edwin A. "A Study of Upward Influence in Organizations." *Administrative Science Quarterly,* Volume 27, 1982.

Spivey, Austin W., Munson, Michael J., Locander, William B. "Improving the Effectiveness of Persuasive Communications: Matching Message with Functional Profile." *Journal of Business Research,* 1983.

Yerys, Arlene. "How to Get What You Want Through Influential Communication." *Management Review,* 1982.

CHAPTER 7

Benne, Kenneth D., and Sheats, Paul. "Functional Roles of Group Members." *Journal of Social Studies,* Volume 4, Spring 1948.

Cartwright, D., and Zander A. *Group Dynamics.* New York: Harper & Row, 1968.

Doyle, Michael, and Straus, David. *How to Make Meetings Work.* Chicago, ILL: Playboy Press, 1976.

Dyer, William G. *Strategies for Managing Change.* Reading, MA: Addison-Wesley, 1984.

Gibb, Jack R. "TORI Group Self-Diagnosis Scale." In J.W. Pfeiffer, and J.E. Jones (eds.). *The 1977 Handbook for Group Facilitators.* San Diego, CA: University Associates, 1977.

Hall, Jay and Williams, Martha S. "Group Dynamics and Improved Decision Making." *The Journal of Applied Behavior Science,* Volume 6, Number 1, January–March, 1970.

Hawley, John A. "Transforming Organizations through Vertical Linking." *Organization Dynamics,* Winter 1984.

Hollingsworth, A. Thomas, Meglino, Bruce M. and Shaner, Michael C. "Coping with Team Trauma." *Management Review,* Volume 68, Number 8, August 1979.

Margerison, Charles, and McCann, Dick. "Team Mapping: A New Approach to Managerial Leadership." *Journal of European Industrial Training.* Volume 8, Number 1, 1984.

Mahoney, Francis X. "Team Development, Part 1: What is TD? Why Use It?" *Personnel,* September–October 1981.

Mahoney, Francis X. "Team Development, Part 6: Variation of Procedure Meetings." *Personnel,* July–August, 1982.

Hall, Jay, and Williams, Martha S. "Group Dynamics Training and Improved Decision Making." *The Journal of Applied Behavioral Science,* January-March, 1970.

Reilly, Anthony J., and Jones, John E. "Team Building." In J.W. Pfeiffer and J.E. Jones (eds.). *The 1974 Annual Handbook for Group Facilitators.* San Diego, CA: University Associates, 1974.

Rosenberg, Sheila. "The Power of Team Play." *Management World,* August 1983.

Sanders, Bruce D. "Fine-Tuning Team Spirit." *Supervisory Management,* June 1980.

Weisbord, Marvin R. "Team Effectiveness Theory." *Training and Development Journal,* January 1983.

CHAPTER 8

Alderfer, Clayton P. "Improving Organizational Communication Through Long-Term Intergroup Intervention." *Journal of Applied Behavioral Science,* 1977.

Blake Robert R., and Mouton, Jane S. "Overcoming Group Warfare." *Harvard Business Review,* November–December 1984.

Blake, Robert R., Shepard, Herbert A., and Mouton, Jane S. *Managing Intergroup Conflict in Industry.* Houston, TX: Gulf Publishing Co., 1964.

Bolton, Robert. *People Skills,* Englewood Cliffs, NJ: Prentice-Hall, 1979.

Caffarella, Rosemary S. "Managing Conflict: An Analytical Tool." *Training and Development Journal,* February 1984.

Filley, A. C. "Some Negative Issues in Conflict Management." *California Management Review,* Winter 1978.

Fisher, Ronald J. "Third Party Consultation as a Method of Intergroup Conflict Resolution." *Journal of Conflict Resolution,* June 1983.

Grove, Andrew S. "How To Make Confrontation Work For You. *Fortune.* July 23, 1984.

Hall, Jay. "Decisions, Decisions, Decisions." *Psychology Today,* November 1971.

Herman, Ronald H. "Resolving Differences." *Supervisory Management,* May 1983

Janis, Irving. "Groupthink." *Psychology Today,* November 1971.

Labovitz, George H. "Managing Conflict." *Business Horizons,* June 1980.

Lippitt, Gordon L. "Managing Conflict in Today's Organizations." *Training and Development Journal,* July 1982.

Mitroff, Ian I., and Kilmann, Ralph H. "Stories Managers Tell: A New Tool for Organizational Problem Solving." *Management Review,* July 1975.

Rahim, Afzalur M. "A Measure of Styles of Handling Interpersonal Conflict." *Academy of Management Journal,* June 1983.

Rahim, Afzalur, and Bonoma, Thomas V. "Managing Organizational Conflict: A Model for Diagnosis and Intervention." *Psychological Reports,* 1979.

Robbins, Stephen R. " 'Conflict Management' and 'Conflict Resolution' Are Not Synonymous Terms." *California Management Review,* Winter 1978.

Sherif, Musafer (ed.). *Intergroup Relations and Leadership.* New York: John Wiley, 1962.

Stimac, Michele. "Strategies for Resolving Conflict: Their Functional and Dysfunctional Sides." *Personnel,* November–December, 1982.

Thomas, Kenneth W. "Conflict and Conflict Management." In Marvin D. Dunnett, (ed). *Handbook of Industrial and Organizational Psychology.* Chicago: Rand-McNally, 1976.

Weisbord, Marvin T., and Maseido, James C. "Learning How To Influence Others." *Supervisory Management,* May 1981.

CHAPTER 9

Bradford, David L., and Cohen, Allan R. Managing for Excellence. New York: John Wiley, 1984.

Byers, John B. "Five Step Checklist Helps Communicate Goals." *Supervision,* June 1982.

Morrisey, George L. *Management by Objectives and Results for Business and Industry.* Reading, MA: Addison-Wesley, 1977.

Ordiorne, George S. and MBO II. Belmont, CA: Fearon Pitman Publishers, 1979.

Ordiorne, George S. "Setting Creative Goals." *Training and Development Journal,* July 1979.

Peters, Tom and Austin, Nancy. "A Passion for Excellence." *Fortune,* May 13, 1985.

Santavicca, Gary, and Jewell, Sandra F. "Goal Setting: How to Work Smarter." *Supervisory Management,* September, 1984.

CHAPTER 10

Drucker, Peter F. "How to Manage Your Boss." *The Journal of Accountancy,* November 1977.

Gabarro, John J. and Kotter John P. "Managing Your Boss." *Harvard Business Review,* January-February, 1980.

Hegarty, Christopher. *How to Manage Your Boss.* Mill Valley, CA: Whatever Publishing Co., 1982.

Larsden, Martin. "How to Manage Your Boss." *Computer Decisions.* September 1984.

Levinson, Harry. "Getting Along With the Boss." *Across the Board,* June 1983.

Neilsen, Eric H. and Gypen, Jan. "The Subordinate's Predicaments." *Harvard Business Review.* September-October, 1979.

Peters, Tom and Austin, Nancy. *A Passion for Excellence.* New York: Random House, 1985.

St. John, Walter D. "Successful Communications Between Supervisors and Employees." *Personnel Journal,* January 1981.

CHAPTER 11

Baker, H. Kent and Holmberg, Steven R. "Stepping Up To Supervision: Coping with Change." *Supervisory Management,* March 1982.

Beckhard, Richard and Harris, Reuben. *Organizational Transitions: Managing Complex Change.* Reading, MA: Addison-Wesley, 1977.

Berry, Waldron. "Overcoming Resistance To Change." *Supervisory Management,* February 1983.

Bridges, William. *Transitions.* Reading, MA: Addison-Wesley, 1980.

Brown, John L. and Agnew, Neil M. "Corporate Agility." *Business Horizons,* March-April 1982.

Burack, Elmer H., and Torda, Florence. *The Manager's Guide to Change.* Belmont, CA: Wadsworth Publishing Co., 1979.

Connellan, Thomas. "Personal Success Is Only 10 Steps Away." *Data Management,* March 1983.

Connor, Daryl R., and Patterson, Robert W. "Building Commitment to Organizational Change." *Training and Development Journal*, April 1982.

Hunsaker, Phillip L. "Strategies for Organizational Change: The Role of the Inside Change Agent." *Personnel*, September-October, 1982.

Hunt, Richard E. and Rigby, Marilyn K. "Easing the Pain of Change." *Management Review*. September 1984.

Miller, Dennis E. "Coping with Changes: Blending the Olds With the New." *Supervisory Management*, July 1983.

Nadler, David A. "Managing Transitions to Uncertain Future States." *Organizational Dynamics*, Summer 1982.

Quinn, Rober E., and Cameron, Kim. "Organizational Life Cycles and Shifting Criteria of Effectiveness: Some Preliminary Evidence." *Management Science*, January 1983.

Winokur, Scott. "Psychologists Zero In On What Sends An Executive To Top." *San Francisco Examiner*, January 7, 1985.

CHAPTER 12

Anderson, Stephen D. "Planning For Career Growth." *Personnel Journal*, May 1973.

Burnett, Robert S., and Waters, James A. "The Action Profile: A Practical Aid to Career Development and Succession Planning." *Business Horizons*, May–June 1984.

Canning, Roy. "Management Self-Development." *Journal of European Industrial Training*, Volume 8, No. 1, 1984.

DeLong, Thomas J. "Reexamining the Career Anchor Model." *Personnel*, May–June 1982.

Kaye, Beverly L. "Performance Appraisal and Career Development: A Shotgun Marriage." *Personnel*, March–April, 1984.

Louis, Meryl Reis. "Managing Career Transition: A Missing Link in Career Development." *Organizational Dynamics*, Spring 1982.

McEwan, Bruce E. "The Risk Management Approach to Career Planning." *Supervisory Management*, January 1984.

Near, James P. "Reactions to the Career Plateau." *Business Horizons*, July-August 1984.

Scott-Welch, Mary. *Networking*. New York: Warner Books, 1981.

Wilhelm, Warren R. "Helping Workers to Self-Manage Their Careers." *Personnel Administrator*, August 1983.

INDEX